Writing for Film

The Basics of Screenwriting

Darsie Bowden
DePaul University

LAWRENCE ERLBAUM ASSOCIATES, PUBLISHERS
2006   Mahwah, New Jersey   London

Copyright © 2006 by Lawrence Erlbaum Associates, Inc.
   All rights reserved. No part of this book may be reproduced in any form, by
   photostat, microform, retrieval system, or any other means, without prior
   written permission of the publisher.

Lawrence Erlbaum Associates, Inc., Publishers
10 Industrial Avenue
Mahwah, New Jersey 07430
www.erlbaum.com

Cover art by William D. Marvin

Cover design by Tomai Maridou

Library of Congress Cataloging-in-Publication Data

Bowden, Darsie.
   Writing for film : the basics of screenwriting / Darsie Bowden.
      p. cm.
   Includes bibliographical references and index.
ISBN 0-8058-4258-6 (alk. paper)
1. Motion picture authorship.   I. Title.
PN1996.B675   2006
808'066791—dc22   2005052760
                                                                  CIP

Books published by Lawrence Erlbaum Associates are printed on acid-free paper,
and their bindings are chosen for strength and durability.

Printed in the United States of America
10 9 8 7 6 5 4 3 2 1

*For Dave Johnson
and my students
at DePaul University*

Contents

Preface

One of the first things my professors told us at the University of Southern California film school was that most of us probably would never make it in the film business. We would never be successful, and we might never even get a job. This was not because they did not expect us to be talented, creative, and ambitious. Rather they wanted us to be very aware of our prospects: Jobs—good, fulfilling, and lucrative jobs—in the film business are very hard to get. Success, if you measure it in terms of star quality (big salaries, name recognition, consistent work), comes to the very few.

Thousands and thousands of people in Los Angeles alone will tell you they are working on a screenplay. They are working at other jobs while writing. Some are waiters, hairdressers, secretaries, or bouncers. Others are lawyers, doctors, and accountants. For every 100,000 writers, 1 or 2 will actually become successful. To tell you otherwise would, I think, be unethical. This said, I offer this book on screenwriting for a number of reasons.

First, for those of you who still believe in pursuing your dream (as I did), this book is designed to help you understand what it is to write for films. It will help you structure your drama, refine your characterization, craft your language, and learn screenplay format. Second, it will help you to understand what you are getting into, introducing you to the complexities of writing for the screen and the contradictions inherent in the process. There are ways of getting films made. Sometimes you will need to look to alternative markets: documentary, independent, non-Hollywood films, experimental films, and films for the marketplace. I hope this book prepares you for a range of possibilities. For those of you who are persistent enough, you will find a way, and you'll need to be prepared.

The one arena that this book does not treat is writing for the TV market (other than cable, which tends to cover everything!). Writing for TV (sit-coms, dramas, TV specials) is a huge topic; it is varied, complex, lucrative, and often exciting. To adequately explore it would require another book (or two), and there are already some good books out there. If TV is the medium you would like to write for, take a look at some of these other books. I have included a list in the appendix.

Regardless of your ultimate goal, this book is intended to introduce you to a kind of writing that will help you see the world in a different way and write about it using a different genre and medium. If anything, this skill is the most valuable; it transcends the conventional definition of screenwriting success, which is to make money, be famous, and win Academy Awards. Success at screenwriting lies in being able to heighten your perceptive abilities about the world and communicate those perceptions in a way that is highly cinematic.

One of my former students, Michelle Sydney Levy, articulated quite nicely what learning to write for the screen can do for you as a writer:

> From the outset, I was determined to improve my ability to write organic and captivating dialogue. The simple direction to write what the audience will see and hear demanded that I anticipate what the audience of my films would experience. I think the screenplay format lends itself to learning how to analyze events in terms of their visual, audible, human, and material components. Learning new formats is equivalent to learning new forms of thought. Writing for the screen has increased my powers of observation. I am more attuned to the pacing of conversations, the significance of people's eye movements and gestures, the objects people touch and how they handle them, all with a view to what, besides time passing, generates forward motion, and stimulates human response.

It is my wish that this book will help all writers, but especially those who have an eye on the cinema.

ACKNOWLEDGMENTS

Any writer of a textbook owes an enormous debt to her students. My case is no exception. My graduate and undergraduate students at DePaul University have been among the best students a teacher could have: motivated, interested, talented, and passionate about writing. I also am grateful to DePaul University and Western Washington University for allowing me to teach screenwriting so often. I am likewise indebted to my first teachers: Mort Zarcoff, Dave Johnson, Ken Evans, Irwin Blacker, and Peter Rothenberg of the University of Southern California film school; to Eric Sears, my collaborator and friend on numerous film projects, and our partner Zachary Feuer; and to Vahan Moosekian, Bruce Block, and Patrick Gregston for their friendship and expertise in my film-making days. Thanks to Robert L. Joseph for inviting me to collaborate on his writing projects for TV and giving me my first introduction to the Hollywood film business in all its glory. Thanks also to John Holland, Betty Bamberg, Jack Blum, Ross Winterowd, and Lawrence Green who taught me how to teach writing.

Marisa L' Heureux first took an interest in the project and gave me a contract and the time to write. Lisa DeMol and the reviewers at The National Textbook Company (NTC) provided discerning critical comments and advice on various drafts that have proved invaluable. My editor at Lawrence Erlbaum Associates, Linda Bathgate, urged me to write the book I wanted and then helped me get it into print.

Finally, I thank my parents who gave me the support to do with my life what I wanted. And to my daughter, Elisabeth, who gave me the motivation to write the best book I possibly could.

—Darsie Bowden
DePaul University

PART I

THE DRAMATIC FILM

The Rhetoric of the Screenplay

A book is easier to write than a film, because you can get away with murder. You can write around all kinds of situations and characters, whereas in a film you have to be much more concise. Every line has to work very hard. Writing for film is much more exposing. It has to move forward at a much more driven pace. Writing a book is a great luxury, because all you do is write it and hand it in. It doesn't matter how much anything costs. You can write any location you want. You don't have to worry about casting. You have the luxury of producing the finished product whole. But making a film is like making a cake. There are so many different factors involved, like recipes, temperature, ingredients and utensils. You don't know, until it comes out of the oven, what kind of cake you've got. A screenplay is more like a map of the film, whereas a book is the end product itself.

—Novelist Helen Fielding, writer of *Bridget Jones' Diary*, interviewed by Alan Waldman for the Writers Guild of America (www.wga.org).

INTRODUCTION: WHAT DOES IT MEAN TO WRITE FOR THE MOVIES?

The screenplay is one of those anomalies that does not fit neatly into a precise literary category. Although screenplays can be very poetic, creative, and imaginative, they are rarely considered to be "literature." You do not often find them in libraries, literary critics do not analyze them (rather, *film* critics tackle the films themselves), and screenplays seldom stand alone as pieces of "art." Although they can be well crafted, persuasive, and compelling, they are not considered essays or arguments. Since the development of the film and TV business—and hence the development of the film and TV script—screenplays have rarely been considered worthy of much focused attention and have only recently been deemed worth reading in their own right.

One of the reasons for this is that, generally speaking, screenplays are *templates* for a film, and therefore, unlike novels, poetry, or essays, they are not ends in themselves. In other words, they are intended to serve as instructional manuals or maps to guide filmmakers and actors in the work of making a film. Yet the skill and art of the writer and the "literariness" of the script is often what captures the imagination of the reader (often a producer or director) and helps to get the screenplay sold and, ultimately, produced. Without the screenplay—or a script in some form—there would be no film.

Despite the lack of attention, the contention of this book is that the screenplay is indeed literature. But it is also a sales tool, evaluated both by what is present on the page and by what kind of potential it seems to have for being made into a good, marketable film. In other words, many of the most important readers of screenplays look at it with two minds: Does it move me (Is it good)? Will it sell (Will it make a successful film)?

It is important for writers to be aware of this tension between creativity and profitability, both when they write and when they begin to look for a buyer for their work. Writers who believe their work is already a masterpiece—that is, so perfect that the slightest change will destroy its integrity—are doomed to suffer considerable torment. Films are almost always different, sometimes drastically and unrecognizably different, from the screenplay from which they are made. Often these differences improve the final film; occasionally the film is worse than the screenplay. For a screenwriter, belief in one's own creativity is extremely important, but part of the creativity involved in screenwriting is the flexibility to accept the flux that is characteristic of the medium and the business.

At the same time, writers who work only to make a profit—that is, simply to get a sure and quick sale—are also destined to fail. They may find themselves trying to second guess the film-viewing public, which can be very fickle in its tastes. Or they might try to second guess the film producers, who are trying to second guess the film-going and fickle public. Moreover, what is popular today may not be popular by the time the script is finished and ready to market, or by the time it is purchased and ready to be made.

Make Money or Tell a Story?

Film making is an expensive business, and screenplays are only the first step in a process that can cost a large fortune. Because of this fact, many writers, directors, producers, and investors in the film business naturally must try to determine what will produce a return on their investment—in other words, what will make money. If they did not, they would not be in the business very long.

But to use this as the sole criterion in writing is a mistake. Film critic for the *Los Angeles Times*, Kenneth Turan, laments that so many films today go for the gimmick—the stunning special effects or the savagely bloody, sex-laced action-adventure plot—to attract the youth segment of the film-viewing population. Unfortunately, in the process, Turan argues, film makers have lost the knack of making broad-based entertainment. They no longer trust that the well-crafted, well-written, old-fashioned story will appeal to general audiences. Ironically, it is the old-fashioned story that people still love to watch: a good love story, a good western, or a good mystery. But as Turan explains, the cost of films today may be one reason that producers fear that a good story will not be enough: "The size of the budget is a problem. When a film costs a lot of money, producers want everyone in the U.S. to see it. The results are films that are not too sophisticated, that don't offend anybody. In fact, they are so bland, they ultimately don't really please anybody either" (Turan, personal communication, December 12, 1998).

Although it is relatively easy to think up a gimmick, writing a well-crafted story takes time, energy, and skill. This book is directed to those who are interested in practicing the craft of good storytelling for the movies.

Trust Yourself and Your Ideas

Most professionals advise students of screenwriting to write about what they know: their lives or experiences. This is because the best writing is that which opens a whole new world to the reader or viewer. To engage an audience in this world, you must be intimately familiar with its details—the look, the feel, the taste, the smell, the action—of that world and use those details to create a world for the screen. These details are best uncovered by those writers who know them by having lived in that world. For example, James Dickey (1982), who wrote the screenplay *Deliverance* from his own novel (1970), can include details about rural Appalachia—the landscape, characters, conflicts, and concerns—that an audience having other kinds of life experiences cannot know about by virtue of the fact that he was born and raised in the South. The result is a film that is rich in detail, has the ring of truth, and creates an environment about which most people only have superficial knowledge.

Perhaps as important is the **insight** that a writer who is intimately familiar with his subject brings to his writing. Lawrence Kasdan, who wrote *Grand Canyon* (1991) from a story that he and Meg Kasdan authored, knows from his own experiences a lot about life in Los Angeles. This in and of itself would not make a good screenplay because many people know a lot about Los Angeles. What makes his film worth watching is the insight about some of the problems that

Angelenos face (crime, racial tension, human relationships, and money) that the Kasdans offer in their script. As with any good script, the issues they take up are in some way universal; they are problems that many of us can identify with even if we have never visited Los Angeles or never care to.

Does this mean you have to have lived in exciting places like the deep South, Los Angeles, or Viet Nam; know exciting people; or have had exciting life experiences to write a good screenplay? This helps, for sure. Even so, most professional writers do a lot of research even when they know a place well. They read, view films, visit places, and talk to people. Often they live in a place for a while so that it becomes part of their subconscious. In other words, you can come to know a place well. We might well frame this, then, as a maxim: *Good characters and plot situations grow not only from your imagination but also from an imagination that is well informed.*

We have all had a variety of life experiences, the most interesting of these being the ones that involve *conflict*. Most of our lives have been filled with conflicts; many of these are small and petty, but some are significant or overwhelming. A difficult life is usually what provides the opportunity for insight, and this insight is usually what makes people want to write. Consider the points of conflict in your life. Do you have something to say about them that would interest or intrigue a wide audience?

One way of looking at this notion of conflict is to liken a story to an argument in expository writing. You have something—a point, an insight, a thesis—you want to get your audience to believe. But to do so, you need to persuade your readers that you are the expert, that you know more than most people about the subject, and that you have insight. Consequently, you can consider your screenplay as support for your point; you will take your audience on a narrative journey through plenty of conflict, and by the end of the story they come to the same conclusion; they see your point. (There is much more on effective drama in chap. 2).

Finally, good writers write about something they feel is important to convey to others. Be aware (and beware) of the current trends because they are just that: trends. By the time you finish your screenplay or your screenplay becomes a film, the popularity for fantasy or futuristic films may have evaporated to have been replaced by stories about broken homes or child abuse; trust yourself and your instincts first.

Creative Genius and Talent

Some people would argue that good writers are born and not made. There is a long tradition in Western culture that upholds the romantic view that the best writing, especially but not exclusively literary writing, requires *genius*. Clearly, no one can help someone else be a genius. But genius is worthless if you don't have the tenacity, proficiency, and knowledge of your craft to get the work—the writing—done.

This romantic tradition also holds that "real" writers hole themselves up in their garret, smoking cigarettes, and living the solitary life of a recluse while they are engaged in the creative process of "writing." This tradition suggests that the only voice you should hear as you work should be your own, and you should avoid any kind of feedback until the work is finished, complete, and, in a word, wonderful. Although much writing tends to be a solitary experience, good writing is a very social event. Good writers consider their audience; their minds are populated with voices: voices of characters, viewers, other writers, people they have known, seen, and heard. They listen to these voices, responding to them and incorporating them into their story.

In film making, much of the work is genuinely collaborative. One person has an idea, another person writes up a story, a third does the screenplay, a fourth rewrites that screenplay, a fifth decides to produce it (with changes), a sixth directs the picture, a seventh interprets the words and actions through her acting, and so on. It is one of the ways in which screenwriting is unique.

This rich, noisy, collaborative process should be celebrated and honored, rather than rejected or ignored. Write with others, get feedback from people you trust, and welcome working with other creative people who can give you intelligent responses. Do not depend on your "genius" to make you successful.

Talent is another difficult term. Many people believe talented writers just have this mysterious "gift"—that some of us are born with it and others of us are not. From my years working with writers, I have developed a different view. Although it is quite likely that certain people are born with certain innate abilities and proclivities, talent in writing takes work. Good work—good writing—requires a healthy attitude about one's craft, preparation, and perseverance.

SOME GENERAL GUIDELINES

If genius and talent are overrated factors in becoming a good screenwriter, then what qualities *do* you need to write successfully. How can you best prepare yourself to write? Here are some suggestions.

Determine if You Have What it Takes

Most good writers agree that success in screenwriting is like success in all kinds of writing, whether literary or nonliterary. It is mostly hard work or, as the tired cliché puts it, good writing is the result of a combination of 1% inspiration and 99% perspiration. Many people can come up with wonderfully inventive ideas, intriguing characters, or interesting situations. But only a small percentage of those people can actually sit down and work through the messy, often monotonous day-to-day struggle of bringing a piece of writing to completion, especially if there is no particular deadline attached. Writing includes thinking, selecting, organizing, drafting, and revising—not necessarily in this order—and these are highly complex intellectual activities. It is not easy and often it is not very exciting. Writing also involves developing a system, a space, and a frame of mind to do the work. Even skilled writers encounter writer's block from time to time; they simply know how to break through it. It is very important to know yourself well enough to know what you need to get the job done.

A good screenwriter, first and foremost, must have the will and ambition to write. Because almost all screenwriters start out as freelancers, writing screenplays in their spare time among jobs, family obligations, and other responsibilities, bringing a screenplay to completion requires a good deal of self-discipline; you must have the ability to sit down and hammer stuff out. Sometimes what you write will be good and sometimes it will be awful. To get past the awful times requires the need to write. Do not write because you want to be a famous screenwriter; write because you *have* to write.

Second, because screenwriting implies potential partnerships among producer, director, director of photography, actors, and a host of others, a good screenwriter must have the ability to sit down and listen to others criticize his work, pulling it apart, belittling it, and changing it. Through it all, he must find ways to retain psychological and professional integrity and be able to work to find ways to incorporate the inevitable comments of others and make things better rather than worse. This skill at negotiating creative territory is also part of the craft; it is one of the elements that makes a writer a "professional."

Prepare to Write

How can you determine what is good writing and what is awful? A good part of this ability to evaluate and assess the quality of your work is to prepare. Here are some ideas that could be valuable parts of an ongoing program of self-education:

   1. Read everything you can, particularly narrative literature. Hone your language skills. The more you read, the more vocabulary and syntactical alternatives you pick up, much of it subconsciously. You can also learn on a

conscious level by taking note of phrasings and words you particularly like—especially for their clarity, color, and freshness.

2. Read screenplays—everything you can get hold of—good ones, bad ones. Read for readability (how it looks, sounds, and feels) and to familiarize yourself with the format and internalize its rhythms.

3. Listen to the world around you: sounds, conversations, music. Listen to how people talk, to what people say and do not say. Develop your ear for good and bad dialogue and for good and bad prose. Listen especially to the silences.

4. Write often. Take up journal writing, letter writing (including e-mail and instant messaging), editorial writing, essay writing, novel writing. Get in the practice of translating your thoughts into print, revising them, writing more, and then revising again. Practice writing for different audiences or, as some would say, in different "voices." Being able to style shift will help as you develop characters and create point of view.

5. Speak less. Listen, read, and write more.

6. Do your research (on characters, plots, history, settings, etc.) before you begin (and keep doing it as you write). As you take up work on a particular project, try to get as close to it as you can for as long a period as is feasible. It will show.

Writing Time.   Most screenwriters have full- or part-time jobs. Many have families and other demands on their time. Reserve part of each day for writing. It may be as little as half an hour the first thing in the morning or the last thing at night.

If you are able to write full time, set up a workable schedule. Full-time writers' schedules vary. Some people work best in the morning and so will work for 4 or 6 or 8 hours at the beginning of the day. Some writers work best at night. Still other writers write best on a crunch schedule in which they plot, plan, and think for weeks, months, or years and then churn out a draft in 48 hours. If you do this, reserve plenty of time for revision; your piece will probably need it. Think about when you do your best work. Set up a schedule and stick to it.

Embrace Screenwriting as a Balancing Act

The screenplay must first be a selling tool. It stimulates imagination, emotion, and vision of a producer with money to invest. Money ensures that the movie gets made. Many, if not most, of the words you write will be

changed, and your ideas will be enhanced, diluted, and sometimes en-
riched or cheapened by:

- the producer or studio executive (who finances the film and controls the
budget)
- the story editor (who may also be a writer and serves the producer or studio)
- the director (a man—usually—who has a "vision")
- the actors (more people with "visions")
- the editor (who shapes and often reduces the "vision" so it makes sense
and is dramatic, exciting, and meaningful)
- the film censor (who might be a member of a concerned parents group,
the government, or the film-rating agency, who further reduces the "vision," regardless of whether it makes sense)
- everybody else who can change it: the producer's lover, child, hairdresser,
secretary, or dog.

Although this may sound a bit cynical, these kinds of collaborations are actually exciting and necessary parts of the film-making process. Writing involves
people talking to one another and shaping what they say to appeal, persuade,
move, and inform their listeners. As I mentioned earlier—and it is worth repeating several times—the film-making process, from idea inception through
the writing, directing, and producing to the final screening, is always a group effort; as such, it is conspicuously and gloriously collaborative.

In summary, work hard on your screenplay, but develop a philosophy of language that is neither possessive nor protective. Try to avoid being defensive
when your readers are analyzing, criticizing, or responding to your work. The
words you have written are not entirely your own even though you have labored over them to select just the right words, phrases, sentences, and rhythms
to develop your characters and plot.

As you know or will come to learn, writing is a difficult process. Coming up
with ideas and making those ideas work is almost never easy. People are very
sensitive about what they consider to be their own language and their own
ideas. Hence, when you work with others or others work with you—in a story
conference, for example—treat people and their ideas with respect even
though others do not always give your ideas the same consideration.

Know What a Good Story Is

Although this book and many others provide suggestions and advice about
how to put together an engaging story, ask *yourself* what you like about good

stories. What does a good story entail? To what degree must it have some universality?

When you see films or read fiction, be critical about what you like and do not like about the narrative. Do you find the characters interesting? Why or why not? Do you find the story captivating? Why or why not?

When you see films, try to look at them as a writer, asking yourself the following questions:

- How is it put together? A linear story, flashbacks, multiple subplots?
- How are the characters developed?
- Where are the characters in conflict? How?
- How many minutes did I have to sit there in the theater without knowing what is going on before I got bored and wanted to get up and leave?
- What is the visual appeal of the story?
- What is the most exciting part of the film? Where does it occur? Is it predictable?
- How does the film end?
- What is the point of the film? What are its themes?

See a wide variety of films—traditional Hollywood films, independents, foreign, old, new, documentary, experimental—and ask yourself these same kinds of questions. How do they "work"?

Familiarize Yourself With the Business of Film Making

The Hollywood film business is, in particular, highly speculative, and with star salaries climbing to the heavens that speculation is very costly. Producers will pay lip service to the value of a good story, but the potential for making money is the primary motivator for investors, including production companies and studios. At the very least, theatrical films must make their cost back, and sometimes even this does not make financial sense for the backers. Keep this in the back of your mind as you evaluate your own work and the work of others.

Emily Dickinson could write poems in her attic, save them, and gain celebrity for them many years after her death. But old screenplays get tossed, and sometimes they are "old" in a matter of minutes. That said, there are many other alternatives to the big studio-produced, traditional theatrical film, and more and more films are made outside the system.

Independent Films.   There is a reasonably healthy market for films that are made outside the Hollywood system, and this is especially good news for the novice screenwriter. The variety here is enormous, ranging from films made on a shoestring budget (*El Mariachi, The Blair Witch Project*) to cult films (*The Rocky Horror Picture Show*) to films by film makers who for whatever reason have chosen to work "outside the system" (*Husbands, Miller's Crossing, Sling Blade, Boyz in the Hood*). Budgets are usually smaller—sometimes much smaller. There are fewer stars or, if there are stars, they work for far less money. Because they operate outside (or even alongside) the system, independent film makers are among those who take chances and invigorate the feature film business. But these films still cost money and must attract audiences.

Nontheatrical Films.   There is a huge market for nontheatrical films—both documentaries and marketplace films (covered in more depth in chaps. 8 and 9). Films made for these markets, however, follow the same principle. They must be worth the cost, either in revenue or in result. In other words, if the film is designed to solicit funds for an AIDS foundation, answer questions about crime, or persuade people to vote for a candidate, it must achieve these goals.

Fortunately, because the documentary business does not generally engage in salary wars, documentary films are a good deal cheaper to produce than the Hollywood film. Thus, although concessions must be made in terms of expensive movie magic and special effects, there is ample opportunity for good drama and storytelling. Furthermore, the documentary audience is on the rise. People want to see these films, and the markets for them are only increasing. Because documentary films are relatively inexpensive, many more documentary films can be made than for the theatrical market. In the past, one of the biggest film producers was the U.S. government. But with the proliferation of cable TV, there is a wonderfully healthy market for documentaries.

Art Films.   The last chapter in this book covers the "art" or experimental film. Unfortunately, for the health of the film medium, up until relatively recently there has been no stable market for the experimental or art film in this country, other than films festivals and the rapidly disappearing "art" movie house. But this is unquestionably changing. We now have new markets for music videos, Internet films, and gaming. The expansion of media studies programs provides a wonderful arena in which art films can be both studied and created. In the past, art films usually made very little money and needed to be produced on a shoestring budget, but developments in technology are rapidly revolutionizing the process of putting a film together. Ultimately, this is a welcome shift because the art film helps the film medium develop as an art form. I spend some time on this topic in chapter 10.

Be Keenly Aware of Your Audience

Whether you are making art films, documentary films, or theatrical films, you need to know whom you are writing for. In the next few chapters, I provide information on screenplay format, selling screenplays, and dramatic form. But there is other information you need to find out for yourself. Consider the following questions at some point in your writing process:

What Kinds of Films Are Being Made? What Kinds of Stories Are Being Told? This does not mean you need to follow a science fiction or spy thriller craze. The best advice is still to follow your own interests and instincts. But you should be aware of trends because this awareness gives you more information about how to structure and market your film. The answers will not solve everything, but they may help you select a workable idea and discard those ideas that do not have much chance of being made. For example, for the past 10 years or more, it has been very difficult to get Westerns made—not impossible, just difficult.

Who Makes up Your Target Audience? Are you writing for children, teens, young adults, or a general audience? Study your target audience. What appeals to them and what turns them off? What kind of language will you use in your shot descriptions and dialogue? Should it be simplified or sophisticated? Will you need a lot of action to keep your audience's attention or can emotional conflicts sustain interest?

Who Might Buy or Option Your Screenplay? Who are the producers or investors who might get involved in your project? What are they like? What do they tend to produce? This will also give you an idea about the language you use in your writing and the structure you provide.

Learn to Be Comfortable With Inconsistency and Conflict

Writing for the film medium will engage you in a maze of quirks and conflicts. The most frustrating of these conflicts is the one between retaining your integrity as a writer/creator and becoming a collaborator in the making of a film. Do not lose sight of your initial ideas in creating, but in working through your screenplay, especially in revision, try not to hold on too dearly to your ideas or words.

Another struggle involves making choices. At what point do you want to relinquish dearly held beliefs about your craft and the results of some very difficult creative work to get your screenplay sold? Sex, violence, and special effects wizardry work very well in some screenplays, but are highly inappropriate for others. Yet you may be prevailed on to include elements in your story that are clearly wrong for it. What do you do and how will you handle it?

The preceding guidelines are practical and general in nature. A more difficult concept to grasp is the unique quality of writing a story that will be seen and heard instead of one that will only be read. The following sections provide information on how to conceive of writing for the screen with this essential difference in mind.

SCREENWRITING VERSUS LITERARY WRITING

When we think of "creative" writing or literary writing, most people think of poetry, novels, or short stories. It is well worth taking a moment to explore the important distinctions between writing for films and writing other forms of literature.

First, the obvious: Film is a visual medium, whereas screenplay is a print medium. How are the film and print media similar and how are these different? A good way to answer this question is to look at the difference between a novel and a film. Consider the following passage from Larry McMurtry's (1966) novel, *The Last Picture Show*.

```
When Sonny kissed Mrs. Popper outside the Legion
Hall it seemed to him that a whole spectrum of
delicious experience lay suddenly within his
grasp. No kisses had ever been so exciting and so
full of promise, neither for him nor for Ruth. She
felt as if she were finally about to discover
something she had somehow missed discovering
twenty years before. Neither of them foresaw any
great difficulties, just the minor difficulty of
keeping it all secret. (p. 127)
```

This passage contains some elements that are fairly typical of a traditional novel. The verbs are in past tense as McMurtry narrates what is going on between Sonny and Ruth Popper. McMurtry avails himself of the novelist's prerogative of revealing what his characters are thinking about and what went on earlier and in intervening scenes. As such, the narrator is all knowing or omniscient; he has access to thoughts and feelings, the past and the future. McMurtry's narrator describes things that someone simply watching the interaction between Sonny and Ruth would probably never know. Moreover, the narrator gets inside the minds of both his characters so that we see the points of view of both Sonny and Ruth.

In films, unless there is explanatory narrative or voice-over, we know *only* what the characters tell us and what we see. Everything we learn about the character must be conveyed to us by the characters in present tense, present time action.

The novelist can also cover a lot of ground very quickly by summarizing the action or what the characters said or thought, whereas the screenwriter and film maker cannot. For example,

```
When Sonny and Ruth met again, the Tuesday after
the dance, they both expected things to be simple
and wonderful, and they were both disappointed.
(p. 128)
```

Here, McMurtry covers in one sentence what it might take a film a 10-minute (or longer) sequence to cover.

The Last Picture Show also provides an example of how a novel can be translated for the screen. McMurtry wrote both the novel and the screenplay, so one could argue that the film—which closely follows the screenplay—may be closer to what the original author might have envisioned than if the screenplay had been adapted by another writer. Here is a scene that occurs a few pages after the passage cited previously.

```
The wallpaper in the bedroom was light green, and
blotched in places. It was the bedroom where Ruth
and Herman had spent virtually all their married
nights: on one wall there was a plaque Herman had
been given for taking a troop of Boy Scouts to the
National Jubilee. Two or three copies of High
School Athletics lay on the bedside table.
   "Are you sure he won't come?" Sonny asked.
The room seemed full of the coach.
   "You know he won't," Ruth said. "He's just
starting basketball practice." (p. 129)
```

Here is the same scene from the screenplay (McMurtry & Bogdanovich, 1998–1999).

```
INT. POPPER BEDROOM - DAY

On one wall is a plaque from the Boy Scouts
National Jubilee; some copies of High School
Athletics lay on the bedside table. Ruth and
Sonny enter awkwardly.

                    SONNY
          You sure he won't come?

                    RUTH
          You know he won't—he's just
          starting basketball practice.
```

In the film, the copies of *High School Athletics* are on the table, but they are barely noticeable because the camera pans (moves) off them very quickly to record the action between the two characters in the scene. So although the scene remains essentially the same in both novel and screenplay, different elements are highlighted (history and setting in the novel vs. dialogue in the screenplay). These become the focus of our attention.

In the novel, the words must create the mood of the scene; thus, the novel tends to be very descriptive, much more than a screenplay would. However, the mood in the film is created by the interpretation by the actors, the direction, the lighting, the set, the pacing, and so on. The only elements that can be specified in the screenplay are the dialogue and a brief description of the scene and action. Consequently, the screenwriter needs to get the most out of these passages, carefully selecting what to say in dialogue and description so that it is both explicit and evocative.

Writing for the Eye and Ear

In significant ways, the novelist or fiction writer has a great deal more freedom than the screenwriter. As we have seen with McMurtry, the fiction writer can choose to include interior monologue; he can summarize thoughts and feelings of the characters and describe past and future events; he can set a tone (angry, objective, cynical) and inject his own point of view much more fully than a screenwriter mostly because he has more time and space to sketch out his plot. He is freer to use language as he would like. By the same token, he is expected to do more in prose fiction, adding more linguistic and stylistic complexity by working the language, extending the characterization in ways that are much more explicit, detailed, or descriptive and complicating the plot line or lines by adding subplots, characters, and actions. This is not to say that screenplays are not highly complex; in fact, the good ones are. But generically the screenplay must do its work within more stringent limitations.

The conventional screenplay is about 120 pages long. Novels range from a few hundred pages to nearly 1,000. Novels are divided up into chapters, which can be relatively short or interminably long; these chapters may include a great deal of action or they may be entirely descriptive without a line of dialogue. By contrast, screenplays are divided up into scenes. These scenes describe only what we are to see on the screen; they provide no history, summary, or character's thoughts or opinions. They usually include dialogue. In other words, the message in a screenplay must be conveyed through a description of the **image** and a transcription of the **soundtrack** (mostly dialogue and sound effects). In addition, the novelist can describe a range of other elements, including what he thinks, what the characters think and feel, and so on.

Reading and Reading for Viewing

Consider, too, the differences between watching a film and reading a book. In general, reading is a private matter. We can read at our own speed in our own time. Usually a person does not read a book from cover to cover in a single sitting. She can stop whenever she wants, later picking the book up again at the same place, or she can reread passages she has read earlier or skip sections, moving to read what happens at the end of the book. Although the VCR or DVD can enable a film viewer to do essentially the same thing, very few people really bother to view films this way. Further, many film audiences generally watch films in public—at movie theaters—with others who often laugh, complain, gasp, and cry together. In theater situations, film goers watch a film in one sitting, usually lasting from 90 minutes to 2 hours. They cannot go back to review something they missed. If something is confusing, they tend to ask their neighbor or hope it will somehow be resolved in the course of the film. The screenplay must take this into account by being as clear as possible.

The consequences of these differences are important. First, dramatic tension becomes much more crucial in the success of a screenplay than in the success of a novel. Although novels may be expensive to purchase, ranging in price from $1 at a garage sale to $20 or $25 in the bookstores, the reader *has* something in her hands when she reads. She owns the book, can read it whenever she likes, can lend it to others, and can come back to it again and again. Similarly, if she borrows the book from a library, she can return to it whenever she wants until it is due. Film audiences pay upward to $9 or $10 for 2 hours in a theater; in general, they expect to be entertained; many viewers go to "escape." They take nothing home with them except the memory of an interlude in another world created by the cinema (and perhaps an upset stomach from the overpriced junk food).

An unwritten maxim in the film business is that any audience will sit for 20 minutes waiting for something to happen, waiting for the conflict to develop, or waiting for the plot to be clarified. After that, they become annoyed; many leave and most feel disgruntled and cheated. In other words, you have lost them. Novelists do not work with that 20-minute constraint.

Second, if film viewers learn about the characters and story as it is unfolding and have no recourse to go back and recheck things as readers do, the characters in films need to be clearly and sharply defined, especially in their roles as protagonists and antagonists; the tension must build to a climax at a specific point, usually toward the end of a film (although there are "mini-climaxes" throughout), and the resolution has to follow. Although films vary widely, there is a more rigid structure—a more conventional format—that needs to be adhered to both because of the nature of the film and of audience expectations. In other words, the dramatic structure of screenplays is determined, at least in important part, by a combination of convention and pragmatics.

There are a few other ramifications. Novels can have many more characters and plot turns than films because readers do not need to keep track of them all. They can go back and remind themselves about Holden Caufield's family or the relatives and acquaintances of a character in a Dostoyevsky novel. Thus, another maxim for the film writer: **Use only as many characters as you absolutely need to carry the plot; the fewer, the better.**

Visualizing

One of the biggest challenges for the novice screenwriter is to write so that the reader cannot help but get a clear picture. Figuratively speaking, you must paint your scenes using words. How does a writer do this? What does it mean to write visually? In general, it means to use language that is so concrete and so specific that the reader sees exactly what might be on the screen. It means describing as precisely and clearly as possible the following elements:

- Characters (e.g., age 18, blond hair, blue eyes, unshaven)
- Setting and locations (outside, inside, in a black sports car, in an alpine forest)

- Time of day (evening, broad daylight, night)
- Context (outside a stadium before a baseball game, in a working garbage dump)
- Mood or atmosphere (dark, eerie, electric)
- Elements in scene (strong, blustery wind, a small revolver, a red dress on the couch)
- Actions (reaches up tentatively to caress a cheek, runs hard to catch a train)

Dialogue is a bit easier; by the nature of the screenplay, writers must be specific about what is said. Even so, take care not to paraphrase or summarize conversations. Description of sounds and sound effects should include what we are to hear, nothing more. Visuals should include what we are to see, nothing less. **In other words (another maxim), you must write to create an explicit image so that it appears clearly in the mind's eye and ear.**

THE ROAD TO SUCCESS

As we have seen, the screenplay must accomplish a lot of quite different tasks. It must be well enough written (creative, dramatic, exciting, well crafted) not only to engage a reader, but to move him—to stimulate his emotions and intellect. It must be marketable enough to entice an investor to sink a lot of money into a project that is based on it. In practical terms, a screenplay must serve as a guide for the film makers, providing dialogue and action as well as indicating location, time of day, production requirements, and, in general terms, shot setups. These dissimilar functions make the screenplay something that both borrows from many other writing genres (poetry, short fiction, novels, essays) and is, itself, a very unique genre.

Becoming a successful screenwriter is a combination of luck, connections, and knowing what you are doing. You need to make your connections and get lucky on your own. But you can do quite a bit toward knowing what you are doing. Perhaps the most significant thing this book can provide is some thorough instruction on screenplay format (see chap. 4) and information about dramatic form and ways of talking about films (chaps. 2 and 3). The rest is up to you.

APPLICATIONS AND EXERCISES

1. *Set aside time to write.*
   Even if you have not started a screenplay yet, find a little time each day—

preferably the same time—that is exclusively reserved to work on writing. Stick to it.

2. *Set realistic expectations.*

   Assume that there are days when you will not get much—if any—actual writing done. Assume that for every good page you write, you will throw away many more. You will have setbacks and delays, and you will have days when it seems effortless. Set a deadline or deadlines for yourself that you can realistically meet. Honor those "thinking" days, in which you still were at work but for which there is no tangible evidence.

3. *Join a screenwriting group.*

   Because film is such a collaborative enterprise and because getting useful feedback is so valuable for all writers, from the least experienced to the most, meeting regularly with like-minded writers working on similar projects can be extraordinary productive.

   A writing group provides moral as well as critical support. Writing can be a lonely and humbling experience. Writer's block occurs with even the best of writers. Meeting with a group of people you respect and who respect you can be beneficial in a number of areas, providing moral support, story suggestions, and marketing ideas.

   For those of you who have had less than positive experiences working in groups, there are a number of guidelines that can be followed that may make working with others a much happier experience:

   a) Work with a small group—from three to five persons.

   b) Meet at regular intervals (once a week, twice a month, once a month).

   c) Before you get to work, discuss with each other your background and goals. Try to decide whether your interests are compatible. Note: It is often preferable to work with people whose background and experiences are different from yours because they add different perspectives, but the writers in the group must be familiar with and respect the goals of all group members. For example, a writer working on theatrical screenplays for the standard commercial market may have trouble working with a writer who considers writing for the theatrical market to be "selling out" and who insists that the art or experimental or "independent" film is the only genuine cinematic form.

   d) As a group, decide on some ground rules for reading each other's work. For example, in my screenwriting classes, we observed the following rules, drawn in part from the Robert Brooke et al. (1994) *Small Groups in Writing Workshops*—at least for the first couple of meetings:

- No one will be subjected to negative criticism of his or her writing.
- No one will be forced to use the advice and response of the small group.
- The writer who is presenting should run the session. Writers should prepare three or four questions you want the group to address.
- Reviewers should use only "I" statements in their comments ("I didn't understand this part," "I'm confused here," "I lost track of the conflict here," or "I'm not sure who the antagonist was"). Here are some helpful questions for reviewers:
    — What did/will you remember the most and why?
    — What struck you the most forcefully and why?
    — What did you like the best and why?
- Writers should *listen* to all responses before they respond (and they need not respond at all).
- At the end of the workshop, each group member should jot down what was helpful to him or her and what was unhelpful. Share these responses with each other before the next group meeting.

e) Read professional screenplays, novels, and short stories as well as see films so these can be discussed as well.

f) Pause from time to time (at the end of each meeting or every few meetings) to evaluate the process. How are things going? Are writers getting what they want or need from the process? How can things be changed to better accommodate the needs of individuals or the group?

4. *Take a course at a local community college or art school.*
Although you have much less control over the other writers you work with, courses can be great refreshers: for ideas and feedback. These courses can keep you writing or jump start your writing when you get stalled. They are also a good way to find others who may later want to join a small group.

SUGGESTED READING

Brooke, R. (1994). *Small groups in writing workshops: Invitations to a writer's life.* NCTE.

Dunne, J. G. (1997). *Monster: Living off the big screen.* New York: Random House.

Goldman, W. (1989). *Adventures in the screen trade.* New York: Warner Books.

McMurtry, L. (1966). *The last picture show.* New York: Touchstone.

McMurtry, L., & Bogdanovich, P. (1998–1999, Winter). *The last picture show* screenplay. *Scenario: The Magazine of Screenwriting Art*, pp. 59–97.

Question: What advice do you have for young writing students?

Pierson: Two things. One is to have a story to tell that's worth telling. That really requires doing something besides going to high school and college. It requires maybe a couple of failed marriages and a short jail term or something like that, so that they've got something under their belt that gives them something worth telling to the world. And then beyond that, they must learn how to tell that story.

—Frank Pierson (writer of *Dog Day Afternoon* and *Presumed Innocent*), interviewed for wga.org by Alan Waldman. http://www.wga.org/craft/interviews/Pierson.html

The Film Drama

The art of telling a good story is not necessarily an art that can be taught. That said, there *is* a considerable amount to learn about what makes a story work. Being able to recognize the components of good drama, both in one's own writing and in the writing of others, is an extremely important part of learning the craft. This chapter explores what constitutes good drama, focusing particular attention on plot, conflict, and premise.

The heyday of classical Greek civilization was a period rich in the arts, particularly the poetic arts, including drama. One of the best-known theorists of the day was Aristotle (384–322 B.C.), who took the time to analyze what good drama is and how it works; he chronicled his analysis in the *Poetics*. Because many of his discoveries and precepts are directly applicable to drama today, and to a large extent influence how we perceive good drama, it is quite useful to be familiar with what he had to say. One of the best ways to do this is to get hold of a copy of the *Poetics* and read it. It is accessible and insightful for the modern reader and should be part of the necessary education of a writer for any kind of drama. The following discussion draws on much of what Aristotle set forth and applies it directly to writing for the screen.

WHAT IS A GOOD IDEA?

There are good ideas everywhere: in your life, in the lives of people you know, in newspapers, magazines, talk shows, short stories, novels, poems, myths and legends, jokes, even dreams. Some people argue that good ideas are "in the air," just waiting for someone creative to come along and make them their own. Other people maintain that good ideas are very hard to come by; everything good has already been done, and there is nothing new under the sun. Although it is probably true that there are very few good ideas that are completely original, there are ways of taking an idea, concept, or story and handling the material in original ways. So while a love story between a living person and a ghost, a war story where a group of soldiers fights against overwhelming odds, a story about child abduction, or a falsely convicted prisoner on death row may not be new ideas, your way of handling them could be. And should be.

New writers may have the impulse to pursue an idea—perhaps taken from real life—that is so unusual and original as to not to be believed. About this, Aristotle has useful advice. In Book 24 of the *Poetics*, he maintains that good dramatists "prefer probable impossibilities to improbable possibilities." What he means is that we should avoid the outrageous—even though it may occur in real life—and stick to what is believable to an audience, regardless of whether it could ever happen. Art should represent life, but this is a representation, not necessarily an accurate portrayal. If anything, this representation should be more intense than a real experience, even more beautiful, so the experience of watching the film is utterly memorable.

Aristotle also argues that good ideas must have a certain magnitude. Good ideas deal with events that can evoke strong emotions or passions in the viewer. They do not necessarily need to involve "big stories" (earthquake, war, epidemic). Even small stories (a boy and his dog, a love affair between a man and a married woman, a woman returning to visit her mother who abandoned her at birth) can have magnitude when they deal with strong feelings.

Good ideas in film writing are ones that lend themselves to the medium of film. A good idea is highly visual and blends image with sound in ways unlike a novel or a painting; it is one that involves action that can be seen on screen. This action should be nested in a context that is visually arresting. It may involve an evocative setting: an old mansion, the Arabian Desert, the Irish countryside, Harlem in the 1930s. It may involve a highly charged situation: a man awaiting execution for a crime in a cellblock of unusual characters. Good ideas involve people, places, and things that are not static; there must be strong interactions; *something must happen.*

A good idea will engage your targeted audience. If your goal is to write for a general audience, you need to understand the tastes of that audience and come to terms with what will induce a film-going public to spend $10+ for a ticket to see the film or buy a DVD for even more.

Last but not least, a good idea is one that enables you to tease out of it a good story. We spend the bulk of this chapter discussing the components of a good story.

WHAT IS A GOOD STORY?

There is considerable debate about which is more important in a good drama: character or plot. I subscribe to Aristotle's theory that character is revealed through *action*, that plot is the essence of good drama, and that character comes second. You cannot know a character—even the best, most engaging of characters—unless you see him interact with the world and with others. Jake Gittes, the lead character in *Chinatown*, is a very engaging character. Played by Jack Nicholson in the film, he is a dapper private detective; he is cynical, good looking, proud, and clever, and he is clearly good at what he does. But everything we know about him comes from seeing him in action. He takes on City Hall, the police, Evelyn Mulwray (played by Faye Dunaway), and assorted other characters, and it is through these interactions, and only through these interactions, that we are able to understand Gittes and empathize with him. Only in action does he reveal himself and become human.

The very first scene in *Chinatown* is a typical example. Curly, one of Gittes' clients, is reacting to photographs that Gittes has taken of his wife having a torrid affair with another man. Curly, angry that he has been cuckolded, slams his fist against the wall and begins to sob, sliding along the window and biting into the blinds in anguish. Gittes pours him a glass of cheap scotch that he takes from his well-stocked liquor stash and then says,

> GITTES
> All right, enough is enough
> —you can't eat the Venetian
> blinds, Curly. I just had 'em
> installed on Wednesday.

Then Gittes tries to console Curly, clearly wanting him to calm down and get out of the office. As they are leaving, Curly indicates he cannot pay Gittes immediately, to which Gittes replies,

```
            GITTES
    I don't want your last dime.
    What kind of guy do you think
    I am?
```

Then he ushers Curly out of the office. In this short scene, we have learned a considerable amount about Gittes. He is tough and calculating; his sensitivity is tempered with a pragmatism that will make him a formidable protagonist in the scenes to come. And now Curly owes him a favor. In other words, Gittes' character is revealed through his actions, which include what he does and what he says.

Action is especially important in a film's screenplay where we are not privy to what goes on inside a character's mind; we only know what he is thinking or who he is by descriptions of what he does and by reading what he says. Ultimately, however, action is useless unless the screenplay has some organizing principle. The chief element of that organizing principle is the premise.

Premise

The difference between a good idea and a good story is that a good story always has a premise. A premise is a difficult concept because—much like a thesis in expository writing—it means different things to different people. Furthermore, in some of the best movies, a premise is difficult to articulate because it requires an answer to the following question: What's the point? Good films prove or illustrate their points without stating their premise or thesis outright.

One way to simplify this notion of a premise is to look at the screenplay as an argument. When a writer sets out to write an editorial or an essay, she has something she wants to get across to an audience. It may be that she wants to persuade her readers that affirmative action is a good thing, that doctors who assist patients to commit suicide are menaces to society, or that one political candidate is better than another. Crucial to the success of her essay is the degree to which her intended readers already agree or disagree with her thesis or premise. If most of the people who read her article agree, then there is little point in making the argument. The essay is only valuable if she is working to persuade an audience who either does not agree or who has no opinion (or

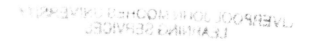

who does not care). Through her essay, she will attempt to make them agree or care. In other words, a good essay "does" something. It has a function; there is a reason for its existence.

The same principles apply to a screenplay. A screenwriter is trying to get across something to his audience that his intended viewers may or may not agree with, may not understand well, or may not be able to articulate. The premise may come in the form of an insight that will help a viewer see a side of an issue or personal dilemma he has never experienced before or understand an aspect of the human condition in terms that make it more comprehensible. In other words, the audience must <u>learn</u> something through having seen the film.

Here again, Aristotle and his *Poetics* are of some help in understanding how drama works. The world we live in is a chaotic, often incomprehensible place. As human beings, we generally desire some kind of stability and security, but more often than not we find that stability lacking. Or if there is stability, it is largely temporary or illusory. But because we must live, make decisions, and select our paths through this chaos, we are always searching for some kind of truth about particular situations, human nature, or the world that will help us decide. Sometimes we find this truth in religion; sometimes we find it in discussing our problems, insights, or lives with others. But we also find it through the experience of drama, wherein we *live through* a character or characters and, as observers of their struggles, we can potentially come to a new insight that will help us make sense.

This insight almost always arises from the climax of the film—the moment of catharsis when the main character comes to some realization about her life. This is also the moment where, in successful drama, we feel the most attuned to the emotions of the character. In fact we have those same emotions—fear, anger, love, release—except that we experience them vicariously. It is this vicariousness that helps us see more clearly, that helps to crystallize the truth that the main character has uncovered, precisely because we do not have to live through it ourselves; we can be more objective because we can eventually detach ourselves from the strong feelings.

As anyone who has undergone a traumatic event knows, it is often confusing and baffling in its complexity. We are too involved in it to have any insight about it. However, seeing someone else go through an experience (and sharing this vicariously) gives us both the experience and the objective distance to understand that experience more clearly and gain valuable perspective that helps us learn from it.

A good way to get a feel for how premises work is to try to locate them in films we see. To do this easily, we should make some distinctions. First, the premise should not be confused with the subject matter or theme. For example, *Out of Africa*, a film written by Kurt Luedtke and based loosely on the stories of Isak Dineson, tells of the trials and tribulations of a Danish woman, Karen, who goes to Africa and tries to raise coffee on her plantation. She falls in love, loses her plantation, and eventually must return to Denmark. The *subject matter* of the film is the adventures of a Danish woman in Africa.

Furthermore, there are numerous important *themes* that are embodied in the conflicts that the film portrays: the problematic British relations with the native Africans, the law of the wild versus the rule of civilization, and propriety versus spontaneity. Both the theme(s) and subject matter of a film are important, both to the story and the film as a whole, but they are not necessarily premises.

So where do we look for the premise? One way to find the premise is to ask yourself what the main character learns from the experience she has gone through. Karen learns something very important about control. She has lived a life where she has tried to tame the African landscape, the natives, and her lovers. At the end of the film, she comes not merely to accept the lack of control all humans have over life, but to value—even celebrate—it. This is the point and premise of the film. In this case, the premise also pulls together the themes, and, consequently, theme and premise may seem inseparable.

In the case of *The Piano*, a film by Jane Campion, theme and premise are more distinct. The main character, Ada, travels with her young daughter to the outback of 19th-century New Zealand to marry a man she has never met. She fights the life that has been mapped out for her by others—primarily men—by an incredible strength of will, manifested in one respect by her refusal to speak. There are recurring themes, much like in *Out of Africa*, about the conflict between the "civilized," Anglo world and its native counterpart. There are also themes involving the distinctions between silence and communication. But the premise of the film revolves around Ada. The woman she was at the beginning of the film is not the same woman she is at the end. She *learns* something; she changes. She falls in love and takes steps to change her life. We could say that she has learned both the value of her own passion and, in her own vulnerability, she finds her strength and her voice.

Clearly, other viewers will find other messages or premises in these pieces, and this demonstrates the richness of the work. Whatever premise one comes up with, however, its key component is character change, and that change is based on the character learning something or coming to some insight about life. As the character finds that insight, we do too.

Determining the premise for your own work is not always easy, nor does it necessarily have to be the first thing you decide on as you set out to write. In fact, many screenplays begin with an intriguing image, an interesting scene, or a character that probably should be developed before you have determined a premise. Ultimately, however, the best films have premises, and you need to know what that premise is as you structure your work.

Making the Premise Work for You.   Many of the problems writers have with screenplays have to do with the lack of a coherent premise. For example, a student in my graduate class, Tracie Ponder, wrote a potentially powerful screenplay about a young black man, Darryl, living in a housing project in Chicago who was getting ready to attend college at an Ivy League school. The first part of her story dealt with the trauma of Darryl's girlfriend dying suddenly and Darryl's turmoil at leaving his life in the projects. The second part covered some of his struggles with racism at college.

Tracie was troubled because she could not figure out how to end the screenplay. When we searched for the premise, we discovered there were two separate points she wanted to get across—one arising from Darryl's conflicts at home and the other stemming from his conflicts at college. The screenplay seemed like two stories in one, and it was difficult to tie both stories together with one climax and one ending. Although both stories showed promise, Tracie decided to cut the second half and focus on Darryl's traumatic departure from his neighborhood; the result was a stronger, more coherent screenplay, with a single antagonist, a single climax, and a single premise.

Universality

For a story to be effective as a dramatic experience, it should also express universal experience in some important way. What is universal experience? Regardless of differences in personal wealth, social class, race or ethnicity, gender, health, and so on, we all, as human beings, experience in our lives some degree of physical and emotional pain, joy, heartbreak, jealousy, romantic love, family love, self-doubt, confidence, confusions, ambivalence, and so on. Some people have more of one kind of experience than another. For example, some people, notably people of color, suffer the consequences of racism more than others do; they may feel excluded and ostracized in ways that Whites do not or cannot feel. But most of us know what it feels like to be left out or in some way stigmatized, and this enables us to empathize. If we cannot empathize, we are usually incapable of understanding. If we cannot identify with the characters in the film on a personal level or if the story is so improbable that we feel removed from it, the drama will not work, no matter how action-packed the film is.

Aristotle points out that "poetry tends to express the universal, history the particular" (Book 9). This is a useful distinction. History tells us what really happened, regardless of whether we can feel compassion or whether it engages us. Poetry (and Aristotle includes drama within this) expresses things we can understand at both an emotional and intellectual level—things that can truly engage us.

This does not mean, however, that your characters must represent Everyman or Everywoman. Certainly there have been successful films about idiosyncratic people. For example, Bill Harris, the lead character (played by Bill Murray) of *Lost in Translation*, is a fairly unusual guy: he is an aging actor contracted to do a liquor commercial in Japan. But his character, as revealed through the story, has a commonality—he is a person who feels at odds with his environment—that many members of the audience can both identify and empathize with.

PLOT

Plot has to do with the selection and structuring of the incidents or scenes and should, according to Aristotle, be constructed so that the hearer of the tale will "thrill with horror and melt with pity." In other words, the audience must be moved. To achieve this, good drama consists of several fairly constant dramatic (and sometimes overlapping) components:

1. Conflict
2. A point of attack
3. Foreshadowing
4. The locking of the conflict
5. Tension arising from the conflict that builds to a climax
6. A climax that leads to a resolution
7. A resolution or dénouement.

Let us explore each of these elements in detail.

Conflict

In real life, as in drama, conflict arises when one person wants something that puts her in opposition with the needs, desires, or goals of another person. Conflict can also arise between a person and a thing (a virus, volcano, alien), but these nonhuman elements frequently take on human characteristics. In other words, they tend to be personified.

For the sake of example, let us consider conflict between people. Let us say that you want to live in the country and your spouse wants to live in the city. The result is conflict. Either you resolve the conflict through negotiation (e.g., you compromise by agreeing to live in a place that is not quite in the city, but not quite in the country) or one of you capitulates. If neither of you gives in, the conflict continues and may even escalate depending on how important this issue is to each of you.

Although this could be a significant conflict for the people involved, it may or may not make for good drama. If it can be resolved through some minimal amount of negotiation, it is not a very good conflict; it will not make for the kind of powerful drama we are working toward here. But let us say that one spouse, the wife for example, gives in and then harbors a resentment for her husband that increases as time goes on. Then, let us say, that their life in the city infringes more and more on her sense of security and well-being (because of an incident or series of incidents involving crime, pollution, crowding, or expense), and her husband responds to her angst by ignoring her. Maybe she eventually files for divorce. The conflict has become more dramatic. If her husband becomes abusive and refuses to grant her the divorce on the grounds that she has been unfaithful to him (which she has not), she may even be driven—because she feels so trapped—to want to do him harm. Then we may have the makings for a good drama.

Let us look at another example. Suppose that a conscientious scientist wants to find the antidote to save the world from a deadly virus that is threatening to wipe out the entire population of a town on the West Coast. On one level, the conflict is between the scientist and the virus. The virus "wants" to kill, and the scientist wants to save. On a more human and, one could argue, more complex and interesting level, the conflict is between the scientist and his superior—an ambitious general wants to save the virus to use it as a chemical weapon. Both men have goals that are in direct opposition to one another. Both believe strongly—on moral and intellectual levels—about the rightness of their positions. There is conflict, and it is a strong one because there is a lot at stake for both men.

If, in his discussions with his superior, the scientist sees the rightness of the general's position and decides that preserving the virus is the correct course of action, the conflict disappears. There is no more dramatic tension; the story is over.

If, however, the scientist insists on his own position on moral grounds (because he is a highly moral person) and the general will not give in because he believes that *he* has the moral advantage—and there are lives and reputations at stake—then you have the conflict for a very good drama; in fact, you have the conflict for the film *Outbreak*.

Our everyday lives are filled with conflict—between loved ones, between people in the workplace, between the store clerk and customer, between parent and child, between teacher and student, between politicians, and between one ethnic group and another—that grow out of competing desires, needs, and aspirations. Some conflicts are easily resolved or have limited consequences, whereas others have much more at stake—lives, livelihoods, and well-being—and have no easy solution. The latter make for the best dramas because, with so much on the line, these are powerful conflicts.

Be Careful of Internal Conflict.   One of the biggest pitfalls for new screenwriters is portraying conflict that is largely internal. A man struggling to determine what to do with his midlife crisis, a woman who cannot decide whether to kill herself, a person going through culture shock but cannot talk to anyone about it—all these may have dramatic potential, but their struggle is very difficult to portray unless we see it played out with other people. One character should not be both the antagonist and protagonist of a film—in other words, be his own worst enemy. The battleground, then, is only in his head. If you find yourself in such a situation, you may have to do some serious rethinking about your conflict and your premise.

Powerful conflicts, then, emerge from characters who:

- have goals that are in direct opposition to the goals of other characters;
- strongly believe in their positions and are willing to fight for them;
- have personal attributes that make them strong opponents;
- have character traits, problems, and goals that are universal; and
- reveal themselves through action.

The following plot components are directly related to the conflict. They make your conflict, and thereby your story, work.

Point Of Attack

Films that begin slowly usually take time for *exposition*. Exposition is what provides the audience with groundwork to understand how the story came to be and what the motivations of the characters are. It typically includes:

- events that occurred previous to what we see on the screen,

- background on characters and setting, and
- character traits.

In the first four pages of *Schindler's List* by Steven Zaillian, we see the following: Jews from rural Poland getting off a train and lining up as their names are called out and their papers stamped; Oskar Schindler in a seedy hotel room, dressing meticulously in a silk tie with a gold swastika; and Schindler carefully watching high-ranking German officers as if they are prey, then carefully getting their attention by wining and dining them. Although we do not yet know how the two strands (Jews and Schindler) will intersect, we know they will simply by virtue of the cross-cutting in the opening scenes. We learn a lot about Schindler—that he is not rich, but that he is a hustler; we quickly identify where we are—Cracow, Poland, during World War II; and we bring to the scene what we already know about prewar Poland, about the roundup of Jews and their internment at concentration camps.

Although these exposition scenes are fraught with tension, exposition can also be unexciting if it serves merely to provide background and bring us up to date as to where we are. To avoid long, drawn-out exposition, attend first to your *point of attack*. A good point of attack is where the conflict begins or, at the very least, where it is revealed that something is at stake. Rather than engage characters in conversations that are entirely dedicated to getting across exposition, a writer is better off providing exposition as the conflict unfolds. That way a viewer learns what he needs to know to understand the characters and plot while becoming engaged in the story.

In *Deliverance*, the film opens with images of a beautiful, bucolic river. Then we hear an explosion from dynamiting at a construction site for a dam as Lewis (in voice-over) complains to his buddies, Bobby, Ed, and Drew, about the "rape" of the land and this beautiful river, the "last wild unfucked-up river in the South." We quickly learn they are about to take a trip down this river. This is the point of attack; it is the very beginning of a journey. We do not know much about the background of these characters or about the environment that they are entering, although writer Dickey does establish some conflict between Lewis and the others. But we soon learn as they embark on their trip. Note that the film does not begin at their homes; it does not provide flashbacks of Lewis' military background or Drew's family life. It begins right as the conflict begins and provides exposition as the conflict unfolds.

It is a good idea to begin your film with a crisis or a problem. In dramatic films, most audiences will be patient, waiting a relatively long time before the conflict begins; they expect things to move a bit slower. In action-adventure films, however, a strong point of attack is crucial. For example, six pages (or 6 minutes) into the screenplay for *The Fugitive* by Jeb Stuart, the lead character, Dr. Richard Kimble, returns home to find his wife dying of a vicious attack by an intruder. Major crisis. On the next page of the script, he is convicted of murder, and in the few pages that follow, he escapes from a prison bus. The man has a big, big problem, and he is on the run; there is hope and there is tension. The rest of the film is the manhunt for Kimble and his desperate attempt to elude the authorities and find the murderer of his wife. The point of attack is the murder because that is where all of Kimball's troubles begin. The film is launched by an exciting and violent scene that catapults us into the action.

Foreshadowing

Related to point of attack is *foreshadowing*. The first thing on the screen in *Outbreak* is the following title: "The single biggest threat to man's continued dominance on this planet is the virus—Dr. Joshua Lederberg, Nobel Laureate." Here the writer, before the conflict is fully developed, drops strong hints at trouble that will follow. In this case, the title portends that what will follow will be a battle between man and his greatest enemy, the virus.

The title is then followed by a tour-de-force title sequence in which we see a military unit blowing up a mercenary camp in Zaire, populated by very sick and dying inhabitants—including some Americans—followed by a long traveling shot through the research institute of the U.S. Department of Infectious Diseases. At the lab, the camera tracks through the research laboratory of "Biosafety Level 1," where an on-screen title lists the low-risk viruses, such as salmonella, pneumonia, and so on. The camera then tracks through "Biosafety Level 2," labeled moderate biohazard with viruses such as hepatitis, Lyme disease, and influenza. "Biosafety Level 3" is extreme biohazard with HIV, typhus, and anthrax. At each level, the personnel seem to be taking increasingly more precautions about how they handle equipment, how they are dressed, and how the rooms are accessed. Finally, worse than typhus and HIV are the viruses in "Biosafety Level 4." A title lists the Ebola, Lassa, and Hanta viruses and adds the title, "No Known Cures or Vaccines." Scientists in this section of the laboratory are covered top to bottom in protective suits. This lab has very high security.

This is a superb example of *foreshadowing*. We are provided with a clue that at least one of the antagonistic forces will probably be a virus with "No Known Cure or Vaccine." We know that some agent of the military is perfectly willing to destroy people to control the disease caused by the virus. We know that somehow monkeys will be involved, having seen numerous monkeys in and around the mercenary camp. And we know, by having seen the sick mercenaries and villagers, of the terrifying effects of the virus on the human body. We are primed for a potentially thrilling adventure.

Foreshadowing is a wonderful way to prepare your audience for what they are about to see. This and intriguing characters will keep the filmgoers not only in their seats, but sensitized to the volatile mood and threatening situation that will soon be developing as they watch.

As you work to create some foreshadowing, remember that foreshadowing should grow out of your story. It should be an essential part of it so that it does not seem superfluous or gratuitous. In *Outbreak*, for example, the traveling shot through the laboratory functioned both as a title sequence and to introduce the main characters, Sam (Dustin Hoffman) and Robby (Rene Russo), a recently divorced couple who snipe at one another as they work in the Biosafety Level 4 Lab.

Locking the Conflict

In the film *Deliverance* (novel and screenplay by James Dickey), four men from the suburbs take a weekend canoe trip down one of the last untamed rivers in the rural American South. As they begin their journey and conflict looms—through veiled threats from the local inhabitants, the potential danger of the river, the conflict among the four of them—the men consider the option of whether to continue on or quit, turn back, and go play golf. They opt to continue. But at a certain point in the film, there is no turning back. This is where the conflict is locked, and locking the conflict is an essential part of good screenplay structure. If the protagonist, or main character, can quit or bail out, then you do not have a strong conflict.

In *Deliverance*, although there is plenty of conflict in the first 20 minutes, the conflict is locked only when Lewis, one of the protagonists (played by Burt Reynolds), shoots one of the local men who sexually molested Bobby (Ned Beatty) and threatened Ed (Jon Voight). At this point, there is no way to back out; the men—both because of the kind of characters they are and because of the situation in which they find themselves—are embroiled in a problem that they must confront head on.

In *Chinatown*, the conflict is locked when Jake Gittes discovers he has been duped—that the woman he thought was Mrs. Mulwray (the woman who asked him to find out if her husband was cheating on her) is not Mrs. Mulwray at all. The real Mrs. Mulwray is now threatening to sue him. Because Gittes' pride is wounded (and we have been led to understand from earlier scenes that he puts a high value on his professionalism), he now has a personal *and* professional interest in this case and cannot let it go. This pits him against the corrupt officials in city government and wealthy real estate tycoons, not to mention Mrs. Mulwray. He has no option but to fight.

Green Card, a dramatic comedy by Peter Weir, starring Andie MacDowell and Gerard Depardieu, is about an American woman and a Frenchman in New York who marry for convenience. He marries her to obtain a Green Card, which will permit him to work legally in the United States, and she marries him so that she can lease a garden apartment that is only available to married couples. Early in the film, the conflict is primarily between Bronte (MacDowell) and Georges (Depardieu) because of the radical difference in their personalities. They manage to make it through the marriage ceremony and then go their separate ways. End of conflict. But when officials from the INS (Immigration) call up and demand to meet with them, the conflict reemerges and is locked. Bronte and Georges must work together to deceive the INS or lose what they each have desperately wanted, and they may even go to jail.

Getting the conflict locked fairly early in the film is essential for keeping your audience interested and involved in your story. If your characters are in a situation from which it is easy to walk away, then you need to work harder to put them in a corner.

Jumping ahead for a moment, notice again how important character is in locking the conflict. In the earlier examples, the personalities of the characters (established early in the films) are such that they cannot quit. In *Deliverance*, Lewis has killed a local man from a very tightly knit mountain community. The four outsiders must cover up the murder or face homicide charges, which would surely affect their comfortable lives in the suburbs that are so important to them. In *Chinatown*, Gittes prides himself on being too clever to allow himself to be duped. In *Green Card*, the garden apartment means everything to Bronte, and getting the Green Card means everything to Georges. Note that I say "means everything." In the best dramas, *the goal must be all important and all consuming to the characters.*

Note also that the characters with these strong goals are protagonists or main characters, and that the conflict is locked between them and the antagonist or antagonistic forces (see Protagonist, Antagonist in chap. 4). Important to locking the conflict is that the antagonist is equally committed to triumphing over the protagonist. In *Deliverance*, the local population does not like outsiders who they blame for threatening to destroy their homes and livelihood. In

Chinatown, power and millions of dollars are at stake for one of the real estate tycoons who happens to be Mrs. Mulwray's father, played by John Huston. In *Green Card*, the INS agents are completely dedicated to exposing Georges, who they feel is attempting to defraud the U.S. government.

Building Tension

This battle between opposites is also crucial in building tension. General McClintock (Donald Sutherland) is temperamentally the converse of Sam (Dustin Hoffman) in *Outbreak*, and he is just as—if not more—resourceful. In fact the tension arises from the fact that he is not only as talented, committed, and charismatic as Sam is, but the cards are still stacked in his favor and against Sam. McClintock is, after all, in charge of the U.S. armed forces. He has the ear of the President of the United States. He has resources, information, and power at his disposal, and he can conceivably use it to get rid of Sam at any given moment.

Or can he? What makes for the tension is while the opposition seems overwhelming and omnipotent, Sam has some resources in his own right. So as the pressure builds against Sam, Sam is also increasing the pressure on the general. *If you have constructed a good conflict, one in which the pressure on both the protagonist and antagonist increases as the story evolves, then you have the potential for an excellent tension build.*

Building tension can be likened to watching the fuse burn. The fuse is lit as the conflict begins (preferably at the beginning of a film); it is subsequently locked; the flame then works its way slowly and steadily toward the bomb as the audience squirms in their seats.

The Verdict provides us with another good example of tension build. Frank Galvin (Paul Newman) is an alcoholic lawyer who was nearly disbarred years before for jury tampering—a charge that was never proved. At the beginning of the film, he takes on a malpractice case that he thinks he can win. As the story progresses, we see Frank in a fight to win this case against overwhelming odds. Every time he seems to gain a small advantage, it is snatched away from him. In fact, the situation gets worse and worse. Finally, when we think it could not get any worse, it does, only more so. This film is a wonderful example of excellent tension build. Again, the lead character (Frank) faces overwhelming antagonistic forces (the best legal team in town, the Church, even at one point the people he is trying to help). But there is tension because Frank, despite his problem with alcohol, despite the fact that his legal skills are rusty and that he is on the verge of a total mental breakdown, is not without resources. He still has an excellent legal mind (he used to be highly regarded as a lawyer); he has a faithful friend, another lawyer who helps him; he is a good man at heart; and, perhaps most important, he wants desperately to win this case, for personal and professional reasons.

Climax

The entire film should build toward the climax, where the opposing forces, represented by protagonist and antagonist, meet for the final and decisive time. The climax, or *catharsis*, is the moment in the drama where the excitement and tension peaks and, as a consequence, it is the moment of learning, where the protagonist comes to some realization about the battle he has been waging. By virtue of this recognition—and only if the audience has in some way empathized with the protagonist—the film viewer should suddenly understand, in a substantive and profound sense, something about his life in particular and our lives in general.

In *The Poetics*, the term *catharsis* can be interpreted in several different ways, and these definitions can be instructive in thinking about the climax. First, a climax can be accompanied by a sense of *purgation*, which results if the drama can sufficiently intensify emotions of the character and audience through the rising conflict to bring them to an explosion point. At this point of release, we cry, laugh, and feel vindicated or relieved; then the feeling fades away or is expurgated. As such, the viewer is inoculated against the thing that caused the pity and fear because the danger or threat is tamed or domesticated.

Catharsis can also result in *purification*, in the sense of cleansing oneself of the passions and emotions stimulated by the conflict. The result is a kind of ritualizing or containment of experience that also tends to lead to a new comprehension of life or human nature. Related to both purgation and purification is the notion of *illumination*, wherein the viewer comes to some realization about what is happening, why it is happening, and how it is happening. These are the kinds of learning that are possible through the climax. Regardless of whether you ever use the terms *catharsis* or *purgation*, you should strive for illumination. Your audience should learn something, either intellectually (e.g., about racial injustice) or emotionally (e.g., about hatred or love, joy or sorrow).

Perhaps most important, the climax is where you have proved your premise. In *The Verdict*, the climax occurs at Frank's final day in court where he gives the closing argument of his life and wins his case over incredible odds.

His closing argument, as much about his own life as it is about the case, asks the jury to believe not in the convoluted machinations of lawyers and the high and mighty trappings of the laws and the courts, but in themselves and the sense of justice in their hearts—in the kind of victory that the little person can have against the powerful. The jurists do find that sense of justice, finding for Frank's client and against the powerful doctors and lawyers, illuminating the power of human compassion.

In *The Piano*, the climax occurs when Ada, having pushed her piano into the ocean from the boat in which she is riding, knots the rope attached to the piano around her leg so that she is pulled in with it as it plummets to the ocean depths—an apparent effort to commit suicide. But instead of choosing to go down with her piano, she suddenly chooses to live and fights her way back to the surface. One could say, then, that she purges herself of the emotions of victimization with which she has lived all her life, and if we have empathized with her, we do as well, at least temporarily. She discovers a different way of living, one that will eventually lead to her learning how to speak again.

Resolution or Denouement

After the release from tension that occurs at the climax, the resolution tends to allow the audience a moment to breathe. Sometimes—although not always—resolutions tie up loose ends. More often than not, however, they provide an opportunity for the audience to see the results of the climax. In *The Verdict* (the screenplay differs slightly), Frank is sitting in his office, refusing to take a call from his lover, Laura, who had betrayed him. He no longer needs her. In *The Piano*, the resolution shows Ada giving a piano lesson, playing with a prosthetic finger that George has fashioned for her. She is also learning to speak, which, one might argue, is symbolic of her return to the world of speech and speakers—a very powerful world. Key to the resolution is the principal character's sense of *recognition*; that is, we see that both Frank and Ada have recognized where they have been and have learned something indelible from the experience.

Graphing the Conflict

A graph is a useful way to consider tension build and filmic structure—useful both in analyzing films you see and films you write. Starting at the left side of the graph, plot the conflict or tension as you perceive it. One way to consider this is "excitement level," which is a fairly subjective analysis. A more telling and effective way might be to consider the degree of tension or conflict intensity at each point in the script or film. Figure 2.1 is a typical example.

Most films begin with a degree of tension, which is low only relative to the rest of the action. Foreshadowing and a strong point of attack, which both involve some level of tension, help interest the viewer and involve her fully from the opening frame. From that point on until the end of the film, there should be a consistent rising tension line that peaks at the climax (the highest point on the line) and drops slightly to a resolution at the end of the film. There should be no point in the film that is higher than the climax. If there is more tension after the climax, you may need to reconsider your climax—you have either identified it incorrectly or there is a problem with the drama at that point.

The line is almost never a straight diagonal line. As in the graph, there are dips in the tension—like resting points—where the energy and tension diminish temporarily, only to build back up again. In *Outbreak*, there is a moment of calm when Sam and his wife, Robbie, believe they have contained the virus. Moments later, they discover it has simply gone "airborne" or into a more destructive, dangerous phase. In *Thelma and Louise* (screenplay by Callie Khouri), the two female leads get into more and more trouble, but it is punctuated now and then by scenes that are both funny and poignant, and not as fraught with tension. Often highly dramatic pieces need this "rest" period to allow a relaxation in the tension so that it can rebuild at a higher level.

Moments of rest are especially important in comedy. Just as tension sustained nonstop has the unfortunate tendency to exhaust itself and the audi-

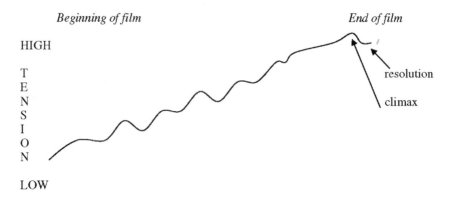

FIG. 2.1.   Tension line graph.

ence, thereby undermining its function, so a laugh-a-minute may result in a kind of tedium in which eventually nothing seems particularly funny. Energy needs time to rebuild so that it can return in greater force.

A graph can help pinpoint problems. Films can be episodic in ways that destroy the dramatic build and create problems for the film. For example, the film Mr. Holland's Opus portrays various periods (arranged chronologically) in the life of Mr. Holland (played by Richard Dreyfuss), a composer/music teacher at a high school. The plot seems to climax several times (at the end of each school year—1965, 1966, 1980, and 1995) before the film actually ends. Each year has a particular conflict, which is resolved at the end of the school year. In the next school year portrayed, the tension must build all over again, rising to a climax and then a resolution, which the film does successfully, many times. This kind of *episodic plot* runs the risk of distancing an already fidgety audience; the viewers may even prepare to leave, only to discover there is more—yet another story. Although it is true that the film has a consistent theme or motif—Mr. Holland's struggle between his own composing of music and the teaching of it—the theme permeates the film at a low level, especially when the composing is apparently altogether forgotten. Because the dramatic tension line seems to fall to the bottom of the graph and has to rebuild tension and often introduce new conflicts and new characters, the audience must reengage.

Figure 2.2 is how a graph of the conflict in Mr. Holland's Opus might look. Note the fairly low climax point, or rather a series of climaxes:

1965—Glenn Holland begins a new job and struggles to get students interested in music, particularly one student who seems to have no talent.

1966—Mr. Holland must help a student with no rhythm learn how to play the drums so he will not be forced to drop out of school.

1985—Mr. Holland falls in love with the leading lady (a student) in the school play, who asks him to run off with her to New York and be a composer while she tries to make it in musicals.

1995—Mr. Holland is laid off when the principal of the school eliminates all programs in the arts. His students, past and present, get together for one last concert.

Certainly the film is more complex than this, and with the presence of Richard Dreyfuss and the interplay between historical events and high school drama, it has some charm and appeal. However, if the audience feels the film has ended and it has not, this is a problem. Although the characters reunite in

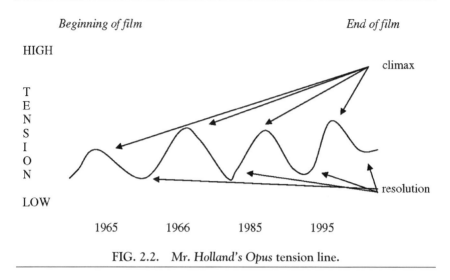

FIG. 2.2.   Mr. Holland's Opus tension line.

the last section of the film, we have pretty much lost the dramatic imperative that might enable us to reach catharsis.

Sometimes episodic films work well enough, especially when there are subplots or highly appealing characters, and the audience seems happy enough to sit through the episodes. But often the episodes move in different directions, sapping energy from the overall tension and diffusing the premise or message.

FILMIC STRUCTURE

I usually start with just a list of scenes that will illustrate the story I want to tell: "These are the things I want to do." Then I start to number them, and I say, "Jesus, this is supposed to be a two-hour movie. If I keep 50 scenes, each one is going to have to be no more than two pages long." And that's a lot of little, choppy scenes, so I start combining them, exploring ways to meld them together. With Lone Star, there are basically three plots, and I had to think of what those were, and when to reveal each thing in them.

(John Sayles, writer of *Lone Star,* interviewed by Tod Lippy for *Scenario: The Magazine of Screenwriting Art,* Summer 1996)

There are as many ways to structure a film as there are films. Films can be structured chronologically with events portrayed in the order they occur, films use flashback and flash forwards, films can portray the same events from the point of view of different characters, and so on. But there are also commonalities based on the nature of the film genre. A good story has a beginning, middle, and ending. For most films, this story must be told in less than 2 hours. You must get your audience's attention, embroil your viewers in the conflict, have tension rise to a climax, and move to resolution—all in a very limited amount of time. Here are some aspects of structure to consider.

Point Of View

Point of view is a cinematic concept that impacts both plot and character. Before you decide how you want to structure your film, it is often a good idea to settle on the point of view. Should we see the film through the protagonist's eyes, from the perspective of a minor character who plays the role of observer, from the vantage point of an all-knowing entity completely outside the piece, or a combination of all of these?

There are numerous advantages to each. The omniscient point of view gives us a glimpse into the lives of all the characters and may convey a seemingly more objective narrative. *The English Patient*, although you could hardly call the point of view omniscient, jumps around among the points of view of the patient, the nurse, and the soldier in its steady and slow revealing of the story. Films like *Thelma and Louise* or *The Green Mile* tend to focus on one or two characters, viewing what happens in the film through their eyes.

In a screenplay, point of view is created in a number of ways: through shot selection, narrative voice over, or focus on a particular character. In *Chinatown*, for example, the point of view belongs to Jake Gittes by virtue of the fact that Jake is in almost every scene. What we know about the characters and what we subsequently learn is through Jake's discovery. In other films, such as *American President*, the point of view is ostensibly more objective. We see scenes featuring, among others, the President (played by Michael Douglas), Sydney (played by Annette Bening), and Senator Rumsen (played by Richard Dreyfuss), with the stories of the characters coming together periodically.

In a novel, point of view can be much more complex, with the author's point of view mingling with the character's point of view, sometimes in the same paragraph. For example,

```
She took his hand again and they kissed standing
up. Neither of them really believed what she
```

> said: as they kissed both of them kept imagining
> the coach walking in. They were so conscious of
> him they hardly felt the kiss, but Ruth was
> determined to go on however dangerous it was, even
> if Herman did walk in. (*Last Picture Show*, p. 117)

Here, in the space of two sentences, we move from the narrator's point of view, into the thoughts of both characters, then into the mind of Ruth, a perfectly acceptable literary device.

In films as well as novels, point of view helps situate the viewer. Should she identify with Thelma and Louise or with Jake Gittes? Or should she get the sense that she is seeing things "as they are." Ultimately, she will never see things objectively. You, the writer, are in charge of the vision, whether it seems to be one character's perspective or an objective perspective.

Structural Commonalities

What follows is traditional wisdom for structuring your screenplay. Although the pattern is fairly conventional, it is important to learn because even structural variation plays off the traditional organization. Furthermore, it is a good idea to follow the rules before you break them because you will be a better, more versatile writer for it

1. *Begin at a crisis point, when there's something at stake for the characters.*
   Outbreak begins with a flare-up of the deadly Motaba virus in Africa. Sam, the main character, in the midst of a divorce, must fly to Africa to check out the situation. Although we do not yet know the extent or magnitude of the problem, we know something is wrong. The fuse has been lit. We just do not know how big the explosion will be.

2. *Reveal background information through action and conflict.*
   I have mentioned this frequently in this chapter, but it bears repeating. *Exposition* provides information about character personalities, relationships, and motivations. But exposition should never be the only reason for a scene or dialogue. To have characters reveal something to each other that they would have already known about—just so the reader or viewer will know it too—is a sure sign of an amateur writer. Furthermore, it can be dull and deadly boring. Instead, try to fill in background material at the same time as you develop the conflict.
   Out of Africa begins with an episode in which Karen, clearly seeing the failure of her romance with her lover, asks his brother, Bror, to marry her and move with her to Africa. In the course of this decision to marry, which is crucial to the plot, we learn about Karen's life—that she is get-

ting too old to be comfortable as an unmarried woman in her society, that she is impetuous and strong-willed, that she is relatively wealthy, and that Bror is an opportunist in his own right. Plot and exposition coincide.

3. *Scenes should be structured to build to a climax, and action within scenes should be structured to build to a climax as well.*

We have discussed in some detail how important the rising tension line is in moving toward a climax. Scenes are the building blocks of that cinematic structure; thus, how they are organized and selected is critical to establishing dramatically effective structure. The action within the scenes should also have a tension build and a climax because this is part of what holds an audience's attention. Take, for example, a seemingly uncomplicated scene from *Out of Africa*:

```
INT. DENYS'S ROOM - NIGHT


We hear Karen's VOICE: "Excuse me?" The door
opens; she enters. A bamboo filament light on a
desk. A gun rack, some sheet music by Schubert,
many books, a print of the Montgolfier balloon.


                    MAN'S VOICE (O.S.)
               My God, these people drink!


Karen whirls to see BERKELEY COLE, delicate,
gently drunk, leaning against the door, holding
the other tusk.


                    KAREN
               I'm sorry, I was just— you've
               caught me snooping.


                    BERKELEY
               He won't mind. That's a thing
               about Denys. He doesn't mind.


                    KAREN
               Are you Berkeley Cole?


                              (CONTINUED)
- - - - - - - - - - - page break - - - - - - - - - -
```

CONTINUED:

      BERKELEY
  Um.

      KAREN
  I brought the ivory with me—
  on the train.

      BERKELEY
  Thank you then. Are you
  taking your quinine?

      KAREN
  Yes.

She ought to leave, but her eyes linger on a small
framed photo of a woman.

      BERKELEY
  An actress. Mad for each
  other but her husband found
  them out. Denys had to kill
  him. It's the gallows if he
  ever goes back.

      KAREN
  No ...

      BERKELEY
  His sister actually.

      KAREN
   (laughs, then)
  He's got lovely books. Does
  he lend them?

Berkeley puts down the tusk, ambles over to the
couch.

          (CONTINUED)
 - - - - - - - - - - page break - - - - - - - - - - -

CONTINUED:

>   BERKELEY
> We had this friend, Hopworth
> He'd got a book from Denys and
> didn't get it back. I said,
> Denys, you wouldn't lose a
> friend for the sake of a silly
> book, would you? He said, No,
> but he has, hasn't he?
>   (then)
> Did you come out through London?

>   KAREN
> No, I came through Rome.

>   BERKELEY
> I thought you might have a
> newspaper.

>   KAREN
> No ... I'm sorry.

>   BERKELEY
> Nothing in them anyway.
>   (beat)
> I had a friend ... for the
> dances at Oxford. They're in
> June, along the river. She
> always had a new silk dress ...
> I think you're wearing
> her perfume.

Moment. Sympathetic, she holds her wrist close to
his cheek. SOUNDS of party; someone LAUGHS.

                                        (CONTINUED)
- - - - - - - - - - page break - - - - - - - - - -

CONTINUED:

> > > BERKELEY (CONT'D)
> > (quietly)
> No. It's very nice ... but not the same.

> > > FARAH (O.S.)
> Msabu.

ANGLE ADJUSTS to include Farah at the door,
judgmental.

> > > FARAH (CONT'D)
> We can go now.

This is the first meeting between Karen and Berkeley Cole (whom, she later tells Bror, she would not mind marrying). Their meeting begins awkwardly because Karen has entered the room uninvited, but this potential conflict between the two dissipates immediately because Berkeley does not mind at all (nor would Denys). Nonetheless, tension returns in the form of sexual tension, which culminates when Karen lets Berkeley smell her perfume. Then Farah arrives and quickly realizes that he has caught them in the midst of a flirtation. The tension rises, peaks, and rises again to a mini-climax, and before we are on to the next scene, something has happened.

Here is another, from *Shawshank Redemption*:

EXT. WOODED FIELD - DAY (1965)

A ROAD-GANG is pulling stumps, bogged down in mud.

> > > RED (V.O.)
> 'Course, Norton failed to mention
> to the press that "bare minimum of
> expense" is a fairly loose term.
> There are a hundred different ways
> to skim off the top. Men,
> materials, you name it. And, oh my
> Lord, how the money rolled in ...

> > > > (CONTINUED)
- - - - - - - - - - page break - - - - - - - - -

CONTINUED:

Norton strolls into view with NED GRIMMS at his side.

> NED
>
> This keeps up, you're gonna put me
> out of business! With this pool
> of slave labor you got, you can
> underbid any contractor in town.

> NORTON
>
> Ned, we're providing a valuable
> community service.

> NED
>
> That's fine for the papers, but I
> got a family to feed. The State
> don't pay my salary. Sam, we go
> back a long way. I need this new
> highway contract. I don't get it, I
> go under. That's a fact.
> (hands him a box)
> Now you just have some'a this fine
> pie my missus baked specially for
> you ... and you think about that.

Norton opens the box. Alongside the pie is an
envelope. He runs his thumb across the thick stack of
cash it contains.

IN THE BACKGROUND, a winch cable SNAPS and whips
through the air, damn near severing a man's leg. He
goes down, screaming in mud and blood, pinned by a
fallen tree stump. Men rush over to help him. Norton
barely takes notice.

(CONTINUED)
- - - - - - - - - - page break - - - - - - - - - -

```
CONTINUED:
                         NORTON
            Ned, I wouldn't worry too much over
            this contract. Seems to me I've
            already got my boys committed
            elsewhere. You be sure and thank
            Maisie for this fine pie.
```

Here, Ned, a road-building contractor, takes issue with Norton's policies (Norton is the prison warden). It rises to a kind of climax (where Ned pays Norton off) and resolution, punctuated by what is going on the background.

Not all scenes have a climax, but the best scenes do. They are, in many ways, mini-scenarios within the web of a larger drama. They also have rising tension and often a short resolution, helping to create the nice step-like structure we see on the graph: tension rises to a climax, releases, and then rises again in the following scene. Tension within scenes keeps us engaged and interested.

4. *The climax occurs near the end of the film; it should be single in issue and importance.*

    Ideally, all the elements of the film should build toward a single finale for the film to maintain its sense of an organic whole. What is an "organic whole" in drama? It is where all elements seem naturally and logically interconnected and where each element contributes either directly or indirectly to the premise. Nothing is extraneous or beside the point. There is one point and one central climax. This is not easy to achieve; this is part of the screenwriter's craft. We will consider this more fully in chapter 5.

5. *The resolution should be short and relatively tranquil.*

    It should be a moment of calm, devoid of tension. If there is any tension in it at all, the audience may think that the drama is not finished or may think that you are alluding, perhaps inadvertently, to the possibility of a sequel.

The Three Unities versus Leaps in Time and Space

One of the elements of drama that Aristotle describes in his *Poetics* is "the three unities": unity of *action* (a main action with few subplots), unity of *place* (one location), and unity of *time* (no jumping ahead or backward in time). In classical and neoclassical drama, the best plays adhered to these unities, rarely deviating. The unity of action—because action is the heart of a drama—is still very fundamental. If some element does not link up to the whole, it probably does not belong in your screenplay. Avoid "red herrings"—story elements that lead the viewers off-track; avoid loose ends—subplots that do not eventually tie to the main action; and avoid wandering characters who lead viewers down a garden path that relates only vaguely (or not at all) to your premise.

However, the unities of place and time are less important to screenwriters; modern audiences are used to dramatic shifts in place and time, and it is often difficult for novice writers to understand the latitude they have for jumping forward, around, and back, both temporally and spatially. Characters can age (naturally) in the space of a screen minute or two. They can be in Africa in one sequence and in Boston a second later in the sequence that follows.

Related to this is the fact that an audience does not have to see everything. We do not have to see the full aging process or the airplane ride. We do not have to see the preparations for Sara's birthday party in *The Little Princess* (by Richard LaGravenese and Elizabeth Chandler) or how her wounded father gets to the hospital from the battlefield. Audiences are very willing and eager to fill in what they do not see. Because audiences are extraordinarily film savvy, they have no problem figuring out what might have happened to land them where they are next in terms of both events and reasons, unless your moves are so unexpected that they are confusing and bewildering.

How do you know if your ellipses (gaps in time or space) baffle your readers or viewers? Mostly this sense comes through experience. That is why it is so useful to have readers' feedback before you send your screenplay off to an agent or producer. Even readers who do not have much experience with film drama can tell you where they are confused, can ask telling questions, or can advise you if they missed crucial steps or felt misled.

More difficult is anticipating whether you have underestimated your audience by telling them too much. Often this results in a slow or sagging conflict or, worse, a boring film or sequence. Sometimes this is a symptom of a lack of conflict; other times it is simply overkill. If you are fairly confident you have compelling tension in your film, then your task is to cut things out: dialogue, actions, even whole scenes (see chap. 5).

Structural Options

There is, of course, infinite variation in filmic structure. Often quite good films seem to break rules of drama and still work very well. Independent films, in particular, are more apt to take dramatic risks than studio or Hollywood films. In general, however, most successful feature films follow (to some degree) the dramatic structure outlined earlier. The best way to get a feel for your options is to see a variety of films that work with structure in different ways. Do not depend on your memory of them; memory of story is consistently unreliable. See the films with the express purpose of attending to structure. The following are some examples.

Thelma and Louise by **Callie Khouri**. This film has a fairly traditional structure following two characters, Thelma and Louise, in a relatively short period of time (about 1 week). Their lives quickly take turns they did not expect, and this works chronologically. As they are pursued by the police, the sequences of Thelma and Louise are intercut with brief shots of their pursuers—Thelma's husband, police, and a detective named Hal who has some sympathy for the pair. The main plot follows the protagonists, however, as the conflict escalates to a climax.

The Piano by **Jane Campion**. This also follows a conventional dramatic structure as things seem to get worse and worse for the main character, Ada. What is interesting about this film is that the primary conflict shifts from between Ada and George (who keeps her piano hostage) to Ada and Stewart (her husband) when she falls in love with George. Still, the steadily increasing tension keeps the structure unified.

The Shawshank Redemption by **Frank Darabont**. This story is told chronologically, but spans more than 20 years—from 1946 to 1967. We see men age, develop, and change dramatically, including the protagonist, Andy Dufresne who is in his mid-20s as the film begins. The opening scene places Andy outside a cabin, listening in desperation to his wife making love with another man. He is holding a gun. The scene jumps to a courtroom where Andy is on trial for the murder of his wife and her lover, to which charge he has plead not guilty. Most of the rest of the film takes place in prison. We are guided through this by subtitles and by the narration of Red, one of the other inmates and Andy's friend. This film is a good example of effective leaps in time and space.

Lone Star by **John Sayles**. This film moves chronologically at one level, but makes use of flashbacks and multiple subplots. Sam Deeds is a sheriff trying to unearth the truth about his late father and previous sheriff, Buddy Deeds, and a murder and theft that he suspects Buddy of committing. As Sam uncovers the facts, we move into flashback to see the actual events.

Subplots include, among others, the conflict between Sam's girlfriend, Pilar, and her wayward son, Amado, and the conflict between Chet, a Black teenager, and his father, Del, an overbearing Army colonel. Both Otis and Pilar are directly or indirectly involved with Buddy Deeds. The subplots eventually link together as they should at the end.

Out of Africa by **Kurt Luedtke.** This film could be criticized as being episodic. It is another film that spans the lifetime of a main character, Karen, but her goals are clear and omnipresent, and the conflict is consistently about the same thing. She is trying to domesticate Africa, to make it her own, while Africa, represented by her farm, the natives, and her lover, resist the domestication. The film moves chronologically and is clearly nested from Karen's point of view. The jumps in time (the ellipses) are interspersed with periods of intense psychological or physical action (Karen takes supplies to her husband in the desert, she comes down with syphilis, her coffee plantation burns down, and she and Denys, her lover, fight). Over the course of the film, Karen's turmoil becomes worse and worse, climaxing in her departure and the death of Denys. Interestingly, this film is based on a true story, and it is quite illuminating to determine how it works as an adaptation (see chap. 6 for more on adaptations).

Subplots

Many good screenplays have subplots. Sometimes subplots involve the main character, and sometimes they do not. As I mentioned earlier, *Lone Star* has several subplots (Pilar's conflict with her son, Del's conflict with his son), and the main character, Sam, is only marginally involved in these subplots. The best subplots both parallel some of the themes and actions in the main plot line and weave in and out of the central action. Ultimately (as I have said and this bears repeating), they also come to some kind of closure. In *Lone Star*, Pilar resolves her conflict with her son by the end of the film, and Del comes to understand himself and his son.

Shawshank Redemption contains a moving subplot about an elderly inmate who does not want to be paroled. He has lived most of his life in prison and knows no other way to live, except within the structure of the prison. When he is finally released, he tries to survive for a short time, but then commits suicide. This subplot does not parallel the main plot, but it does provide us some valuable information on what prison life does to one's ability to make it on the "outside." This contributes to an audience's understanding of what the main character, Andy, is going through.

Although working subplots into your drama can enrich an audience's experience of the principle story and can demonstrate a sophistication with dramatic writing that will mark you as a pro, subplotting is also quite difficult. It is best to get comfortable working with fairly simple plot lines first. Later, you can enhance your work with subplots. In fact, as your facility with the genre becomes greater, plotting at various levels and with increased complexity will probably come naturally.

READY TO GO

Expressing your ideas dramatically is not easy. Good ideas often come easily whereas good stories are more difficult. Translating good stories into good screenplays is even tougher. The best way to begin is to start writing up an idea for a short screenplay (20–30 minutes). Consider it as an analogue to a short story, with limited characters, limited scope, and limited actions. Try not to pay attention at first to premise, to tension build, or to market considerations. Just write. As you get more comfortable, begin to pay attention to dramatic form and structure. Most likely, the screenplay will be terrible, but this is how you begin and learn. Next time may be as difficult and the result as disappointing, but if you keep at it and begin to attend to dramatic principles, you will improve.

At the beginning it's torture. You've got a lot swimming around in your head, but that's a long way form getting it down on paper. But it's that initial process that feeds the home stretch. The more I write, the more the story takes over. The characters and the situations dictate where the story goes.

—John Patrick Shanley (1993)

APPLICATIONS AND EXERCISES

1. Over the course of a week or two, rent five films of different types of genres (a good sampling with a mix of traditional and nontraditional might be *Pulp Fiction, The Green Mile, American Beauty, Die Hard, The Pianist,* and *Fargo*). With pen and paper in hand (or on a laptop), chart the point of attack, locking of the conflict, tension rise, climax, and resolution. Where do these occur?

2. Create a graph of the tension rise in these films. Based on the impact the film had on you, does the tension rise work? Where does it falter or even

fail? Where were you bored? Where were you tensely gripping your seat (and unable to take notes)?

3. Find the premise of the same five films. When in doubt, look for the climax and/or character change. What does the main character learn? What do you learn? What insight does the film provide?

4. Pick a scene in one of the films you watched. Check it against the guidelines for film structure in this chapter. Does it follow the suggested film structure? Should it?

5. Select one of the worst films you remember seeing. Rent it and subject yourself to it one more time. Purely in terms of plotting, where does it fail? Where does it succeed?

6. Graph the tension line in one of your own screenplays. Where is the point of attack, the locking of the conflict, the tension build, the climax and the resolution? What is the premise? Could the script benefit from a more standard rendering of plot structure?

SUGGESTED READING

Aristotle. *The poetics.*
Blacker, I. (1986). *The elements of screenwriting.* New York: MacMillan.
Darabount, F. (1996). *The shawshank redemption: The shooting script.* New York: Newmarket.
Lajos, E. (1960). *The art of dramatic writing.* New York: Simon and Schuster.
Mehring, M. (1990). *The screenplay: A blend of film form and context.* Boston: Focal Press.

I know there are a lot of people who are successful by giving the public what they want or giving the producers what they want. I think that's a mistake for the soul. I think that the best films are those that are written by people who care about what they write and who aren't trying to figure out what it is that people want to see. They're not trying to second-guess what an audience wants to see. The truly great films are those that are original and can't be second-guessed or predicted. So that's a very long-winded way of saying that I think you should write about what you care about.

—Steve Zaillian, writer of *Schindler's List* and *Searching for Bobby Fischer,* interviewed by Alan Waldman for wga.org.
http://www.wga.org/craft/interviews/zaillian.html

Character

Once I have thought out the action of the story, and have a handle on the charac-
ters, I'll go out in the backyard in the morning, and just sit there and try to open
myself up and let the characters come to me; let them talk to me. So much of writ-
ing is about getting quiet enough so you can hear your characters talking. Some-
times I feel they choose you because they know you're listening. You just have to
shut up and listen.

—Callie Khouri (writer of *Thelma and Louise*), interviewed by Syd Field for
SydField.com (Interviews with Writers).
www.sydfield.com/interviews_calliekhouri.htm

In the course of discussing plot, we have also necessarily discussed character because the two are inseparable. Although you can have a film with good characters that fails miserably because of an inane or ill-conceived plot, you cannot have a good plot without good characters. It makes sense to spend time creating rich, interesting characters. Much can be said about characters and characterization that will help make your good plot much better than it would otherwise be.

WHAT IS AN EFFECTIVE CHARACTER?

An effective character is capable of strong passions and emotions. It could be argued that effective characters can be easily labeled. They can be stereotyped as having a certain kind of personality—for example, a loud bully, a shy wallflower, a handsome rake, or a prostitute with a heart of gold. But the best characters deviate from the norm in some significant way. In other words, when we encounter effective characters, we both recognize ourselves in them (they are ordinary people like us or people we know or have met) and we see their extraordinary qualities; they are in some way "better" than we are. At the very least, they are like us when we are at our best. They are stronger, more focused, and more talented; they are, in a word, ordinary people acting extraordinarily. The same applies to characters who take on the role of villain. The best villains are extraordinary villains.

TYPES OF CHARACTERS

Protagonist

The *protagonist* is the character in a drama who drives the action and tends to be the main character. This is also the character who undergoes some kind of character change during the course of the film. In *Shawshank Redemption*, the protagonist is Andy. The action revolves around him; he is the reason the film is made; he is central to the film's premise. In *Deliverance*, although there are four main characters, Ed (Jon Voight) is the protagonist. He begins the film as a guy out for a good time with his adventuring friend, Lewis. But when Bobby is raped, Drew is killed, and Lewis breaks his leg, it is Ed who confronts his demons and takes over the situation. It is Ed who changes from a conservative suburbanite who wants some excitement in his life to a man who has lived life, has killed, and has overcome some significant personal shortcomings. He has gained wisdom in a way the other characters in the film did not or perhaps cannot.

As in *Deliverance*, the protagonist often emerges from a group of leading characters. In *American President*, there are two potential protagonists—Andy, the president, and Sydney, his love interest. Although Sydney is a catalyst, Andy is the protagonist because he makes things happen. He invites Sydney out on a date, he refuses to make public his relationship with her, he works at continuing the relationship when Sydney gets nervous, and, ultimately, he comes to understand that his love for Sydney outweighs some of the pragmatic concerns of getting reelected to office, and he says as much in a press conference at the climax of the film, risking his political future.

Most often it is the protagonist with whom audiences identify. Therefore, he should have qualities that make him human. Jake Gittes in *Chinatown* is a good protagonist because he not only drives the action, but he is very sympathetic. He is tough, calculating, and slick, but he is also vulnerable and susceptible to the emotions that motivate us all (pride, desire for control, insecurity). For the climax to work effectively, the audience must empathize with the main character so that we travel the route to the climax with him, and then feel the release—and learn something—when he does. Jake learns that life is a bit like

Chinatown—utterly unpredictable and out of anyone's control, even his own. He has, with us, attained a kind of wisdom.

Antagonist

The *antagonist* is the character or characters (or elements) who threaten to prevent the protagonist from achieving his or her goals. Often the antagonist is embodied in a single character. In *Outbreak*, for example, General McClintock is dedicated to stopping Sam from finding a cure for the deadly Motaba virus that threatens the people in a town (and potentially the world). He is constantly in Sam's way, confronting him indirectly through others, such as Sam's friend and superior officer, Billy (Morgan Freeman), and directly, as in the helicopter battle where the General tries to shoot Sam down, thereby preventing him from returning to the laboratory with the monkey who holds the key to the anti-serum. In *The Fugitive*, Dr. Kimble's central antagonist is Gerard, the detective in charge of the manhunt who is determined to bring Kimble in.

In both these films, the antagonist also represents a cluster of antagonistic forces, making them much more powerful as adversaries than they might be as individuals. For example, in *Outbreak*, General McClintock embodies the industrial-military complex whose primary goal is to retain power. The Motaba virus is key in their plans for developing their chemical warfare capabilities. In *The Piano*, Stewart represents the civilized, male world that has thrust Ada into a foreign and hostile environment. One could also say that characters often share antagonist roles. For example, Ada's antagonists are actually quite numerous. At first it is her husband, Stewart, his partner, George Baines, and, to a lesser extent, the native Maori population; later Baines takes her side and Stewart is able to turn Ada's daughter, Flora, against her.

In many films, the antagonist is more complex. In *The Verdict*, Edward Concannon, a high-powered attorney, is the chief antagonist, but he is not the only one. The principal antagonist for Frank (Newman) is the powerful establishment, represented variously by the Bishop of the Archdiocese who manages St. Catherine's Hospital, the legal team that tries to beat Frank, Laura who betrays him, and alcohol, which, along with his past, plagues Frank. But for antagonistic forces to work well in a drama, *they must be represented by characters* so we can see the conflict in action. In other words, it is smart to prefer external conflict to internal conflict. Alcoholism is not a good antagonist because it is a man fighting a disease; the conflict is largely internal. One's past is not a good antagonist because it is largely intellectual and therefore internal. But people who use Frank's alcoholism and Frank's past against him help make the film dramatic.

Finally, antagonists do not necessarily have to be human. Hence, we have antagonistic forces in the realm of natural disasters (viruses, volcanoes, tornadoes, earthquakes, storms), man-made disasters (airplane crashes, atomic bombs, scientific mutants), or aliens from another world. As we have mentioned, these antagonistic forces often take on human characteristics. So, for example, a storm may attack its opponents' weak spots (when or where the protagonist is least able to defend herself); a virus or a tornado may retreat to marshal its forces for a stronger assault. But in any case, they are extraordinarily powerful and threaten the protagonist to the utmost.

It should be said that antagonists are not necessarily "bad." Although Gerard (*The Fugitive*), McClintock (*Outbreak*), and Stewart (*The Piano*) are all in conflict with the protagonist or character whom audiences tend to identify with, they are not necessarily evil. Gerard functions ultimately as a supporter of the fugitive, and McClintock and Stewart both have their likable qualities. After all, McClintock's goal is to save humanity. Stewart simply wants to be loved; in his own way, he loves Ada. The best antagonists have texture; that is, they are multifaceted in ways that enable us to understand their motivations (although not necessarily agree with them) and see them as both humans and individuals, not stereotypes.

Supporting Cast

Supporting is a misnomer for characters who do not serve the dramatic function of protagonist and antagonist. They are only supporting in the sense that they should—like the protagonist and antagonist—help further or "support" the plot. There are not necessarily minor characters. Robby in *Outbreak* is not minor at all, and, in fact, Rene Russo, who plays the part of Robby, is given star billing. Although not the protagonist, she has a critical part in the plot as she is at times part of the antagonistic force against Sam and at other times is his biggest fan. Red, who narrates the story in *Shawshank Redemption* and is played by Morgan Freeman, is neither protagonist nor antagonist, but plays such a key role in the film that he was nominated for an Academy Best Actor award. Even though one could argue that categories dreamed up by the Academy should be treated with some skepticism because they are highly controversial even in Hollywood, in this instance, the label of *Best Actor* is accurate. One might even argue that he shares the protagonist role with Tim Robbins (who plays Andy), although Andy is clearly the one who moves the action.

The following list suggests the range of dramatic functions for secondary characters:

- **Confidante**—Someone to whom the central characters can reveal themselves: their emotions, fears, or doubts. In *American President*, A. J. (played in the film by Martin Sheen), a member of the President's cabinet and an old friend of the President, takes on this kind of role. The President can let his guard down in front of A. J. and talk about his personal problems and concerns.

- **Observer**—Red, in *Shawshank Redemption*, takes on this role. Although he is also a character in the drama and a friend to the lead character, Andy, he is also narrating the tale, explaining, elucidating, and giving the perspective of an insider. As an insider, he can also point out the workings of the prison to Andy.

- **Catalyst**—This is a character who, although not the antagonist or proponent, makes things happen or helps to force an issue. In *The Piano*, Ada's daughter, Flora, serves this role. She discovers that Ada and George are having an affair, and she tells Stewart, escalating the conflict.

- **Comic relief**—Some of the supporting characters in *Out of Africa* provide a nice contrast to Karen's serious character. For example, Karen's servant, Farah, displays a mixture of wisdom and naiveté about the customs of the White Man in his responses to Karen.

- **Foil**—Although not necessarily an antagonist, a foil has the role of working against the protagonist and often serves to intensify the conflict and tension. In *Out of Africa*, Karen's husband, Bror, is not really the antagonist; he both helps Karen escape her life in Denmark (by marrying her) and makes her miserable (by planting coffee instead of raising cattle, by being unfaithful, by giving her syphilis). Opposite to Karen in character, easy-going, and adventurous, Bror is very effective as both contrast and conflict with Karen's desire for control.

Be careful of categorizing your supporting characters too rigidly, however. None of these categories is discrete; there are, in fact, overlapping roles for characters, both supporting and main. The previous discussion merely suggests that equal time should be spent with all your characters, regardless of whether they play key dramatic roles. Although it is important to understand who your protagonist and chief antagonist are, certainly other characters have important dramatic functions.

HOW TO CREATE A GOOD CHARACTER

The most common advice is to start with people you know. When I was in film school at the University of Southern California, my first screenwriting professor, Mort Zarcoff, asked us to write up a character sketch of ourselves—one that we might use as a character in a film. Other people advise writers to use family, friends, and people we are intimate with as a place to begin. This is sound advice; because people we know are rarely very simple, using them as models may help us avoid cardboard, stick-figure characters. Most good characters have some similarities to people we know—even if the characters are merely amalgams of different people.

Second, spend time with your characters before you begin to write. You will need to "breathe life" into them. One way to do this is to engage in some prewriting or invention exercises designed to tease out some of their underlying personalities and histories—even if you will not use all this information in your script. Create character sketches or profiles on each of your major characters and your important supporting characters. Students in my writing classes are asked to do two things before they draft their screenplays: create a physical, sociological, and psychological profile (as Lajos Egri, 1960, suggested in *The Art of Dramatic Writing*), and put the characters in a scene so you get used to working with them and seeing them in action.

Egri's model asks writers to consider character elements such as sex, age, appearance, class, education, occupation, home life, religion, race, political affiliation, sex life, ambition, frustrations, temperament, complexes, abilities, and personal qualities. Here is a sample character profile (created by a student in my graduate writing seminar and a published poet) based on Egri's model.

Bob Blanks

Cafeteria manager

Physiology
1. male
2. 43 years old
3. 5'8", 230 pounds
4. dirty blond (greasy) hair, balding a little, blue eyes, pale skin
5. slouchy posture, big round beer belly
6. overweight, not good looking at all; odd shaped—very top heavy, appearance is untidy, with old grease stains on his clothes
7. no deformities—but there is an ugly mole on his right hand

Sociology
1. Middle class

2. Cafeteria manager; works 50+ hours a week; makes $13.00 per hour—no overtime. His work is monotonous; he does not like his job.

3. Has a wife who works a part-time job at a supermarket and two teenage sons who do not want much to do with him.

4. Graduated from a suburban high school in a middle working-class neighborhood; favorite subjects were history and science, poorest subjects were history and science. Possibly dyslexic.

5. Grew up with both parents—very plain people with no aspiration beyond their neighborhood—very content. His father collects baseball cards, but he has never been to a game. His mother watches his father collect cards and categorizes them and binds them for her husband.

6. Catholic

7. White

8. A leader among his friends and a member of the YMCA bowling league in his community.

9. Republican

10. Main hobby—bowling; reads *National Geographic* and watches C.O.P.S. religiously.

11. Rents porno flicks and goes to strip clubs.

Psychology

1. Would like to be ambitious, but he isn't

2. Chief disappointment is working in a cafeteria at 43; he wanted to be a historian.

3. Attitude toward life: resigned

4. Obsessed with appearances

5. Neither extroverted nor introverted

6. He is a family man

7. Average IQ

Although Bob, at this point, does not have goals strong enough to be a protagonist or antagonist, he is an interesting enough character. With more detail, we might have enough information to put him in a scene.

Here is another example that is further along. Here writer Larry Wethington has sketched out profiles for the three main characters of his screenplay (a son and his parents). We can begin to see the potential for some good conflict stemming from personal differences and goals (see chart on pp. 64–65).

This sketch provides some depth over a broad range of attributes, and consequently gives the writer a considerable amount to work with. Although still

Category	Billy Wilson	Sam Wilson	Mae Wilson
P **h** **y** **s** **i** **o** **l** **o** **g** **y**	• White male • Gay • 26 • 6' • Fit: gym-toned • Blonde, blue-eyed, freckled: average looking • Wears business suits at work and dresses preppy outside of work	• White male • Straight • 56 • 5'8" • Strong and muscular, but overweight; carries it all in his belly • Wears bifocals • Dark, handsome, hairy, a "bear" • Jeans, leather boots, and "recycled" (i.e., shirts that are faded and worn from evening/social use and repurposed for farmwork) knit shirts • Knit shirts, sans-a-belt pants, and sport coats for evenings/socializing	• White female • Straight • 55 • 5'7" • Fit: muscular, thin, and healthy, until suffers stroke • Wears bifocals • Gets her teased hairdo done every Friday at the beauty parlor, except during harvest season when she can't keep it clean • Natural beauty, not augmented by makeup. A little plain • Paints her toenails once a month or so. Occasionally wears lipstick. Keeps fingernails short because work requires it • "Recycled/Repurposed" clothes for farmwork • Casual wear, sometimes dresses for evenings out
S **o** **c** **i** **o** **l** **o** **g** **y**	• Middle class • IT manager at a prestigious consulting company • BA in Accounting, MBA • Agnostic. Attends mass when his parents visit • Lives in heart of Chicago. Is simultaneously repulsed and drawn to pace/activity of city • Has few friends because he is devoted to work • Frugal • Risk averse • Still in the closet. Doesn't lament lack of friends because	• Lower middle class • Farmer • High school diploma, but barely managed it Spelling/English skills are atrocious • Devout Catholic • Well respected in the community • Funny and popular. Spends a lot of time gossiping with friends in town during weekday morning and socializing (dances mostly) with them and their spouses on weekend evenings • Extremely hardworking, but doesn't work as hard as his wife: no one does	• Lower middle class • Farmer, housekeeper, gardener, sole caregiver for children when they were at home; calls herself a "housewife" • Worked in secretarial-level job at bank when met Sam • High school diploma Would have liked to have gone to college and pursued BA in History • Devout Catholic. Converted to marry Sam. Prays a lot • Does a lot of volunteer work, donates blood regularly

Category	Billy Wilson	Sam Wilson	Mae Wilson
S **o** **c** **i** **o** **l** **o** **g** **y**	*(continued)* doesn't want to expose/explain himself, yet he is lonely • No hobbies beyond the gym and running (alone) • No sex life • Keeps a meticulous apartment. Cleans it every Friday.	• Mother died when he was a teenager • Father is a misogynist, egomaniacal bastard, whom Sam can never please • Frugal • Risk averse • Always drives when he and Mae are in a vehicle together • Never allows anyone to run the planter or harvester. Others can/do/ must help, but those machines are his.	• Well respected in the community • Funny and popular. Spends time with friends on weekend nights with Sam. Weekdays are all work • Met/fell in love with Sam at a dancehall • Rarely socializes without Sam, but volunteers alone • Workaholic • Parents are wealthy and generous. Help/ helped out financially, babysat kids, etc. • Frugal • Risk averse • Fantastic cook. Makes traditional "homestyle" meals, always from scratch.
P **s** **y** **c** **h** **o** **l** **o** **g** **y**	• Leads a successful and productive life in Chicago, but cannot communicate with his father • Avoids conflict (in his personal life) at all costs. He learned this coping device as a child to avoid Sam's wrath • Introverted; feels inadequate; pessimist • Meticulous • Dotes on his mother: He's a mama's boy • Feels desperate to help his mother when she's abused by Sam, but cannot muster the courage.	• Macho: takes responsibility of being head of household seriously. Feels he is obliged to fulfill his manly duties. Teaches kids how to drive a nail, change a tire, etc. • Hates his son's girlishness. Wonders why he doesn't have a girlfriend • Perfectionist. Is hard on himself when he doesn't meet his own expectations. Calls himself a dumbass, but can't tolerate others doing it or even tolerate others' mild playful teasing • Explosive temper.	• Belittles herself in response to years of belittlement/abuse from Sam • Works hard to please everyone. Wants everyone to always "just get along" • Sacrifices her own needs and always puts others first. Is everyone's caregiver • Sees the good in every situation: optimist • Feels all of her children are without fault • Feels strongly (partially because she has always been counseled as such by clergymen and family) that marriage is forever, even if Sam hits her or berates her.

preliminary, we can see that these characters have some stereotypical ele-ments in their backgrounds (the brawny, abusive father and passive mother), and yet they also exhibit character traits that are not as common (a successful businessman who lives a solitary life). That is, the characters begin to exhibit shades of gray; they are different, unique, and in some ways unusual. The fact that Billy and Sam are nearly polar opposites opens up enormous potential for conflict.

There are several lessons here. First, try to create characters who are both recognizable and familiar, but who also break that mold. In other words, you want characters who are like people we have met, but are, at the same time, quite different. You want to demonstrate that you are quite familiar with human psychology and yet know how to be creative in designing character. Your characters will then be seen as "fresh," "interesting," and "unusual." Be careful, however. It is not easy for a truly offbeat character—one who exhibits few universal traits—to hit it off with an audience. There must be something familiar for the audience to identify with, and there must be something original for the audience to be intrigued with. This is anomaly, for sure, but it is one of the reasons that screenwriting is such an exciting challenge.

Second, you want characters with strong motivations to pursue their goals. This enables you to determine the role each will play in the drama and helps you construct a dynamic plot.

Moving from Character to Scene

To demonstrate how a character sketch can evolve into a plot, let us look at a character sketch of Jake Gittes from *Chinatown*, drawn after the fact.

Jake Gittes

Physiology
1. He is a male in his late 30s, average height and weight, with a dark complexion. He keeps his dark brown hair neatly oiled and combed back. He wears very stylish suits, usually light-colored linens, and is meticulous about his appearance. It is important to him to always be neat, dapper, and smart looking. Sometimes this comes across as "natty"; he is a natty dresser.
2. He is fit.
3. He constantly smokes nonfiltered cigarettes.

Sociology
1. Jake is from a working-class background, joined the police force as a young man, and served on one of the more difficult beats in Los Angeles—

Chinatown. He got into some trouble on the beat—he does not much like taking abuse from authority figures and likes to handle things in his own way—so he quit. Now he runs a successful detective agency and oversees a secretary and two male assistants.

2. Was never married, but fell deeply in love with a woman when he was a beat cop. She was killed, and he feels responsible for her death.

3. No other immediate family; his parents died when he was in his 20s. Does not have a lot of close personal friends; does not really need them. Has some fairly reliable office employees.

Psychology

1. Jake prides himself on his professionalism. He hates failure and those who are losers, although he makes his living off them, and he does not mind taking advantage of them. He certainly does not like losing a case, and he despises people who look down on him. He will not be made a fool of.

2. Likes to tell a good (dirty) joke.

3. He is stubborn; can be quick to anger.

4. He is smart in the sense of street smarts; he is clever, but not brilliant. Works hard at his job—as hard as he needs to.

5. Cannot stand hypocrisy, but is not about to worry himself about it unless it directly affects him.

6. Cynical. Has seen it all and is slightly bored by it.

7. Has a strong sex drive and likes women, but he is not about to let himself get emotionally involved. He has been hurt before.

Obviously, some of the details of Jake's life have been extrapolated from the screenplay and the film—in other words, we have gone at this task backward. But the sketch illustrates the importance of craft in the creation of good characters. To be a good protagonist or antagonist, a character needs to want something so badly that he or she is willing to go to extremes—that is, to go beyond what an average person would—to get it. Second, he or she has to have the emotional, sociological, or even physical qualities to do so. In the previous sketch, neither Bob nor Billy seems to have those powerful desires—although both of them—especially Billy—have potential. Jake, however, is confronted with something that challenges his personal ethic and will (and does) fight the good fight. He will do just about anything to avoid being duped, including risking his life. That kind of drive is what makes a good protagonist (and often antagonist) and separates him from the other characters in a drama.

Here is where knowing a lot about your character can help you craft that character. For example, Billy, the prior character, in some ways may seem like a loser. But his dedication to his mother might be the character element that will help him be "interesting" or even intriguing because it could motivate him to tap into his strengths. Sam seems like a good antagonist because he is strong willed and capable of brutality. What might induce Billy to go up against Sam?

Introducing Your Characters

Once you have created your characters and sketched out a plot, you need to introduce them in a way that conveys the crucial aspects of their personalities. The best way is for your reader to meet them in action, but you also have some minimal leeway to describe them. Description should focus primarily on what we see, but you can also get away with some minimal reference to your character's state of mind, psychology, and social position.

Here is an example of a character introduction by Frank Darabont in *Shawshank Redemption*:

```
ANDY DUFRESNE, mid-20s, wire-rim glasses, three-
piece suit. Under normal circumstances a
respectable, solid citizen; hardly dangerous,
perhaps even meek. But these circumstances are
far from normal. He is disheveled, unshaven, and
very drunk. A cigarette smolders in his mouth.
His eyes, flinty and hard, are riveted to the
bungalow up the path.

He can hear them fucking from here.

He raises a bottle of bourbon and knocks it down.
The radio plays softly, painfully romantic,
taunting him.

              Darabont, Frank. The Shawshank Redemption: The
         Shooting Script. New York: Newmarket Press, 1996.
```

What do we know? Aside from his age, we have learned that Andy is middle class, normally mild mannered, fairly well off, and "a respectable citizen." He is also in a tough spot; he is drunk, he is angry, and he is feeling reckless. He hears two people having sex, and presumably one of those people has been involved romantically with Andy. He is a character who we can visualize and remember. He is also a guy with a problem—a big one.

Here is another introduction from Francis Ford Coppola's *The Conversation*. The scene is San Francisco's Union Square. A mime is imitating unsuspecting people as they come down a walkway.

```
VIEW ON THE MIME

Imitating a middle-aged, slow, bobbing walk. But
precise and purposeful. He sips coffee out of an
imaginary cup.

THE VIEW ALTERS revealing the subject: a rather
ordinary-looking man in his middle forties, with
a thin moustache, dressed immaculately in an
out-of-fashion suit, with a slow, bobbing walk.
He sips coffee from a steaming cardboard cup
wrapped in a paper bag. THIS IS HARRY CAUL.
```

Adapted from Francis Ford Coppola.
"The Conversation." Scenario: The Magazine of
Screenwriting Art, 5.1 (Spring 1999), 12.

Both descriptions work well because they reveal characters in interesting situations. Andy is about to take out a gun. Harry is doing undercover work and is, ironically, himself targeted (and mocked) by the mime. These are interesting ways to introduce characters because they immediately engage as well as inform the audience.

WHAT IS EFFECTIVE DIALOGUE?

Good characters, a strong conflict, and a solid dramatic structure are essential to a good screenplay. In significant ways, dialogue lies at the heart of these important components. First, it is central physically. It is located in the center of the page; it is isolated by large margins, and hence lots of white space, calling attention to itself and making it stand out. In addition to its location, there is usually more dialogue than shot description, so it takes up more space on the page. It is easier to read than description. Although dialogue is nested in shot description, and shot descriptions set the scene, create the image, and help establish point of view, **dialogue is often the first—and sometimes only—thing screenplay readers read carefully**. As such, dialogue can make or break a screenplay, so it is worth spending some time honing one's skills at making it sharp, interesting, and lucid.

There is a common misconception that good dialogue must sound real. But real conversation can be erratic, digressive, awkward, interminable, and downright dull. This is because real conversation is unedited; when you speak, you cannot go back and fix up what you said, making it sound better.

Oral language is produced on the spot; often speakers do not have much time to think about what they will say or how they will say it. They must compose it on very short notice and in response to the vagaries of the environment, their moods, and the discourse of other speakers. If speakers had the luxury to revise what they said, they probably would not say half as much of what they do say. The following is an example of a transcribed conversation between two friends getting together for lunch:

A: Oooh, God! [pause] I'm working on this really
hard story, and I'm puttin' too much time for what
I'm getting paid ... an' I wanna make a good
impression 'cause it's a magazine that pays a lot
when you get to write features for 'em, and so I
want to write features for 'em, so I have to do
well on this column, and it's not a good story, and
I'm just— [sighs]
M: What's the story about?
A: It's about water. Did I tell you about this one?
M: Do you want a beer?
A: No thanks. [very low] I gotta work this
afternoon. [Pause] It's about water, and the
consumption of water and ho-, and do people drink
enough and … how is their consumption of water ...
M: [overlapping] You have some dirt on your uh—
[gestures to M's cheek]
A: ... affected by ...
M: [humorously] It's perfect. It's perfect.
A: [laughs] ... affected by, um ... taste or ...
temperature or whatever.
M: [interrupting] Do you like curry?
A: Yeah. How come your red light's on here? Did you
get a new ...
M: [overlapping] 'Cause my machine's on.
A: ... machine?

The topic and flow are constantly interrupted. There are stutters, run-on sentences, vague pronoun references, expletives, and other disfluencies. Because of the way it is produced by the speaker and processed by the listener, spoken language can be characterized as containing the following:

1. *Repetition*—Speakers often repeat themselves to emphasize a point, ensure the point has been clearly made, and allow them more time to come up with what they will say next.

2. *Disfluency*—Because of time constraints, speakers use inappropriate or confusing vocabulary, disjointed or convoluted sentence structure, fillers such as *um, uh,* and *well,* stutters, and errors, such as inaccurate names, places, and dates.

3. *Overlapping*—Speakers often jockey for the opportunity to speak, often talking over another person's speech. They interrupt, overlap, drown out each other's words, and monopolize the conversation.

4. *Prosody*—Linguists refer to the way a stretch of discourse is uttered as prosody. Prosody includes pitch, tempo, loudness, and any other elements that contribute to how language sounds when spoken aloud. These are important at conveying meaning. Although some of these elements are more significant at communicating meaning than others, they all impart important information about the person speaking (e.g., nervous, confident, or moody) and the situation (e.g., tense, peaceful, emotional).

Eventually the dialogue in a script will be spoken; it will have prosody. Then it is up to the actor or director to provide this level of meaning. But apart from some minimal dialogue direction (such as "loudly" or "angrily"), a screenwriter does *not* have the same range of ways to convey meaning. Everything that comes across to a reader must do so from the page.

That screenplay dialogue is read and not "enacted" may seem like a fairly obvious point. But, in fact, it is a crucial distinction. It is one reason that obscenities or slang expressions, although perfectly realistic and meaningful when spoken, are much more offensive or distasteful when they appear the page. It is the reason that dialogue that is indeed "realistic" can fall flat or is utterly boring when it is worked into a screenplay. Writing has a different impact than speech, and writers need to be very sensitive to the differences.

Here are five important tips for writing good dialogue:

Tip 1—The best dialogue is not what a real person actually says at a given moment, but what she wishes she had said.

Because in writing you have the opportunity to edit, use it. Be judicious and artful about everything that appears on the page. This does not mean that all dialogue must be witty and clever, although much of it can and should be.

Tip 2—If you can cut any dialogue out of your piece, do so and then cut 33% more.

When we talk, we usually say much more than we need to. When we write, we tend to write too much partly because there is usually a lot we think we must get across that we do not have to and partly because we often fall back on our essay-writing experience, where everything seems to need an explanation. But writing dialogue is a situation where less is indeed more. Readers are not dumb; they pick up things very fast, and they are always reading between the lines.

Tip 3—Try to be believable and realistic but <u>not</u> authentic.

This distinction recalls what we said earlier about Aristotle ("Prefer probable impossibilities to improbable possibilities"). Believe the truism: "Life is stranger than fiction." Events take place in real life that no one would ever believe. People say things in real life that are utterly incredible, improbable, and, simply, bizarre. Because something actually was said or done does not necessarily mean it sounds believable or that it will play well on the screen. A 4-year-old may actually say things that sound like German philosopher Immanuel Kant or American essayist Ralph Waldo Emerson but if she sounds that way in a screenplay, you risk losing credibility. She may be exceptionally eloquent and her timing may be impeccable, but she should sound like we imagine 4-year-olds *might* sound.

Tip 4—Do some homework. Listen to:
- Conversations—How people you know talk; how strangers talk; how people are affected by what others say;
- Films—How film characters talk;
- Radio talk shows—How people talk when they think they are being listened to;
- Books on tape—How a good reader conveys the talk of characters from novels and short stories. For example, mystery writer James Lee Burke writes wonderful dialogue, and almost all of his books are on tape.

Listen to the differences between dialogue in each genre or between different speakers and writers; take mental (or even written) notes.

Tip 5—Do more homework. Read:
- Screenplays—Get a feel for what is there and not there, for the rhythms of characters talking *in print*;
- Novels and short stories—Pay attention to how novelists portray people talking, what these writers include and omit, and how the dialogue reveals character;

• Contemporary poetry—Attend to how poets use language in new and interesting ways; observe how they use poetic devices such as metaphor and simile, assonance and alliteration, rhythm and phrasing, concrete and abstract language. Compare the language of poetry you read with the language of the prose you read and look for correlations;

• Newspapers—Pay attention to how quotations taken from what people are supposed to have said are actually used. Figure out what makes something worth quoting.

Orchestration

The term *orchestration* is used in drama or screenwriting to refer to the degree and fluctuation of emotional intensity in your characters from one moment to the next. In a well-orchestrated film, characters' passions rise and fall, much like a piece of music or the tide. A character should not jump from being quite calm one minute to quite angry the next. We have to be able to see the wrath building and reaching a climax. Otherwise we will not believe it; the emotions will ring false or seem shallow. Emotions, feelings, and passions have to be motivated.

The following is an example of a poorly orchestrated scene from an early draft of what ended up as a very good script by Katie McConnell. The scene is lifted from a confrontation between a Kosovar father and daughter at a refugee camp. Note how the characters' anger seems to rise suddenly and then disappear just as fast. Tears come and then composure follows almost immediately.

```
                    KARA
          Papa, I loved him, don't you know
          that?


She starts to cry again, but not as hard as before.
She stands alone, but close to her mother and wipes
her tears away.

                    PAPA
          Love? You are too young for love.
          And what time is this for love? We
          are at war. When the war is done,
          you will have plenty of time for love.


                                     (CONTINUED)
- - - - - - - - - - page break - - - - - - - - - -
```

CONTINUED:

                KARA

Papa, it is not my fault we are at war.

                PAPA

But we are.

                KARA
             (getting angry)
What does that have to do with
anything?

                PAPA

It has everything to do with
everything!

                KARA

Papa, people can love each other
during war.

                PAPA

That's absurd! What are you going
to do for dates, stand in the food
line? Wait till the war is over and
you will have plenty of dates.

                KARA

What if the war doesn't end?

                PAPA

It will end.

                KARA

You just said it might not.

                          (CONTINUED)

CONTINUED:

                    PAPA
                (sternly)
        Kara. I was making a point.

                    KARA
        What point?

                    MAMA
                (authoritatively)
        Yes, Papa. What's your point?

                    PAPA
        My point is that there are more
        things to think about than a broken
        heart. You shouldn't be so
        concerned with yourself in a time
        like this.

                    KARA
        So I'm selfish.

                    PAPA
        I didn't say that.

                    KARA
        Yes, you did. You said I'm selfish
        because I'm thinking of Sopi.

                    PAPA
                (exasperated)
        That's not what I meant. I was ...

                    KARA
                (interrupting)
        You just don't understand. You
        think I'm just a little girl.

                            (CONTINUED)
- - - - - - - - - - page break - - - - - - - - - -

CONTINUED:

                              PAPA
                        (with emphasis)
                  Kara. You are a little girl.

                              KARA
                  No, I'm 14.

                              PAPA
                  Yes. A little girl.

                              MAMA
                  Papa, I was 14 when we fell in love.

Papa rolls his eyes. Tears start falling down
Kara's cheeks again. She wipes them away and bites
her lower lip. Papa walks toward Kara and puts his
arm around her.

                              PAPA
                        (exasperated)
                  You can't keep thinking about Sopi.
                  Fine, he broke up with you. Now
                  keep walking. No reason to look at
                  it again.

Part of the problem stems from the fact that the scene is quite long and wordy and could be cut significantly. When it is cut, however, attention should be paid to a more slowly rising passion in both Kara and Papa. Right now the characters seem to whine or pick at one another.

Settle first on the point of the scene. What do you want to convey? In this case, the writer might want to portray the stubbornness of Papa in the face of an impassioned daughter. Perhaps Kara should start out trying to reason with Papa, which leads to her increasing frustration, which leads to her increasing anger, then tears as he refuses to listen and understand. The same might occur with Papa as he tries to reason with her, then angers in frustration. Alternately, it might also be wise to keep Papa at a fairly stable level of inflexibility and pig-headedness so he can act as Kara's foil.

Here is a revision of the prior excerpt that attends to orchestration and narrows the focus of the scene. Note both Kara's and Papa's slowly rising frustration and anger as they fail to understand one another.

                        KARA
        Papa, I loved him, don't you know
        that?

                        PAPA
        You are too young for love. And
        what time is this for love? We are at
        war. When the war is done, you will
        have plenty of time for love.

                        KARA
        What does war have to do with it?

                        PAPA
        Everything.

Kara is silent a moment, biting her lip.

                        KARA
        People can love during war.

                        PAPA
        Wait till the war is over and you will
        have plenty of dates.

                        KARA
        I don't want plenty of dates; I want Sopi.

                        PAPA
                (exasperated)
        There are more things to think about
        than a broken heart. You shouldn't
        be so concerned with yourself in a
        time like this.

                                (CONTINUED)
- - - - - - - - - - page break - - - - - - - - - -

```
CONTINUED:

Kara flushes with anger.

                    KARA
          So I'm selfish?

Papa turns away, shaking his head in frustration.

                    KARA
          You think I'm just a little girl.

                    PAPA
          Kara. You are a little girl.

                    KARA
          No, I'm not. I'm 14. You're not
          even trying to understand!

                    PAPA
          A little girl.

Papa reaches out to touch Kara's cheek and she turns
away in anger and rushes out of the tent. Papa throws
his hands up in exasperation.
```

In the revised version, the tension between Papa and Kara rises to one peak. Kara's anger rises more slowly than in the previous draft and is more clearly motivated both by what Papa says and her increasing frustration with him and the situation that he represents. The scene is more carefully orchestrated. It does not jump from one peak to another. Rather, there is a more interesting dramatic crescendo or rise in emotion.

Subtext

When we converse, a surprising amount of meaning is conveyed. Some of it is communicated directly—this is the substance of what we say. However, some of it is communicated indirectly; it is implied. For example, if a man walks down the street, notices a pretty woman, and says "Nice day" as they pass, chances are he is not just making a comment about the weather. It is likely that she will see his remark as a come-on, a way of beginning a conversation with her as a prelude to getting to know her or asking her out on a date. "Nice day" is the direct communication; the come-on or pick-up line is the *subtext*—that is, what is implied, but not directly spoken.

The same is true in film dialogue. In fact film conversations that contain subtexts are quite rich because there is communication going on at several levels. Here is an example from *Out of Africa*.

```
EXT. TERRACE - DENYS - DAY

A new gramophone plays MOZART. Juma rolls out
drink cart. PAN AROUND to see Karen approaching
past Denys's parked safari truck. Natives stare,
grave.

                    DENYS
          Look here: They've finally
          made a machine that's really
          useful.

She doesn't respond.

                    DENYS (CONT'D)
          It's for you.

                    KAREN
          I can't accept it.

                    DENYS
          Why not?

                    KAREN
          Because Bror's moved to town.

                    DENYS
          That's a private matter, I imagine.

                                    (CONTINUED)
- - - - - - - - - - page break - - - - - - - - - -
```

CONTINUED:

> KAREN
> (beat, even)
> Did you think you'd spend the night?

> DENYS
> Can't thanks.
> (beat)
> I'm going up to the Aberdares. I've taken up safari work, I've got to find a camp.

> KAREN
> (long pause)
> No ...

> DENYS
> There's country there you ought to see. It won't last long now.

> KAREN
> You'd be wasting your time. I won't sleep with you.

> DENYS
> You'll do as you like.
> (then)
> Why don't you just jump the fence? Wait to see what happens.

> KAREN
> I can't afford much, right now.

(CONTINUED)

- - - - - - - - - - page break - - - - - - - - - -

```
CONTINUED:
                           DENYS
                        (beat)
                 Life's not years, Karen. It's
                 just a day here and a minute
                 here—a few fine moments.
                 You've got to collect them.


                           KAREN
                 If you like me at all, don't
                 ask me to do this.


                           DENYS
                        (quiet)
                 All right.


   In profile, they look at one another across some
   distance. HOLD on their figures.
```

There is a lot going on in this scene that is not explicitly stated. Karen is angry at Denys for staying away for so long—not visiting her as frequently as she would like. She expresses this by treating him as a presumptuous suitor. She is in love with him, but does not want to be because it illustrates her lack of control. Denys loves Karen as well, but purposely does not rise to her comment about spending the night, in fact, pretends to misunderstand it, treating it as an invitation to a hospitality rather than a sexual encounter. He won't be drawn in to her argument and she tries to resist his proposal for a trip to a safari camp, a trip he wants her to take so she can see what the wild is really like and perhaps understand him and Africa better.

Individuation and Pacing

Think about how you want your characters to sound and how you might individuate your characters. In the real world, people talk differently. Some people are verbose, whereas others are quiet and reticent, saying little. Some people have a dry, ironic sense of humor; others are silly. Some sound aristocratic; others use slang, obscenities, and colloquialisms. The same variations should be true of your characters, and the way you write them will create distinctive characters that your readers and viewers will remember and be able to distinguish between.

The following scene is taken from a screenplay I wrote with Eric Sears, entitled *Jungleland*. The characters in the scene, Shoulders and Carla, are two cops who work together in Los Angeles. In the previous scene, which took place the night before, they had gone out for drinks, had a little too much to drink, and exchanged a kiss. Both flustered and drunk, Carla drove off, forgetting he had no other ride home. In this scene, Carla sees Shoulders sitting on a traffic stanchion; she pulls up in her car. Carla is Hispanic, Shoulders is African American. In the scene, we tried to create in Carla an assertive, outgoing, and bright cop. Shoulders, in contrast, is a troubled man; he is also impassive and prefers to keep to himself. We also worked on rhythm, slowing the pacing down to let some of the drama play out in the action. It is an awkward encounter, and we tried to let the pacing—in jerks and starts—emphasize this.

                              CARLA
                    Need a lift, Lieutenant?

He looks at her, then the car, then laughs. She
pulls away and parks. She gets out of the car
and moves towards him. In tight jeans and a
bright sweater, she's beautiful. Shoulders gives
her a long study as she saunters up to him.
She's very conscious of his stare.

                              CARLA
                You gave me a headache the other
                night.

                            SHOULDERS
                      (smoking nonchalantly)
                You're over eighteen.

                              CARLA
                So I am.
                          (sheepish)
                You get home all right?

                                              (CONTINUED)
        - - - - - - - - - - - page break - - - - - - - - - - -

CONTINUED:

Shoulders gives her a bemused look.

>   CARLA
>   (going on clumsily)
>   I didn't mean to get you drunk ...

He looks at her a moment, then ...

>   SHOULDERS
>   I felt fine. It was a long walk
>   home.

>   CARLA
>   (uncomfortable)
>   Oh? Yes, well good.Good. I didn't
>   see you around yesterday. Thought
>   you might have been ... well ... you
>   know ...

Shoulders makes no comment. He gazes out into
the street.

>   CARLA (CONT'D)
>   God, you're so immovable! You sit
>   there like a slab of marble while
>   I bumble around from word to word.

>   SHOULDERS
>   (finally a chuckle)
>   "Immovable."

>   (CONTINUED)
- - - - - - - - - page break - - - - - - - - - -

CONTINUED:

>   CARLA
>   Well, yeah. At least that's
>   what you pretend. We did catch
>   a glimpse of the shifting sands
>   the other night.

Shoulders stubs out his cigarette. There is a
long silence. Carla gives up. She starts to
move toward the building entrance. Then
suddenly, she turns back.

>   CARLA
>   Say, listen. I'd appreciate
>   it if you'd get your horny
>   partner off my ass.

Shoulders looks at her in surprise.

>   CARLA
>   Yes. For the little time you
>   two spend around the station,
>   he must feel he has to make
>   up for his lost time. And
>   for everybody else's.

>   SHOULDERS
>   I have no control over the animal
>   instincts of my partner. Not in
>   my jurisdiction.

Pause. Carla looks at him gloomily.

>   (CONTINUED)
- - - - - - - - - - page break - - - - - - - - - -

CONTINUED:

                    SHOULDERS
          (going on)
     Besides, Sergeant, he's a
     great guy. You really ought
     to give him a tumble.

                     CARLA
          (stricken)
     A what?

                    SHOULDERS
          (getting up)
     Hell, he's virile, he's crazy
     about you and he's white.
     What more could you want?

                     CARLA
          (a low voice)
     I really should have taken a
     closer look at your off-
     center underpinnings. You're
     a real bastard.

                    SHOULDERS
     Hey, lady. Handle it
     yourself. The force is a
     man's world. You wanted in.
     It's your problem.

                     CARLA
          (sarcastic)
     Valuable advice. Thanks.

She's off. Shoulders screws up his face in
anguish over his own words. He calls after her.

                        (CONTINUED)
- - - - - - - - - - page break - - - - - - - - - -

```
CONTINUED:
                        SHOULDERS
                Sergeant?

Carla looks back at him.

                        SHOULDERS (CONT'D)
                    (trying)
                What are you Narcs working on
                these days?

                        CARLA
                    (sounding very
                     hard)
                Not much. Just busting
                heads, busting pushers,
                busting butt.

She's through the door. It closes behind her.

                        SHOULDERS
                Shoulders, you asshole.

He throws his cigarette packet into a dumpster.
```

It is important to emphasize that, in a screenplay, dialogue does not stand alone. This is what makes it different from a play. Use your action to help create a rhythm. Use your action to tell as much of your story as you can.

Dialogue as Poetry

Although some people insist that screenplays are not literature and that it is erroneous and misleading to consider them as such, do not believe it. Most good screenwriters do not believe it. Although at present the screenplay remains in the background of the film project and the advertising hype, this will not forever be the case, especially if the Writer's Guild and the screenwriters have any say about it.

To get produced, a screenplay must move people. Most significant, it must move *someone* enough or get *someone* excited enough to think a film can be made from the script—one that is good enough to move and excite millions of other people, whether it be with comedy, drama, adventure, mystery, or science fiction.

Dialogue is a perfect example of how you can use "literariness" to your advantage. By definition, literature uses language in distinctive ways, making use of the range of features we also use in conversation. So treat dialogue as literature. In the next chapter on style, I look at how to craft language so that it maintains some of the features of literature: pacing, rhythm, patterns, metaphors, and figures of speech.

APPLICATIONS AND EXERCISES

1. Character Sketch—After the fact. Pick a character from a film that you particularly like and sketch out a profile on him or her. What makes this character a strong character?

2. Character Sketch—Self-portrait
   a) Do a character sketch of yourself (or loosely based on yourself) that you might use for a film. This should be an informal list of physical, sociological, and psychological features.
   b) Put this character (whom you know so well) in a scene.

3. Subtext
   a) Find a scene in a screenplay or film that has a subtext. Describe what is going on at the various levels.
   b) Write a scene that has a subtext.

4. The Two-Minute Dialogue Cut
One of the most useful exercises in my film-writing classes has been The Two-Minute Dialogue Cut. It is often best done by a trusted editor, fellow screenwriter, or, failing this, a friend you can trust to be sensitive, intelligent, and honest. You can do it yourself, although this solitary approach is generally less effective because writers are quite naturally attached to writing they have labored over.
   a) Have your selected reviewer read the entire screenplay. If the screenplay is incomplete, let him read as much as you have and fill him in on the rest, as appropriate.
   b) Select 10 to 20 pages of screenplay. Give the reviewer a colored pen.

c) Instruct the reviewer to slash the dialogue by one third to one half. Tell him to work quickly, trying to get through the pages in 2 minutes. He should be ruthless and cold-blooded, attempting to cut out everything that is not totally necessary, including words, phrases, sections, and whole scenes if he can.

d) Survey the damage. Chances are that most of what the reviewer has cut can be left out. There may be the odd sentence that has to be put back or replaced to connect one scene with another or for foreshadowing purposes.

e) Try not to be defensive. This is an exercise designed to give you a different and often enlightening perspective on what is necessary and what might be expendable in your dialogue.

Rationale: The quick cutting tends to mirror the speed at which a reader reads. It also helps the reviewer avoid the problem of thinking too long and hard about a specific word or phrase. Remember, elements can always be put back. Although the reviewer may have cut too much, this activity should sensitize the writer to the fact that she does not need to say as much to get across her message. It is quite likely that this shortened version will be sharper, more focused, and more dynamic.

When you have cut out one third of your dialogue, wait a few days and then cut out another third. Then you should be set!

The Nuts and Bolts
of Screenplay Format

One of the most important aspects to screenwriting is professional presentation. It is the first thing that experienced readers notice, and it can mark the writer as a professional or a novice. When writers come across as novices, they increase the chance that their scripts will not be read.

Films are expensive to make; screenplays are expensive to buy or even option. It is cheaper, therefore, for a producer, studio executive, or story editor to say "no" and absolve themselves of responsibility for spending money to acquire a flop. Improper format makes it too easy to say "no."

Many writers have their scripts retyped by professional script typists. Others use computer software programs to make the job easier (see appendix). Still others prefer to cope with formatting on their own using Word, WordPerfect, or another word processing program. This chapter covers the accepted conventions for typing screenplays in a standard format either on a computer or typewriter. This discussion is intended to serve as a general guideline. Although there are certainly deviations, most screenplays follow a format similar to the one described here.

SOME GENERAL RULES

Use Master Scenes

A *master scene* consists of all the action and dialogue that takes place at one location at one moment in time. *Writers work most often in master scenes* and avoid breaking their script down into specific camera angles. In other words, close-shot, medium-shot, and long-shot indications should be used minimally, as should specific camera movements (dolly, pan, track).

Remember that, at this stage at least, you are the writer, not the director. Try to avoid annoying your producers or potential directors by overdetermining the "look" of the film. In other words, do not use too many shots. *Do not overdirect.* That said, when used judiciously, a close shot or a dolly shot can be useful, but only when it is warranted dramatically. For example, using *close shot* for dramatic emphasis to call attention to an element in the story is not only acceptable, but also dramatically effective. When overused, however, camera indications make a screenplay difficult to read and can antagonize many readers, such as directors or producers, who feel that shot selection is not the domain of the writer. In point of fact, you can do some directing by *describing* a scene in a certain way and establishing a point of view through your descriptions. Just do not do it with shot breakdowns.

Describe What Readers/Viewers Are to See and Hear

As mentioned in chapter 1, a screenplay is a description of what a viewer might see on the screen. Therefore, it is important to work toward creating a filmic image (picture and sound) for the reader. All descriptions should be in *present tense* and depict as precisely and clearly as possible what will be seen on the movie screen.

Do not describe what we cannot see or hear. For example, unless the following can be talked about by the characters or in titles or seen on the screen, *avoid* including:

- a character's thoughts
- a character's background
- actions (that we do not see) leading up to the scene described
- actions (that we do not see) that will take place after the scene described
- details about the setting that we cannot see or hear

Use a Standard Script Format and Be Consistent

Some people argue that there is no such thing as "standard screenplay format." Although it is true that formats can vary—sometimes widely—most professional readers of dramatic scripts (story editors, producers, directors, actors) expect the dramatic script to look and read a certain way. Although highly acclaimed writers can get away with odd-looking screenplays, most writers cannot. Novice writers, in particular, should take care that their work looks professional.

Consistency is one of the hallmarks of professionalism. If you write a scene heading in one style, do not change it halfway through your screenplay.

Pay Attention to Standard Grammar, Punctuation, and Spelling

This rule may seem like a given, but it is surprising how many screenplays are filled with errors in mechanics. Although a writer can take some license in creating dialogue for his characters—using sentence fragments, for example, or phonetic spelling (for dialect differences)—scripts are much simpler to read when writers pay attention to mechanics. Most people who read screenplays are very busy people who read hundreds of screenplays a month. If a screenplay is filled with grammatical errors, it takes more time to get through, and this alone makes it easier to reject as a viable property.

In summary, using proper mechanics accomplishes three things. First, it makes the screenplay easy to understand. Run-on sentences, lack of punctuation, and errors in forming contractions all make smooth reading more difficult. Second, one of the highest compliments that can be lavished on a screenwriter is that she has written a screenplay that is "literate." This means a variety of things—many of which we go into later when we discuss the language of screenplay—but a script that is cluttered with mechanical errors cannot, by definition, be considered literate. Finally, proper mechanics demonstrate that the writer is a member of a writing community—that he has control of his medium, of English, and of filmic language. A writer has far less of a chance to be accepted as one of a community of writers if he has created an illiterate persona through sloppy mechanics.

THE MECHANICS OF SCREENPLAY FORM

To begin, let us start with a typical master scene at the beginning of a typical screenplay.

The Basics: Slug Lines and Headings, Shot Descriptions and Dialogue

Example 1: Slug Line or Scene Heading

```
FADE IN:

INT. STUDIO APARTMENT - DAY
```

Explanation

Screenplays most commonly begin with **FADE IN**, meaning that the picture gradually "fades in" or appears out of a black background. **FADE IN** appears at the left-hand margin, is always capitalized, and is followed by a colon. Most films conclude with **FADE OUT**, which appears at the right-hand margin, again in capital letters. **FADE OUT** indicates a fade to black and is followed by a period.

Slug lines always begin with **EXT.**, meaning the shot takes place outside (or exterior) or **INT.**, meaning the shot takes place indoors (or interior); these cues are abbreviated. Every time there is a change in location or time, you must use a new slug line that includes—at the very least—**EXT.** or **INT.**, the location, and the time of day.

Time of day is usually **DAY** or **NIGHT**, but can also be **DAWN, DUSK, EVENING**, and **EARLY MORNING** if these distinctions are important to the story. If two consecutive scenes take place during the same day, an accepted notation is **LATER THAT DAY**. If you have a series of shots that takes place the same day, you do not need to repeat **DAY** in the slug line.

The slug line is always capitalized so that it stands out from the body of the text. Aside from improving readability, this also makes it easier for the director, cinematographer, production manager, and other crew members to do their work.

If the film takes place during a certain time period or if the date is important (such as in the passage of years), the date usually appears in parentheses at the end of the slug line, as in:

```
INT. STUDIO APARTMENT - DAY (1933)
```

If the viewer needs to be aware of the specific date, an onscreen title may be desired. This would appear in the scene description as: **TITLE IS SUPERIMPOSED: 1933.**

If the location needs more specificity—for example, if one scene takes place in the living room of an apartment while the next scene takes place in the bedroom, and this distinction is important—these different locations should be indicated, separated from the overall location (the apartment) by slash marks, as in:

```
INT. JOE'S APARTMENT/FOYER - DAY
```

or:

```
                INT. JOE'S APARTMENT/BEDROOM - DAY
```

Punctuation: Except with slash marks, there is a single space between all words and very often a hyphen (separated by a single space from the preceding and the following words) between location and time of day.

Example 2: Slug Line and Scene Description

```
INT. STUDIO APARTMENT - DAY

The apartment is small and sparsely furnished.
JOHN HOLLAND, an attractive 40-year-old man with
shoulder-length curly hair is seated on a couch,
his hands poised over an electric piano. A HIGH-
PITCHED HUM emanates from the piano.
```

Explanation

The *scene description* (sometimes called *action*) follows the slug line and begins two lines down from the slug line. Scene descriptions are always single spaced.

Characters who are introduced for the first time should be briefly but interestingly described in a sentence or two. This characterization should include age, sex, and a general physical description, and it should avoid any psychological profile or mental state that is not evident visually (see examples in previous chapter). Sharp, short character description is important because it helps create a mental picture for the reader and helps differentiate one character from another.

Capitalization.   All newly introduced characters appear in capital letters the first time they appear. When they appear subsequently, they are often written in lowercase, although some writers prefer to capitalize characters' names all the way through the script. Character entrances and exits are also generally capitalized (e.g., **PETE EXITS**). All salient sounds—sounds that are important plot points (a knock on the door, an approaching thunderstorm)—are capitalized. Ambient noise (dogs barking, the wind in the trees, street sounds) are not capitalized unless they have consequential bearing on the plot. Finally, all camera movements are capitalized.

Capitalization makes it possible for a producer, line producer, script supervisor, or other reader to see at a glance where characters are introduced and what special effects or sounds are required for that particular scene. To summarize, the following should appear in uppercase (capitalized):

1. Scene headings (or slug lines)
2. Characters who are introduced for the first time
3. Character entrances and exits
4. Significant sounds or sound effects
5. Camera movements

Do not capitalize anything in the dialogue. If you want to emphasize a word or phrase, use underlining or italics.

Example 3: Scene Description (Action) and Dialogue

```
EXT. CENTRAL PARK - DAY


Pete and Karen stroll leisurely through the park.
As they near the reservoir, Pete turns to Karen.


                    PETE
         You never told me you were married.


Karen looks intently at Pete, then shrugs.


                    KAREN
                 (softly)
         What does it matter now?
```

Explanation

For dialogue, the name of the character who is speaking (**PETE, KAREN**) should be capitalized and located at a set margin approximately in the middle of the page (see next section for margins). Any dialogue direction (i.e., "softly") should appear on a line of its own and in parentheses. It should be at a margin five spaces left of the character name margin. Dialogue begins on the next line.

Both the dialogue and dialogue direction should be single spaced.

When one character speaks before another character has taken his turn, use **CONT'D** (abbreviated and in parentheses after the name of the character). For example,

```
                    KAREN
          You lout! You common, good-
          for-nothing lout!
```

She takes a swing at Pete and misses.

```
                    KAREN (CONT'D)
          You knew from the beginning!
```

Sometimes you will want characters to interrupt one another. Although there are a number of ways to write this, here is a fairly typical way:

```
                    DEBBIE
          I've made every effort to—

                    BARRY
                (interrupting)
          Don't give me that crap!
```

Note that dialogue is commonly broken up by both action and dramatic pauses that might indicate hesitation, reflection, or awkwardness on the part of the characters involved.

Naming Characters.   You can call the characters by whatever name you choose (first name, last name, nickname, title); just be consistent. For example, if you call a character "ADMIRAL" for a few pages, avoid suddenly calling him "ADMIRAL BYRD."

Also, try to keep character names short, easy to recognize, and easy to distinguish from one another. For example, using "KAY" and "KATE" or "JACK" and "JAKE" in the same screenplay may easily cause confusion because they look so much alike. Avoid the potential for confusion wherever you can.

Dialogue Direction.   The maxim about overdirecting is also true for dialogue direction ("softly," "lovingly," "angrily"). More often than not, the way a line is said can be inferred from the action. *Avoid dialogue direction wherever possible.* Where absolutely necessary, try to keep it at one or two words, and put all action into the scene description instead. For example, "Karen looks intently at Pete, then shrugs" is both action and too long for a dialogue direction; it therefore appears in the shot description.

Margins

Before we go any further, I should say a word about margins. People working in professional and technical writing know the value of blank space. It improves readability and textual design, helping to highlight important points. Blank space in the script is no exception. Centered in the middle of the page with wide margins, the dialogue is surrounded by white space; hence, the format of the film script emphasizes dialogue.

Although margins do vary from one script to the next, use the following as a rough guide:

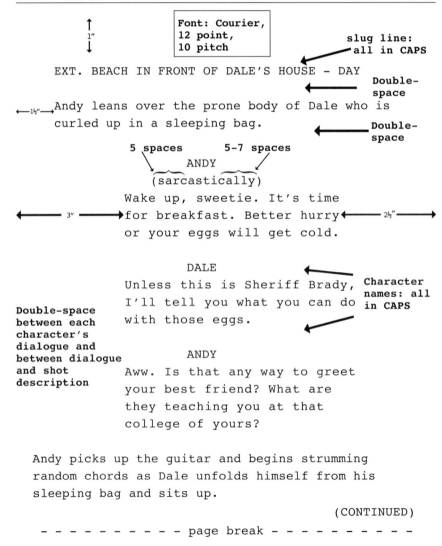

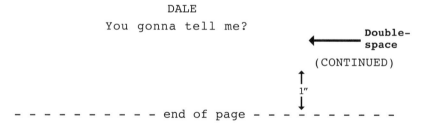

CONTINUED:

                        ANDY (CONT'D)   **No CAPS or**
               When did you get in? ◀━━━━   **boldface in**
                                              dialogue

                        DALE
               Eight.

                        ANDY
               How come you slept out here?
               Did you have another fight
               with mummy dearest?

Dale stands up and starts to brush the sand off.

                        DALE
               You know what time it is?

                        ANDY
               Yep.

Dale stares at Andy through sleepy eyes. Andy
strums   a   chord.

                        DALE
               You gonna tell me?
                                              Double-
                                     ◀━━━━   **space**

                        (CONTINUED)
                                         ↑
                                        1"
                                         ↓
- - - - - - - - - end of page - - - - - - - - - -

Explanation

The left margin of 1½ inches may be widened to include scene numbers. Scene numbers are usually added with the final revision so that scenes do not have to be numbered and renumbered as scenes change through the early drafts. Whatever your margins, *make the dialogue margin sufficiently large so that it cannot be confused with the scene description.* Pay particular attention to the right-hand margin, trying to avoid letting the dialogue extend too far into the margin.

Likewise, do not let the dialogue direction bleed into the margin for the dialogue. The margins for dialogue direction are very wide; often there is only room for one or two words on each line. Again, try to limit your dialogue direction so that you do not take up a lot of space.

Page Breaks

Note that should a page break occur before the scene ends, (CONTINUED)—all caps and in parentheses—appears at the right margin. On the top of the following page, CONTINUED: should appear at the left margin, to indicate that the shot carries over from the preceding page.

Try to avoid breaking dialogue at the page break. If it is unavoidable, use the following format:

```
                    PAUL
          I can't stand up in front of
          two hundred people tomorrow. I'll
          turn purple and ...
                         (MORE)


                                      (CONTINUED)


 - - - - - - - - - - page break - - - - - - - - - -

CONTINUED:


                    PAUL (CONT'D)
          ... break out in hives. Don't
          make me do it. For the love of God.
```

Explanation

Although it is always better to break the dialogue at the end of a sentence, if you must break midsentence, try to break it at a clause boundary (i.e., where the sentence seems to break easily and naturally) and use ellipses to indicate that the dialogue continues on the next page. Note the ellipses (above) as the dialogue ends on one page and as it begins on the next. MORE should be slightly to the right of center.

Each page should be numbered in the upper right corner; the page number should be followed by a period (.).

Camera Shots and Movements

Although indications about camera shots and camera movements should be used sparingly, it is important to know what they are and to use them correctly. Here is a list of the most commonly used camera directions:

AERIAL SHOT—from an extremely high angle, usually from an airplane or helicopter. This shot is usually of landscapes; people, if visible, are quite small in the frame.

LONG SHOT—from a distance of about 200 yards or more. The subject of the shot is very small in the frame. Examples might include a horse galloping along a beach a half mile away or a police car traveling along a dirt road several miles distant.

FULL or **ESTABLISHING SHOT**—from a relatively short distance, including the full subject. For example, the openings of many sitcoms include a full shot (or establishing shot) of the house the characters live in. Full shots show characters in their setting.

MEDIUM SHOT—from a short distance, usually showing a person from the waist up.

CLOSE SHOT—from close up. Close shots are generally face shots or head shots. Should you wish to indicate a very tight close shot, such as of an eye or the muzzle of a gun, generally **EXTREME CLOSE SHOT** is used.

INSERT—similar to a close shot. Writers use insert shots to call attention to an object, such as a photograph, letter, piece of jewelry, weapon, contents of a closet, and so on. Usually, but not always, these objects are static and are used to reveal something more closely.

POV—or point of view. These are used with a character's name, such as **DAMIEN'S POV**, and mean that the camera is taking on the character's perspective for the shot.

Important note—When you break out of a master scene to go to any of the shots above, you need to return to the master scene if you wish to play out the rest of the scene. Typically this is accomplished by the slug line: **BACK TO SCENE**.

There are a variety of different camera movements that are used in screenplays. These are the most commonly used:

PAN—the camera is stationary, but the field of view moves left or right. It is not advisable to indicate direction. Let the director handle that. Example: "`CAMERA PANS TO REVEAL ...`" In a **TILT**, the camera is again stationary, and field of view moves up and down. Note, again, that camera directions are capitalized.

DOLLY—both the camera and the field of view move. The dolly shot is much more common than the pan. Example: "`CAMERA DOLLIES WITH EILEEN as she moves toward the window.`"

TRACK—the camera is (literally) on a track and follows (or "tracks") the subject. "`CAMERA TRACKS WITH THE MOVING CAR.`"

PULL BACK AND REVEAL—the shot widens so that some new character or elements is revealed. "`CAMERA PULLS BACK TO REVEAL JEFF, now standing over Bob with a dagger in his hand.`"

SUPER—abbreviation for "superimposed." Generally this is used in scene descriptions when you want a title to appear over the scene. `SUPER: SIMLA, INDIA ... AUGUST 1914.`

V.O.—abbreviation for "Voice Over." This is used when you hear the voice of a character or narrator, but he or she is not in the scene. Most often this is put next to the character's name in the dialogue column. Example:

```
            NEVILLE (V.O.)
      I was born by a river ... in a little
      tent.
```

O.S.—abbreviation for "Off Screen." This can refer to a voice or sound that is in the scene, but is not visible in the particular shot. For example, "`O.S. crash is heard`" or "`John turns as he hears Donna's O.S. screams from her office.`" If this refers to specific dialogue, this also appears next to the character's name in the dialogue column.

```
            MOTHER (O.S.)
      Are you in bed yet?
```

Scene Heading Variations

There is quite a variety of scene heading possibilities.

```
ANGLE - KEISHA
```

Within the master scene, the focus switches to Keisha. Sometimes this is abbreviated even more to ANGLE.

```
CLOSE - ISABEL
```

This is a close shot on Isabel, often used for dramatic emphasis.

```
TWO SHOT - BOBBY AND JAKE
```

Often used to show two people in Medium Shot, reacting or talking.

```
KEISHA'S POV - BUSY STREET
```

POV is an abbreviation for "Point of View." In this case, the busy street is seen as if through Keisha's eyes.

```
EXTREME CLOSEUP - MOSQUITO
```

This is a very, very close shot and is used to focus complete attention on a small object, which, consequently, appears very large in the frame.

```
EXT./INT. CLEAVER HOUSE - DAY
```

EXT./INT. indicates that the shot involves two locations—either by moving outside (exterior) to inside (interior) or by having the camera located outside and looking inside, such as from the yard into the living room.

Series of Shots or Montage.   Occasionally, a writer will want to show a sequence of quick shots to show a passage of time. Usually these have no dialogue and are used to illustrate a series of sequential events. For example, a sequence indicating the growth of a child into an adult (birth, infant, toddler, child, teenager, etc.) might be best illustrated through a series of shots. A *series of shots* and a *montage* have been used interchangeably, but technically a *series of shots* indicates events in chronological order, while a *montage* may be showing events that occur simultaneously. A series of shots often includes characters in the film, whereas a montage may not and can usually be constructed in postproduction. The following is an example of a series of shots:

```
SERIES OF SHOTS - BILL'S YOUTH

A) Hospital Ward — Newly born Bill cries.
B) Infant Bill cries from his stroller.
C) Toddler Bill on his tricycle cries.
D) Bill, age 7, cries as he rides his bike.
```

A montage might look like this:

```
MONTAGE - L.A. RIOT

A) AERIAL SHOT - Two men beat up a third
B) A storefront burns
C) Riot police stand ready
D) Citizens in line at a grocery store, packing
handguns in their belts
```

Again, camera directions or specific locations should be capitalized, and double spacing should separate each element. Description should be short and to the point.

Intercutting. For telephone conversations or other sequences in which the writer wants to cut quickly between two locations, there are several alternatives. The writer can indicate in the slug line or scene description that scenes are intercut, as in

```
INTERCUT - ELLEN'S GARAGE OFFICE/L.A. TIMES CITY
DESK

Ellen is on the telephone with Phil, who is
staffing the city desk.
```

A second option is as follows:

```
INT. ELLEN'S GARAGE OFFICE - DAY

Ellen is talking to Phil at the Times.

                    ELLEN
          I want the story done my way.
```

```
INT. L.A. TIMES CITY DESK - DAY
```

Phil is shouting angrily into the telephone to
Ellen. INTERCUT their conversation.

>   PHIL
>   But it reads like crap.
>   Get your ego out of this.
>
>   ELLEN
>   Get your ego out of it.

Transition Between Scenes. To indicate that a scene or sequence has ended and another begins, some writers use **CUT TO** or **DISSOLVE TO**, followed by a colon, as in John Masius' screenplay, *Ferris Bueller's Day Off*:

```
INT. FERRIS BUELLER'S BEDROOM - DAY
```

>   FERRIS
>   Dad. Believes the world would
>   be a better place if everyone
>   started the day with a tummy
>   full of oatmeal.
>   CUT TO:

```
INT. KITCHEN - DAY
```

BARBARA BUELLER, forty, dressed in a business
suit, cradles the phone on her shoulder.

>   BARBARA
>   Ferris. It's ten after.
>   CUT TO:

The choice to use **DISSOLVE TO** usually indicates a passage of time, ranging from a few hours to a few days to a few years. Because **CUT TO** is often implied, it is not really necessary, and some writers choose to omit it altogether.

Now that we have gone through the essentials, let us take a look at an extended example of a professional screenplay. This sample is from *Outbreak* by Ted Tally.

```
INT. HOSPITAL CORRIDOR (BOSTON) - MOVING ANGLE -
DAY

Robby and THREE BOSTON DOCTORS, dressed in full
surgical smocks, caps, foot covers, and gloves,
stride briskly down the hall and approach double
doors marked "Quarantine: Protective Clothing
Required" in red letters. COMPUTER KEYS POUND OUT
A TITLE: BOSTON MUNICIPAL HOSPITAL. SEPTEMBER 2.

Robby and the other doctors put on their positive
pressure facemasks, and we hear the sound of
RUSHING AIR.

INT. QUARANTINE WARD

Jimbo Scott's girl friend, Alice, lies near death
in one bed while ...

Jimbo lies near death in another. Plastic drapes
have been placed over both beds, holding the air
inside.

Robby moves closer to Jimbo, sits beside his bed.
She is shocked at his condition. The scarlet
hemorrhagic rash can be seen on both cheeks.
Blood trickles from his nose, mouth, and ears,
soaking his sheets. His chest heaves weakly.

                                        (CONTINUED)

 - - - - - - - - - page break - - - - - - - - -
```

CONTINUED:

>   ROBBY
>   Mr. Scott ... Jimbo ...? Can
>   you hear me? We're trying to
>   figure out how you got this
>   disease. Please try to help
>   us, it's very important. You
>   work at an animal facility in
>   San Jose ... Jimbo?

But Jimbo's eyes are blank; his chest is still.
He's dead. Upset, Robby looks at the other
doctors. Their voices are low, frightened.

>   BOSTON DOCTOR #1
>   What in God's name is this?

>   ROBBY
>   I don't know. We'll need a post.

>   BOSTON DOCTOR #2
>   No way. I'm not gonna slip and
>   cut myself and get whatever the
>   fuck he had.

>   BOSTON DOCTOR #1
>   Me neither.

Robby looks at Doctor #3: What about you? He
looks back at her nervously. Suddenly, from under
her plastic shield, Alice stares over at Jimbo's
bed. A pitiful whisper.

>   (CONTINUED)

- - - - - - - - - - page break - - - - - - - - - -

CONTINUED:

                          ALICE
            Jimbo? Honey, are you all
            right? Answer me, please ...

Alice has just spoken her last words. FADE UP the
WHIR of a SUCTION PUMP, as we go to:

INT. BOSTON MUNICIPAL HOSPITAL - PATHOLOGY LAB -
DAY

We see a plastic autopsy tent, with negative
pressure SUCTION PUMPS WHIRRING. Two shadowy
figures stand inside ...

INSIDE TENT

Boston Doctor #3, in a biosafety suit, stares at
Jimbo's naked body lying on the autopsy table.
The body is appallingly marbled with hemorrhagic
lesions.

Robby, also in a biosafety suit, stands opposite.

                          ROBBY
            Go very slowly. Maximum sharps
            precautions.

Sweat drips off the doctor's face, fogging his
visor. He starts to make the first cut, but his
hand is trembling too much. He looks up at Robby
helplessly.

                                        (CONTINUED)

- - - - - - - - - - page break - - - - - - - - - -

```
CONTINUED:
                    ROBBY (CONT'D)
          It's okay. It's okay.
          Give me the scalpel, and
          you assist.

He turns the blade carefully, giving her the
handle end. Holding it firmly, she hesitates,
swallows hard, then reaches toward a central point
high on Jimbo's chest.
```

Note how easy to read the screenplay is. The slug lines indicate where we are—both generally (Boston) and specifically (hospital corridor)—and the time of day. The scene quickly identifies which characters are being featured, and the formatting (paragraph length, dialogue, and dialogue direction) highlights what we see and hear. The paragraphing is short and easy to follow.

CHECKLIST

After you have completed a draft of your screenplay, run through the following checklist of most commonly made errors:

1. The dialogue margin bleeds into shot description margin. Example:

```
              LESLIE
     I've been in Paris so long that I don't even
     recognize when someone is speaking French or
     English. I've even gotten used to the dog
     poop on the sidewalks.

She goes to the window and looks out at the river
flowing slowly past her 19th floor apartment. It
has started to rain.
```

If this scene stretched out to a page or so, it would be difficult to distinguish between dialogue and shot description. Keep the dialogue margins clearly distinct from the description margin. Revision:

```
                         LESLIE
          I've been in Paris so long that
          I don't even recognize when
          someone is speaking French or
          English. I've even gotten
          used to the dog poop on the
          sidewalks.
```

She goes to the window and looks out at the river
flowing slowly past her 19th floor apartment. It
has started to rain.

2. Too much business is explained in the dialogue direction. Also, the margin is too small.

```
                    PIERRE-HENRI
              (nodding as he fingers a newly grown
               beard which is flecked with gray)
          I don't really understand English that
          well.
```

This should read:

Pierre-Henri fingers a newly grown beard that is
flecked with gray.

```
                    PIERRE-HENRI
                      (nodding)
          I don't really understand English that
          well.
```

3. Characters are not capitalized at all or are intermittently capitalized throughout the screenplay.

It is quite useful for a director, the director of photography, and the production manager to know when a character first appears. It is also useful for a reader to be aware of the point he appears in the story. Use capitalization to improve readability and be consistent.

4. The screenplay is overdirected with too many camera movements and shot indications.

Although you can certainly get away with indicating a shot now and then—and sometimes this can add quite a bit to the reading of your screenplay—too much "directing" can, as we have said, antagonize a reader. For example,

```
INT. ATLANTA TOWNHOUSE - NIGHT


CLOSE SHOT as Guy enters the room and collapses on
a couch. He is drunk. CAMERA PANS with Mimi as she
enters through the same door and glares at Guy with
undisguised hostility. CAMERA ZOOMS IN on Mimi as
she holds up a paper napkin emblazoned with a
bright red lipstick stain.


CLOSE SHOT - GUY


As he reacts. Mimi smirks, tosses the napkin at Guy
then jumps on top of him and pummels him with her
fist.
```

First, the camera directions really do not add anything to the telling of the story. The camera angle in the slug line actually could slow down the reading. Furthermore, Mimi is not in the second shot (according to the slug line), so technically we cannot see Mimi when we are in close on Guy. Whenever you can, simplify your formatting; in most instances, the story is more important than the camera angles. Instead, convey your "vision" of the story or through vivid scene descriptions that help direct and focus the reader's visual imagination. Revision:

```
INT. ATLANTA TOWNHOUSE - NIGHT


Guy enters the room and collapses on a couch. He is
drunk. Mimi enters through the same door and glares
at Guy with undisguised hostility. She holds up a
paper napkin emblazoned with a bright red lipstick
stain.


                              (CONTINUED)
```

(CONTINUED)

```
Guy reacts. Mimi smirks, tosses the napkin at Guy then
jumps on top of him and pummels him with her fist.
```

5. The script provides background and/or a character's thoughts.

```
INT. OFFICE/CHICAGO TRIBUNE - DAY

BILL is a cub reporter assigned to women's news.
He'd prefer to be covering Notre Dame football.
He's from Wisconsin and misses the duck-hunting he
used to do with his father (a Republican), who
died in a hunting accident in Minnesota. Bill's a
gambler; he lost two grand in Vegas last year.
```

This is what we need from the script: his looks, his age, his demeanor (so we might get an idea of what he will look like on the screen). The rest of the information should not be in a screenplay unless it is something we learn by watching him in action.

6. There are too many spelling, grammar, and punctuation errors.

I have said this before. Sloppy mechanics can only hurt the chances of selling your screenplay. Sometimes readers can or will ignore spelling errors or odd punctuation. But you are taking a chance you do not need to take. Use your spell checker or grammar software to make sure the errors you have are intentional. Be aware, however, that spell checkers do not catch every spelling error (especially where the word is wrong, but is spelled correctly), and grammar checkers are notoriously unreliable, especially for dialogue, where you may want sentence fragments or run-ons. Have a friend check your mechanics, and proofread your material well.

Because screenplays vary greatly from one to another, there is a strong likelihood that you may come up with something you want to describe or indicate in your script for which there is no apparent rule. In such cases, you may have to invent your own variation of the format; in so doing, however, let consistency and clarity serve as guiding principles. Try to put yourself in the role of a reader (producer, actor, etc.), asking yourself whether what you have written creates a clear image in the mind of that reader. Keep your format simple and your language concrete and specific, and use plenty of white space.

APPLICATIONS AND EXERCISES

Here are some ways to hone your skills at screenplay form.

1. Sketch out a short scene (2–3 pages) in screenplay form. Give yourself some practice. Then reread this chapter and see what you might have overlooked.

2. Find the errors in the following examples.
(a)
```
    FADE IN

    EXT. CLOSE SHOT

    Craig is chewing on a wad of bubble bum as he
    looks in the drug store window.
```

Key:

1. FADE IN should be followed by a colon.

2. Because this is the first scene of the film or of a sequence, it should begin with some kind of establishing scene so we know where we are (e.g., **EXT. CLARK STREET/CHICAGO - DAY**). If it is not an establishing shot, at the very least, the slug line should include location and time of day. Normally **CLOSE SHOT** and other indications are left to the director.

3. If this is the first scene of the film, "Craig" should be capitalized and followed by a short physical description, including age.

Solution:
```
    FADE IN:

    EXT. CLARK STREET/CHICAGO - DAY
```

CRAIG SMITH, a 50-something man sporting a professorial beard and a bow tie, is chewing on a wad of bubble bum as he looks in the drug store window.

(b)

Interior - Drug Store - Day

CRAIG enters and sits on a stool at the counter.

JOAN, a large handsome woman of thirty-six, nods at him.

>   Joan
>   (wiping her hands on a towel and
>   grabbing a coffeepot)
>   What'll it be, honey.

>   Craig
>   (chomping noisily down on his gum)
>   Espresso. With a twist.

Key:

1. Slug line (**Interior - Drug Store Day**) should be capitalized.

2. If this is not his first appearance in the film, then "Craig" should appear in lowercase.

3. All characters' names should be capitalized when they speak.

4. Joan's action (**wiping her hands on a towel and grabbing a coffeepot**) is too long to put in dialogue direction. In addition, it is all action. It should appear in the shot description; in this case, it could be put before she begins to speak.

5. Joan's dialogue needs to be properly punctuated (with a question mark).

6. Craig's dialogue description extends too far into the right margin. It should end with "down," and the rest should appear on the next line, still within the dialogue direction margin. Because it is action, it would be even better to put it in the scene description.

Solution:

```
INT. DRUGSTORE - DAY

Craig enters and sits on a stool at the counter.
JOAN, a large handsome woman of thirty-six, nods
at him. She wipes her hands on a towel and grabs
a coffeepot.

                    JOAN
          What'll it be, honey?

Craig chomps down noisily on a piece of gum.

                    CRAIG
          Espresso. With a twist.
```

(c)

```
Joan pours him a cup of coffee from the pot and
slides  it  toward  him.

                    CRAIG
          Muchas gracias, baby.
          (Pause) When do you get
          off work?

                    JOAN
          Get a life, Craigie.

                    CRAIG
              (UNDER HIS BREATH)
          I hate it when you call me that.

          cut to
```

Key:

1. Craig's pause is a dialogue direction and should be on a line of its own within the dialogue direction margin. It should be entirely in lowercase.

2. Craig's dialogue direction "`UNDER HIS BREATH`" should be in lowercase.

3. `cut to` should be capitalized and appear in the far right margin. It should be followed by a colon.

Solution:

```
Joan pours him a cup of coffee from the pot and
slides it toward him.

                    CRAIG
          Muchas gracias, baby.
               (pause)
          When do you get off work?


                    JOAN
          Get a life, Craigie.


                    CRAIG
               (under his breath)
          I hate it when you call me that.


                                        CUT TO:
```

SUGGESTED READING

Cole, H., & Haag, J. (1990). *The complete guide to standard script formats.* North Hollywood, CA: CMC Publishing.

Crafting Your Screenplay
(Brilliance With Just a Little Extra Effort)

The best advice on writing I ever got was from novelist Muriel Spark, who said, "Write as if you were writing to a friend. Do not to try to impress an imaginary audience who isn't like you." My experience is that it's always better to write about what you know. I would also say, "Rewrite as much as possible." I believe in showing it to a number of close friends who will be honest with you. Listen to what they say, and rewrite accordingly. I would also warn young writers that everything you do will always take three times longer than you think it will.

—Helen Fielding (writer of *Bridget Jones's Diary*)
interviewed by Alan Waldman for WGA.org.
http://www.wga.org/pr/awards/2002/helen-fielding.html

Revision rarely gets the attention it deserves in screenwriting textbooks. This is because it seems to lack the glamour and panache associated with the initial creation of compelling characters and great stories. It gets a bad rap because it sounds dull and tedious; it requires reworking old stuff.

In fact much of the revision process can be as exciting as the original act of creation (if not more), especially when writers see themselves reworking awkward or untenable plots and drab characters into elegant and exhilarating dramas. Almost all writers—whether journalists, screenwriters, or novelists—will tell you that good revision is what makes or breaks a piece of writing. The following suggestions are geared specifically toward the screenplay and are designed to be relatively easy to implement, enabling you to give your screenplay the polish and art of a professional screenplay—or better.

Constructing a workable drama or creating interesting characters is not easy. Consequently, in the process of plotting your screenplay, you may not have had much time or energy to attend to matters of style. Because revision provides the opportunity to place focused attention on style, this chapter also contains some ideas about looking at your writing in terms of form, function, word choice, sentencing, and organization. Style and content go hand in hand. You cannot write anything without using style. This chapter helps you rework and refine the style of your piece to improve its drama, dynamism, and readability.

ALL-PURPOSE PRINCIPLES FOR WRITING THAT DAZZLES AND IMPRESSES

Most good writing, and most writing that seems like it was written effortlessly and with enormous fluency, has been revised dozens of times if not more. Sometimes these revisions are minor, but most often they involve substantive changes to the script. Characters are changed, tension is reworked, plots are thickened, story turns are adjusted or completely reconceived, and language is revised, often drastically. Revising means "re-seeing" your work and then recasting it in the most rhetorically and dramatically effective way—that is, in the way that will most appeal to your reader.

Often we fall in love with what we have written, or we have worked very, very hard on something to get it to work. Revision means changing things, and this is not easy. But revision almost always makes things better. Despite my cynicism about some of the kinds of revision suggestions you might get in story conferences, scripts almost always improve with revision, especially if that revision is done with thought and care.

Here are two ways to look at revision, both of which involve re-seeing your work with a critical eye toward making it better.

Conceptual Revision—Focuses on global consideration of the drama and includes:
- Seeing new ways to intensify the drama
- Seeing new ways to define and reveal the characters
- Coming to understand your screenplay in a different way
- Using a different strategy to convey your drama

Technical Revision—Focuses on craft and copyediting strategies such as:
- Adding description, characters, and dialogue (expanding, developing)

- Deleting (unnecessary or vague) description, characters, and dialogue
- Rearranging scenes and actions
- Clarifying
- Copyediting—correcting errors and proofreading

Some of the suggestions in this chapter can (and should) be done before anyone reads your work. Other strategies can serve as part of the revision at any time in the process.

Read as a Reader

Role-play. Pretend that you are the kind of reader who will, most likely, be reading your script (an agent or agent's assistant, a producer's assistant, a story editor). Read as someone who is more inclined to say "no" than "yes" to your project. In other words, become someone who is both skeptical and knows next to nothing about your subject.

There are several things that might facilitate this process. The first is to let the material rest for a period of time (days or weeks, if possible) without looking at it or thinking about it so that you come back to the material fresh and more objective. When you do review your work, read fast, as a reader will read.

Second, read the piece *aloud* to yourself. Often you will catch problems with mechanics, grammatical errors, and glitches in rhythm and tone. Alternately, tape-record the piece and play it back, or have a friend read it aloud so you can hear it.

Question Your Work

As you review your work, ask yourself the following questions:

Does your screenplay have enough?

Do you have as much description as necessary for your reader to be able to feel as if she were there, in the scene? Are the characters fully fleshed out? Do you have enough information about what is happening so that a reader can clearly understand with a minimum of effort?

Does your screenplay say one thing?

Are you trying to do too much? Do you have, for example, more than one premise? Certainly good films have subplots, but good subplots either run parallel to the main story or link up with it at certain key points, especially at the end. Subplots and the main plot should contribute to the same premise. Do loose ends get pulled together at the end?

Will the reader care?

This is significant and applies to your characters, your plot, and your premise. Is your protagonist universal enough so that the reader can identify with her in some way? Does your plot have enough tension to carry the reader through to the end? Will your reader become engaged in the story? What would make the reader turn the page?

Does your premise actually say something interesting or provide some insight? In other words, why should anyone see this film? If you do not have a good answer, shouldn't you?

Finally, would anyone believe your story? Are your characters so idiosyncratic that no one will believe they exist? Do you have plot twists, special effects, or dramatic surprises that test the limits of credibility? If you are worried about a plot element or character tag, cut it or change it; if you have second thoughts about something a character does or says, chances are the audience will have them too.

Do you anticipate and answer the reader's questions?

This is difficult to do by yourself because you know what you had in mind when you wrote, but it is a good thing to pay attention to. Are there plot holes—that is, things that do not make sense in the narrative? For example, do your characters live in a studio apartment that suddenly has a bedroom? Do you have characters who appear early on in the script and then disappear without comment? Or does someone get killed in Act I who later reappears in Act III? Will your reader ask—at any point—what happened?

Concentrate on what works first. Chances are that some of your screenplay is stunning; the tension works well and it has strong characterization and great dialogue. Find those scenes or sections and then bring the rest of the screenplay up to that level.

Organization

Because prototypical stories, the ones we hear in our youth, the stories of myth, and the classic stories of our cultural history, are commonly told chronologically, this is the structure we usually expect when we listen to a story or see one on the screen. Consequently, we often perceive chronology as the *natural* order, and because it meets our expectations, it is generally easier to read.

Even so, many wonderful stories do not necessarily proceed in chronological order, and, in fact, are memorably told by jumping around in time (e.g., *The English Patient*). Remember, however, that you should have good reason for breaking with tradition. For example, it is a good idea to avoid flashbacks if at all possible unless they contribute substantially to the style and tone of the film. In other words, are the flashbacks the point? Do they contribute substantively to the message you are trying to get across? Because they usually make a quick read of the screenplay more difficult and potentially confusing, are they worth it? *The English Patient* is about unlocking secrets and revealing identities. Part of the point is the difficulty of sorting out what actually happened to the patient. In *Jacob's Ladder* (starring Tim Robbins), the premise has to do with the confusion between dream world, memory, and reality, so the jumping around in time and place is highly appropriate. But quite often flashbacks not only seem contrived, but bewildering. Because they go against audience expectations about logical chronology, the disruption has to be warranted.

Where possible, keep the narrative lines clean, and let the reader discover the meaning with you. Allow the reader to walk through the scene with you; make her part of the discovery process.

Dramatic Integrity

Finally, tell the truth or at least make it seem like you are telling the truth. Make the piece both factually accurate and honest: about historical and scientific details, about human nature and psychology, and so on. Where appropriate, talk to experts: doctors for details on medical diagnoses and procedures, nuclear scientists about atomic weapons, psychologists on human nature or human pathology. Do your research. Although the research should be done *before* you begin your screenplay, it can also be enhanced in the revision process. *Outbreak* uses a lot of medical jargon, especially to describe the virus and its methods of spreading; it has to seem realistic. Even if your film is futuristic and you must invent terminology, you will be able to make it sound more realistic if you have spent some time on it. *Ghostbusters* authors Harold Ramis and Dan Akroyd came up with a laundry list of invented vocabulary to describe their ghostbusting technology; it works because it sounds realistic. If you do some homework, you will end up with a product that sounds authentic, and you will be better able to invite your reader into a world that she will believe could really happen.

QUICK AND DIRTY TROUBLESHOOTING TIPS

Essentially, you want to try to read your screenplay as a writer or producer would. As you revise your screenplay, consider using the following checklist:

1. *Check for the premise.*
To do so, look for the climax. What does the character learn? What does the audience learn? Is it one thing? Multiple things?

2. *Identify the protagonist and antagonist.* Make sure they are not one and the same.

If you have James G. fighting his own schizophrenia or Cyndy R. confronting her past and these are the principle antagonistic forces, you have internal conflict; the characters are fighting themselves. Internal conflicts are fine in fiction, but they do not work well in drama because we are not privy to the internal workings of a character's mind, only what he says and does.

This is not to say that you cannot have internal conflict as part of the drama, but this works only if it is not the only conflict sustaining the tension. For example, Frank Galvin (Paul Newman) in David Mamet's *The Verdict* has enormous inner conflict. He is a failure, a loser, and has sullied his own reputation as a lawyer. But he has bigger antagonists who are real people—and these characters enable us to see and understand the inner turmoil as we follow the story.

3. *Obey dramatic rules. And when you do break them (good films do it all the time), do so consciously, purposefully, and judiciously.*
Here is **what to avoid** unless it is absolutely critical to your plot.

- Dream sequences. They are tough for audiences to identify with because they are not "real." They do not need to follow logical or dramatic rules.
- Long-winded telephone conversations. Talking heads (see Tip 5).
- Extended scenes with characters who are:
  - ✓ Drunk
  - ✓ High
  - ✓ Temporarily or permanently insane

They do not have to obey any dramatic or characterological rules. They are nuts.

- Quickie murders. Murder is a significant action. Most people in real life do not do it cavalierly, with the possible exception of psychopaths. Psychopaths are hard to identify with, and their stories are not very dramatic unless we can see the tension within them rise and finally explode. Or unless you are writing *Kill Bill*.

4. *Cut pure exposition.*

Revise any sections where you have characters simply laying out background information. It is dull and often looks silly, especially when a character is explaining something to another character that she must obviously already know. That said, there are times when scenes that demonstrate character traits are useful because they may help explain why a character does something later in the film. If you can, keep these to a minimum and, if you find later that you do not absolutely need these scenes, drop them. The first scene in *Chinatown* seems expositional; it sets the scene for the film and lays out Gittes' character. But it also establishes that Curly owes Gittes a favor, which Gittes will later ask him to make good on.

5. *Eliminate flashbacks.*

Unless it is called for stylistically, a flashback often reveals problems in the organization or exposition of your screenplay. See if you can revise to remove any and all flashbacks, especially if there is only one.

6. *Eliminate or reduce talking heads.*

Talking heads are scenes where you have two people talking to one another for an extended length of time. They may say quite a bit, but what we see is tediously the same: two bobbing heads in the middle of the frame. There is little action or movement on screen. Telephone conversations are good examples of talking heads, but they are even worse; there is only one head. It is done in films, but it is not very cinematic.

Grammar

One irritating but important word about the bugaboo that haunts us all: Check to make sure all of your work follows standard rules of spelling and sentence structure. This makes the screenplay readable, and it marks you as a "literate" writer—someone in control of the language. Grammar rules can and probably should be broken in dialogue, but break them judiciously so that your deviations come across as dialogue color, rather than the errors of an illiterate writer.

STYLE

As I mentioned in the first page of this chapter, the style of your screenplay is very important and should be part of your revising plans. There is a range of aspects to style in screenwriting. At one level, smart stylistic changes result in enhancing the readability of your screenplay. But at a more important and perhaps more subtle level, attention to style can turn your screenplay into a well-crafted, highly engaging work of art. Here are some aspects to consider.

Format Style

We have discussed at some length the format for the screenplay. There are some considerations, other than the ones I listed in chapter 4, that help in stylistic revision. Because shot description and dialogue are quite different from one another, I will take each separately.

Shot Description. Long paragraphs are difficult to read; in fact, readers who are in a hurry will either skim them rapidly or skip them altogether. If you think the prose in your shot descriptions is important or powerful—in other words, worth reading—work with shorter paragraphs in your shot descriptions so they may actually get read by a producer. Four or five lines is usually the maximum you can get away with.

Dialogue. The same precept applies to dialogue. Consider the following scene from a screenplay rough draft by Megan Riordan, in which two characters are talking:

```
                    KATY
          No, no, you're right,
          Pascha. God, those
          words, "You're right."
          My old boyfriend used to
          say that there were no
          two sweeter words in the
          entire English language.
          But it's true. You are
          right, you know. It's
          just that, Pascha, try
          to understand me. Here
          I am, in the middle of
          central Asia, a foreign
          country, foreign
                  (MORE)
                                    (CONTINUED)
```

- - - - - - - - - - page break - - - - - - - - -

CONTINUED:

>   KATY (CONT'D)
>   culture. Everything's
>   new: language, people.
>   People—that's the worst.
>   What do you think it's
>   like, Pascha, to leave
>   the house every day and
>   have people staring at
>   you and yelling "Yankee,
>   wanna make babies with
>   me"? What do you know
>   about me and what I
>   feel? At home, Pascha,
>   I could go anywhere and
>   do anything. I was
>   free ... and independent.
>   And here, here I might
>   as well walk around
>   naked wearing bunny ears
>   and a tail because that's
>   how people look at me anyway.
>   And sometimes, I hate it
>   here, and all I want to
>   do is crawl under my
>   covers and hide, and I
>   ... I'm sorry, Pascha.
>   What am I even talking
>   about? I want to
>   understand you, Pascha.
>   I want to know you and
>   what you think and feel.
>   It's just that, well,
>   here, I feel I need you.
>   Feel I need your help
>   and, oh, I don't know.
>   (MORE)

                                    (CONTINUED)

- - - - - - - - - - page break - - - - - - - - - -

CONTINUED:

>   KATY (CONT'D)
>   Just you, okay? You're
>   the only one I can tell
>   this stuff to, the only
>   one I trust.

The obvious passion of this character will be lost in the long block of text. So is any clear message about what she is trying to get across. There is no apparent response from Pascha, the other character in the scene. Some response from him, whether it be a look or a grunt ("Pascha gives her a look of surprise" or "Pascha grunts noncommittally"), would help break up text and make the scene much more dynamic and easier to follow. As it is, a reader may get lost in the monologue of self-absorption.

But the length of the monologue is also symptomatic of another, more significant problem. The character seems frustrated, confused, and unsure of what she wants to say. The impact on the reader is often the same; the reader is frustrated, confused, and unsure of what he is supposed to get out of the exchange. Here is a revision in which I have tried to break up the dialogue and focus the exchange.

>   KATY
>   Pascha. Try to understand
>   me.
>
>   PASCHA
>   I try. But you don't make
>   sense.
>
>   KATY
>   Here I am, in the middle
>   of central Asia, where
>   I've always wanted to be.
>   But I'm lost. Completely
>   lost.
>
>   PASCHA
>   Ah.

>   (CONTINUED)

- - - - - - - - - page break - - - - - - - - - -

CONTINUED:

                  KATY
          And trapped, trapped by
          customs I don't
          understand. No matter
          how hard I try I cannot
          blend in. I've failed
          here. It's time to pack
          it in.

                 PASCHA
          This is not a country
          where Americans blend in
          easily. Perhaps that is
          a good thing. Perhaps
          it is not failure at
          all. You might still
          help.

Katy is silent for a moment.

                  KATY
          How?

Here I have changed the direction of the scene by using Pascha more and by giving the scene more movement. The characters are now clearly listening to one another, and their words have some impact; something happens. Instead of a rather ineffectual word explosion, we see that Katy's frustration and dialogue with Pascha has led her to some decision, and that is more concrete than what we have from her in the original.

Cutting, Shaping, and Sequencing

In real life people say things they shouldn't. They also do not say the things they probably should. In other words, people in real life can be utterly shy or irritatingly wordy and verbose. As I stated in chapter 3, screenwriters do not have to replicate real life in their scripts. In fact, it is dangerous to do so for several reasons. It will fight your dramatic structure, it will make for a long-winded screenplay; it is boring.

Length of Scenes.   You do not have to portray scenes from beginning to end. You do not have to start your scenes with, "Hello, how are you?", and play them out until the final "good-bye." **So, start scenes where the action essential to the plot begins (or even after).**

The feature-length screenplay is a series of scenes, and, depending on the style of the film and length of scene, the number can vary enormously. Scenes can be as short as part of a page and as long as 10 pages. An entire screenplay is about 95 to 125 pages—rarely longer. The rule of thumb is that **one page equals one screen minute.** That is not a lot. Make sure you have used your screen time wisely, both in where you want to start and end your screenplay and where you want to start and end each scene.

As difficult as it is working with the time and page limitations of the screenplay, there are numerous variables you can play with that will directly impact the style, and therefore the reception, of your piece.

Organization of Scenes.   It is an advantage to cut in and out of scenes where you want because it enables you to deal only in the best, most dramatic moments. But you can also juxtapose highly emotional or action-packed sequences with quieter scenes to create a pattern. Sometimes a "quieter" scene is merely a shorter scene; other times this is a scene in which you have allowed your characters (and audience) time to breath, think, and consider the drama thus far. In Jeb Stuart's script for *The Fugitive*, Kimble jumps off a dam in a desperate attempt to escape Gerard, the detective who has been in hot pursuit. The next scene is much quieter, with Gerard and his crew trolling below the dam and searching the shallows for Kimble. They cannot find him.

You can also intersperse uproariously funny scenes with poignantly sad scenes. The contrast is what helps you create a dynamic effect and gives your script the stamp of the pro. You are crafting your film and your filmic language.

Diction

Diction has to do with the choice of words you use to get your point across. Aristotle (330 B.C./1955) argues that:

> Nothing contributes more to produce a clearness of diction that is remote from commonness than the lengthening, contraction, and alteration of words. For by deviating in exceptional cases

from the normal idiom, the language will gain distinction; while at the same time, the partial conformity with usage will give perspicuity. (p. 61)

In other words, although you do not want to use language or diction that calls attention to itself, it is to your advantage to use language that has some distinction. What is language with distinction? It is language that is precise; creates clear, strong images in the mind of the reader; and has color. Distinctive language tends to be more forceful and powerful than common prose. Often distinctive language is very straightforward.

Diction in screenwriting can best be considered in light of the following question: Do you use language that seems appropriate? Does your use of language in your shot description convey what you want it to convey in terms of details, mood, and atmosphere? Do your characters speak both memorably and as one would expect from what we know about their personalities and backgrounds? Here are some elements to think about:

- Size of words—long, short
- Kinds of words—adjectives, adverbs, concrete nouns, abstract nouns, verbs
- Slang—including obscenities and vulgarities
- Jargon
- Academic-sounding language ("intellectual-sounding" words, like *usage* instead of *use* or *facilitate* instead of *help*)
- Common or unusual words (*wicked* or *noisy* vs. *profligate* or *obstreperous*)
- Latinate (*juxtaposition, interrogation*), ethnic (*gringo, gringa*), foreign words (*bonjour, gracias amigo*)
- Proper nouns (names of people, places, businesses, associations)

Diction in Shot Description. Shot descriptions should be detailed enough so that your reader can read quickly with complete comprehension while feeling involved, even immersed, in the world of your story. Concrete nouns (names of things like *wall, building, gun, man*) are usually better than abstract nouns (*feeling, love, universe, intellect*) because they are more likely to conjure up a distinct image in a reader's mind. Metaphors and similes work well. For example, *His face went white as chalk* tends to be more vivid than *His face went white*.

Compare the following passages. The first is a description from an early draft of a screenplay.

```
Kamal is playing the keyboard and humming
different scales. His wife, Nia, walks in and
stands in the doorway for a moment. Kamal is not
aware that she is there because he is in his own
world. The room is located in the basement of
the house and it is connected to a studio Kamal
and his brother, Kyrie, built themselves. The
room often smells of incense and feels very warm
and comfortable.
```

Although we do get a sense of the scene, the paragraph contains some generalized and abstract nouns (*warm, comfortable, in his own world*) that make the setting ill defined. The verbs tend to be forms of *to be* that fail to connote very much action. Furthermore, things are described that we would not be able to see in the film (e.g., who built the studio and the room smelling of incense). Here is a possible revision.

```
Kamal plays the keyboard and hums different
scales. His wife, Nia, walks in and stands in
the doorway for a moment. Kamal does not seem
aware of her. CAMERA FOLLOWS HER GAZE around the
room, which we see is filled with photographs of
Kamal with accomplished jazz musicians—
saxophonist Ari Brown, jazz vocalist, Cavanduka.
The room contains a cluster of amplifiers and
percussion instruments, and a large, comfortable
couch.
```

Note that the revision contains more concrete detail, and the mood that is described so generally in the first passage now has some concrete specificity.

It may be useful to take a look at style elements from good fiction and compare them with shot descriptions in a script. Here is a narrative drawn from a short story, "The Prussian Officer," (1914/2003) by D.H. Lawrence.

The spur of the officer caught in a tree root, he went down backwards with a crash, the middle of his back thudding sickeningly against a sharp-edged tree-base, the pot flying away. And in a second the orderly, with serious, earnest young face, and underlip between his teeth, had got his knee in the officer's chest and was pressing the chin backward over the farther edge of the tree-stump, pressing, with all his heart behind in a passion of relief, the tension of his wrists exquisite with relief. And with the base of his palms he shoved at the chin, with all his might. And it was pleasant, too, to have that chin, that hard jaw already slightly rough with beard, in his hands. He did not relax one hair's breadth, but all the force of all his blood exulting in his thrust, he shoved back the head of the other man, till there was a little "cluck" and a crunching sensation. Then he felt as if his head went to vapour. (etext.library.adelaide.edu.au/1/lawrence/dh/prussian/chapter1.html)

The paragraph is clearly too long for a screenplay, and it is in past tense rather than present tense, but it contains some very good techniques for shot descriptions. It is quite concrete and uses plenty of adjectives (*serious, earnest, hard, rough with beard, crunching*), adverbs, and adverbial phrases (*sickeningly, with a crash*) that contribute to a strong, evocative image. In other words, we can see what is being described.

The third example is from *Shawshank Redemption* by Frank Darabont (1996). Red (Morgan Freeman) is having a nightmare.

```
He [Red] senses a presence, looks over his
shoulder. There's a Rita Hayworth poster on his
wall. He gets out of bed. Rita just keeps
smiling, inscrutable. As Red watches, a
brilliant round glow builds behind the poster,
shining from the tunnel. The poster rips free,
charred to ash in the blink of an eye as a shaft
of holy white light stabs into the cell.
Sunlight. Red staggers back against the glare.

A whirlwind kicks up, whipping everything into
the air. The hole in the wall is like a giant
vacuum cleaner—papers, books, toiletries,
bedding—if it ain't nailed down, it gets sucked
down the hole toward the light. Red fights it,
but the suction drags him closer and closer.
(p. 110)
```

Although both of the previous examples create strong images, one is clearly more suitable for a screenplay than the other. In the first place, the diction is simpler in *Shawshank Redemption*. Darabount uses fewer adjectives and adverbs to get his point across and a lot of simple, short nouns and verbs. His generous use of action verbs (*smiling, rips, stabs, kicks, whips, fights*) helps convey action, which, as we have discussed frequently, is the core of the screenplay. Unlike Lawrence, Darabount also sticks faithfully to what we hear and see, not what the character thinks or feels. He occasionally uses literary devices such as metaphor or simile ("like a giant vacuum cleaner") to make the image more evocative.

When and if it is important to allude to something a character feels or thinks, it is common to use the locution "as if." For example, "Brad looked fearful *as if* he had seen his mother's ghost." Otherwise, describing a character's thoughts and feelings is not only amateurish and inappropriate for a screenplay, it leads the reader to question: "Okay, but what am I seeing on the screen?"

One last suggestion: Avoid "purple prose." Do not get too fancy with your descriptions. The readers are often just working through it quickly until they get to the dialogue.

Diction in Dialogue. Clearly, the rules are a bit different for diction in dialogue. The language used in dialogue should convey the unique personalities of the characters. A highly erudite character (or one that is satirizing a highly erudite person) might use a lot of abstract language, long Latinate words, or even jargon. For another character, you might want to stick to slang or even spellings that indicate an accent, as in, "C'mon, gimme some more o' that chili, dahlin." Different characters will also say the same things in different ways. Although one character may say, "I dunno," another may say, "I haven't got the foggiest idea."

In all cases, you should act with some restraint. Scholarly diction could put your audience to sleep, whereas dialect spellings that may accurately reflect a strong Liverpool accent, for example, may also be impossible to read. Also, as I have mentioned before, obscenities stand out much more in print than they do in speech. If you choose to use epithets and obscene language, be aware that you may be alienating even the most liberal of your audiences if you use them with the abandon common in everyday discourse. Obscenities are best used sparingly and only when they are absolutely called for because they almost always call attention to themselves and away from what a character is saying.

Finally, most problems with dialogue come from vocabulary that is overly formal, stilted, or bland. Use diction to your advantage to help you create characters that sound different from one another, but that represents them (their backgrounds and personalities) in interesting ways. The words characters use often reveal as much about them as their actions. In the following scene from *Jungleland*, Eric Sears and I wanted quite different characters to play off one another. Hecht, a detective, is a talkative, in-your-face kind of guy. Shoulders is quieter and, in this scene, hung over. Jaime is a young informant, taciturn and smart. They are at the impound yard looking at a stolen car.

Shoulders enters and goes over to the Porsche.
Hecht is there, studying the car. Jaime Desoto,
21, a Chicano, is leaning against another car
nearby, smoking. He seems lightly amused by
Hecht and very content to simply watch him work.
He grins broadly at Shoulders as Shoulders
approaches but remains slouched against the other
car. Hecht looks up and sees Shoulders standing
near him.

                    HECHT
         Frank, take a look at this car.

                    SHOULDERS
                 (painfully)
         Don't shout at me, Hecht.

Hecht looks at him more closely.

                    HECHT
         Rough night?

Shoulders shrugs.

                    HECHT (CONT'D)
         I know her?

Shoulders grimaces.

                    HECHT (CONT'D)
         You got to get out more,
         Frank. That greenish
         tint becomes you. Or
         broads, too. Where'd
         you pick her up? Some
         bar? She have any friends?
                              (CONTINUED)

- - - - - - - - - - page break - - - - - - - - - -

CONTINUED:

                       SHOULDERS
                (nodding at Jaime)
          Get that kid to stop
          grinning at me, would
          you.

                       HECHT
          He speaks English. You
          tell him. And be nice
          to him, Frank. He knows
          some things.

                       SHOULDERS
          Like what?

                       HECHT
          Like what this car's decked out
          with.

Shoulders takes a look at the car.

                       SHOULDERS
          Jaime.

                       JAIME
          What man?

As the scene continues, Jaime is finally prevailed on to reveal what he knows about the car.

                       JAIME
          Wide cyclone wheels. A lot of
          money.

                            (CONTINUED)

- - - - - - - - - - page break - - - - - - - - - -

CONTINUED:

                         HECHT
              And?

                         JAIME
                    (gaining speed)
              Racing rubber on the outside,
              a Nardi wheel, Scheel 560
              seats, a 3001 Blaupunkt with
              KLH woofers and tweeters, on-
              board computer ...

                         SHOULDERS
              Christ, kid, where'd you
              learn to talk like that?

Thus, in this particular scene, we worked with personality and mood to create a contrast in diction and linguistic style. Shoulders is reticent and more formal by nature; Hecht is overbearing, his talk salacious and often obscene; and Jaime is smart the ways of the street. Hecht is also in a teasing mood, and Shoulders is hung over.

Syntax

Generally speaking, the simpler the sentence structure, the better. But it is always valuable to at least consider the variety of sentence and phrase structure options at your disposal. Here are some syntactical variations to consider. See if you use the range of types at your disposal; play around with these in terms of variety.

- Statements
- Questions
- Commands
- Exclamations
- Simple/complex sentences

Again what is appropriate for shot description is not necessarily appropriate for dialogue. Generally, dialogue can use the full range of sentence types—de-

pending on context, characterization, and use—whereas shot description
should tend toward fairly simple sentences (mostly statements). Take another
look at the prior example from *Jungleland*, which contains a range of sentence
types and sentence variety.

You should also feel free to use sentence fragments and run-ons to imitate
the way people speak. However, these should look like they have been done
purposefully and not because you did not know what a complete sentence was.

Rhythm

If you can re-create the rhythms of a piece of music, your screenplay can beguile
your reader at a number of levels. First, it will seduce and fascinate your readers
and viewers, often on a subconscious level, bringing them into the action, almost without their realizing it. Second, its patterns will set the reader to expect
more of the same so that if the pattern is broken, the viewer is forced to pay
even more attention than before; breaking a pattern grabs her attention. It is
jolting. Third, you have much more control over a reader and his emotions as
he follows the piece through its dramatic crescendo and decrescendo, through
the pianissimo and pianoforte.

Although this explanation might seem a bit overstated, writing with this in
mind can work in your favor. Consider the following cadence from *Chinatown*
in which Jake Gittes is trying to figure out from Evelyn who the girl upstairs
is—the one Evelyn is trying so desperately to protect. Evelyn has already lied to
Gittes about her and he knows that.

```
                    EVELYN
          I'll tell you the truth.

Gittes smiles.

                    GITTES
          That's good. Now what's her name?

                    EVEYLN
          Katherine.



                              (CONTINUED)

- - - - - - - - - - page break - - - - - - - - - -
```

CONTINUED:

                          GITTES
                Katherine? Katherine who?

                          EVELYN
                She's my daughter.

Gittes stares at her. He's been charged with
anger and when Evelyn says this, it explodes. He
hits her full in the face. Evelyn stares back at
him. The blow has forced tears from her eyes,
but she makes no move, not even to defend
herself.

                          GITTES
                I said the truth!

                          EVELYN
                She's my sister.

Gittes slaps her again.

                          EVELYN (CONT'D)
                She's my daughter.

Gittes slaps her again.

                          EVELYN (CONT'D)
                My sister.

He hits her again.

                          EVELYN (CONT'D)
                My daughter, my sister—

                                    (CONTINUED)

- - - - - - - - - - page break - - - - - - - - - -

```
CONTINUED:
```

```
He belts her finally, knocking her into a cheap
Chinese vase which shatters, and she collapses on
the sofa, sobbing.
```

```
                    GITTES
            I said I want the truth.
```

```
                    EVELYN
                (almost screaming)
        She's my sister and my daughter!
```

Notice how the dialogue bounces back and forth; notice also the use of repetition, which creates a pattern that comes to an ending as the climax of the scene arrives.

The best kind of rhythm makes plentiful use of silence—a concept well used by film masters such as Alfred Hitchcock. Pauses, beats, and periods of silence are powerful tools for communication and are wonderful ways to establish or break a rhythm.

Writing Against the Grain

The grain of a piece of wood tends to follow in one direction. Sections of the wood that go against the grain are what make much of woodcraft (carving, furniture-making, hardwood construction, etc.) interesting. The best writers of the English language write against the grain, in the sense that they avoid clichés, conventionalized idea, and stereotypes in all aspects of their work: description, dialogue, plot points, and characterization.

For example, one of the most interesting elements of the film *Thelma and Louise* was the enormous strength possessed by the two women. Thelma, who starts out the film as a ditz, almost entirely under the thumb of a lout of a husband, turns out to have enormous composure and strength under pressure. The friendship between Thelma and Louise evolves in unusual ways through a series of unfortunate incidents. In addition, the film fights the "happy ending" stereotype as Louise drives the two of them over a cliff to avoid getting caught by the authorities.

The same thing applies to the language you use. To avoid clichés, say things a little differently. Instead of "It is a beautiful sunny day," write, "The day is bewilderingly bright." In dialogue, instead of "How are you, Jim," write, "You look like hell, Jimbo."

Clearly, writing against the grain has to be done with care and with attention to consistency and message. You do not want to confuse your audience or make them shudder or laugh outright. But you do want to intrigue and you do want to sparkle. You cannot do this with hackneyed and overused expressions.

Going against the grain gives your screenplay qualities that not only may help to sell it, but may also make it memorable.

Tone

Almost all of the preceding discussion has to do with creating a tone. Some ways of characterizing tone are terse, florid, ironic, humorous, judgmental, informal, chatty, or stuffy, but overall tone is the writer's use of language that creates our sense of how a movie will play. Because it has to do with the "feel" or "impact" of a script, it is very difficult to define before you start to write and even afterward. Often the creation of an effective or memorable tone comes with experience in writing. But your selection of stylistic features also has something to do with it, and that can be controlled, especially *in the revision* of your work.

Included next are three examples of professional screenplays from different genres (comedy, action/adventure, drama). Each has a distinct tone, created in part by choice of organization, diction, syntax, rhythm, and ways of writing against the grain. The first is from the first scene of the comedy, *The Full Monty*, by Simon Beaufroy (1998).

```
EXT. SHEFFIELD - DAY

A fine rain blankets the council estate. From
somewhere can be heard the noise of a hoover and
a man singing Sheryl Crow's "All I Want to Do Is
Have Some Fun" in a confidently tuneless
Yorkshire accent. Through the drizzle, the Man
and the Boy can be seen crouched behind a wall
watching JEAN, a sturdy woman in her mid-
thirties. She walks out of a council house,
remembers something and shouts up at the open
bedroom window from where the sound of hoovering
is coming.

                                    (CONTINUED)
```

- - - - - - - - - - page break - - - - - - - - - -

CONTINUED:

JEAN
Dave love? Dave!

No response. Jean gives up and walks off down
the road.

INT. DAVE'S HOUSE - DAY

A barrel-chested goliath in his mid-thirties is
giving the upstairs bedroom an incongruously
dainty hoover. With a flowery pinafore stretched
across his impressive stomach, DAVE hoovers up
what looks like a pebble that has appeared on the
carpet. He turns only to find that another,
larger one has appeared. Assiduously, he vacuums
this one up, too. It rattles alarmingly into the
hoover. A third pebble comes through the window,
unseen by Dave until it lands. Becoming
perplexed, Dave picks this one up, stops singing,
takes off his glasses, shakes the hoover,
attributes it to one of nature's mysteries and
carries on. Then a cowboy boot flies through the
window and hits the opposite wall with a smack.
Dave finally clicks and goes to the window.
Outside, amidst the remnants of a Ford Granada
that constitutes Dave's front garden, the Man and
the Boy have come out of hiding: GAZ, a thirty-
year-old magnet for trouble and NATHAN, his son,
who at nine years is the more mature of the two.
Hunched in his ex-army parka, Gaz stands
miserably on one leg using Nathan as a crutch.

As a comedy, this plays off comedic contradictions: a big, strong man wearing
an apron while he vacuums (hoovers), the incongruity of the boot flying
through the window instead of a pebble. Note also the use of detail and juxtaposition. These elements help create the tone.

The second example is from an action/adventure film, *The Fugitive*, by Jeb Stuart (1993). The scene is similar to the prior one in that it covers action with minimal dialogue and is near the beginning of the screenplay.

```
EXT. KIMBLE'S TOWNHOUSE - NIGHT


Snow swirls around the street as Kimble's car
pulls up on the street. On the third floor, we
see a bedroom light still on. He smiles.

INT. KIMBLE'S TOWNHOUSE - NIGHT
     .

Tastefully done. A grandfather clock ticks
softly. It's late, after one o-clock. He tosses
the keys on the entry table. He picks up a stack
of mail on the table and calls up the stairs.

                    KIMBLE
          I'm home.


No answer. He looks upstairs a moment, then goes
into the kitchen. The wall phone shows a line in
use. Kimble notices it. The washer buzzes; he
switches the clothes from the washer to dryer and
starts the machine.

HALLWAY—He starts toward the stairs, stops.
A SMALL WHITE BALL on the stairs. He bends down
and picks it up—a pearl. Two steps farther up—
more pearls.

                    KIMBLE
          Helen?


He hears a NOISE and stops. He looks up the
three flights of stairs. The lighted third floor
landing seems quiet.
                              (CONTINUED)
```

- - - - - - - - - - page break - - - - - - - - - -

CONTINUED:

UPSTAIRS - NIGHT

Kimble tops the stairs. An overturned table and
crystal lamp. He notices a wet discoloration to
the felt base. He touches it—and comes up red.
Suddenly, there is a WOMAN'S CRY FOR HELP.

Adrenal surge. Kimble looks up as ...

... a forearm flattens him.

Going for the stairs, the attacker tries to vault
him. Kimble grabs a leg and twists him down.

The man kicks free and tries again for the
stairs. This time, Kimble catches an arm.

And rips it off the man's shoulder.

Kimble looks bug-eyed at the arm in his
hands ... to the man's unreadable face ... to the empty
sleeve of the man's coat ... and back to the arm.
It's hollow. Electrodes are visible inside.

Before Kimble can recover. The ONE-ARMED MAN
snatches back his arm and wallops Kimble with it.
He whirls and clumps down the stairs. We hear a
DOOR BANG OPEN and feet escaping.

Kimble staggers up and starts to follow but ...

                    HELEN (O.S.)
        He's here ... still in the house ...

Note the choppiness of the description—created by short sentences and fragments, short paragraphs, and sparse description, mirroring the frenetic events

in the passage. These elements create an altogether different impression from
The Full Monty.

Finally, a third example from a drama, *Lone Star*, by John Sayles (1996). This
is a film constructed of fairly short scenes that jump around from location to location, one set of characters to the next. But it is a drama—things happen between people. The following is a scene where Sam, the protagonist, has been
following Pilar, with whom he had a romance as a youth.

```
EXT. WINDOW - PILAR - SAM'S POV

MUSIC CONTINUES. We can see Pilar through the
lighted window of her classroom, preparing
something on the blackboard.

INT. CAR

MUSIC ENDS as Sam leans back to wait -

EXT. PARKING LOT

Pilar digs in her bag for her car keys as she
makes her way across the lot. She sees
something, slows, reacting, then brings us to Sam
in his car. He has parked head-to-foot next to
hers. They look at each other for a long moment—

                    PILAR
                 (softly)
            Follow me.

EXT. MAIN STREET - NIGHT

Nothing stirring. Pilar's car appears, closely
followed by Sam's. The café has closed for the
night—

                            (CONTINUED)
```

- - - - - - - - - - page break - - - - - - - - - -

CONTINUED:

INT. CAFÉ - NIGHT

Sam and Pilar sit on chairs next to each other,
facing the window, talking softly. The
STREETLIGHT shining through the letters in the
front window makes patterns on their faces—

               PILAR
We thought we were something, didn't
we?

               SAM
Yeah.

               PILAR
I look at my kids in school—
tenth, eleventh graders.
That's who we were.
Children.

               SAM
Yeah.

               PILAR
I mean what did we know about anything?

               SAM
Nothing.

Pilar looks at him.

                       (CONTINUED)

- - - - - - - - - - page break - - - - - - - - - -

CONTINUED:

> PILAR
>> When Nando died—it was so
>> sudden—I was kind of in shock
>> for awhile. Then I woke up
>> and there was the whole rest
>> of my life and I didn't have
>> any idea what to do with it.

> SAM
>> You know the other day, you
>> asked why I came back?

> PILAR
>> Yeah?

> SAM
>> I came back 'cause you were here.

Pilar nods. She gets up and we FOLLOW her across
the dark room to the jukebox. She looks at the
selections.

> PILAR
>> My mother hasn't changed the
>> songs since I was 10.

She puts in a quarter, punches some numbers. A
Mexican BALLAD comes on. She crosses back to
Sam, holds her hand out. He stands to greet her.
They slow-dance in the empty café.

The style of this selection can be characterized as understated. There is ample use of silence (through short, unelaborated responses) and ellipses (cutting into scenes that are in progress and out of them before they actually end). The diction is concrete and spare, but there are elements of color and mood—the light shining through the window, the Mexican ballad. Although one might argue that the drama carries the scene, this is not entirely true. The scene has a tone—quiet and low key with underlying sexual tension; two people are meeting again and falling in love.

FINAL NOTES ON REVISING

There is a well-known adage in expository writing that is expressed by the acronym, "KISS," or "Keep It Simple, Stupid." Although I am not a big fan of acronyms, I do believe that simpler is better; it tends to be cleaner, more to the point, and, oddly enough, more impacting. Although quite different from each other in tone, all three of the previous examples follow this same precept. To help simplify, here is another checklist for you as you revise. Check for:

- Extra scenes you do not need
- Extra characters that do not serve a purpose
- Too much dialogue (see Dialogue Cutting, chap. 3)
- Long-winded shot descriptions
- Overly long-winded or convoluted sentence structure
- Ornate, baroque, or flamboyant vocabulary

Check to make sure you have only the shots and dialogue that are necessary. If possible, shorten or omit. If you cannot take anything out, you may be able to break up the paragraph—in dialogue by some bit of business or action, and in shot description by going to a new paragraph.

There may inevitably be some fear of oversimplifying or cutting out the heart of the piece. But this rarely happens, and more often than not writers overstate rather than understate. Overstating may result in an audience feeling like you are *underestimating* them; they may think you are pandering to them or treating them like dummies. Do not oversimplify, but use uncomplicated sentences and language.

Bottom line: *If it can be cut, cut it.*

Everything in the text should develop the point of that text.

Be ruthless. Be wonderful.

Finally, no matter how exciting your drama is, if your style is bland, tedious, or confusing, your audience will not buy into it. Your style will make your screenplay. Now take that drab, mediocre screenplay you have just finished and make it marvelous.

APPLICATIONS AND EXERCISES

1. To work on structure

Post-script Outline: Get a stack of note cards and write each scene with a brief description of the characters and the action on each card. Identify how each scene serves the premise, plot, and characterization. If you have a scene that is unnecessary, get rid of it. If you have two that could be combined, do it. If you feel something needs to be added, think twice about it; if you still think you need it, add it (usually we add more than we need so be cautious).

2. To work on diction and syntax

Translate: Select a passage in a novel or short story that creates a very strong image for you. Identify the features (adjectives, concrete nouns, action verbs) that help make it so strong. Be as specific as you can. Translate that passage into a shot description (in other words, be visual), feeling free to temporarily "borrow" or imitate the prose from the original.

3. Self-analysis—Select a passage in your own screenplay that you feel works especially well. Identify the stylistic features that seem to make it so strong. Again, be as specific as you can.

4. Imitation Exercise A—This exercise involves copying, word for word. Although it may seem mindless at first, this task, when done regularly, can teach you a lot about style and stylistic differences. It enables you to become familiar with the rhythms of a piece in a way that is not otherwise possible. First, find several screenplays that you particularly like, preferably by different authors and genres. Select passages and do the following imitation exercise. Read the entire passage, then:

   a. Copy the passage slowly and accurately, word for word.
   b. Do not spend more than 15 to 20 minutes copying at any one time.
   c. Do the copying with pen or pencil, not word processor or typewriter.

This exercise is most useful over an extended period of time. For example, you might do this once a week for 6 months.

5. Imitation Exercise B—This exercise involves copying patterns, using your own words rather than copying word for word. Similar to the prior exercise, select several passages from different genres of scripts. Especially useful are passages that have ample scene descriptions or action. Pay particular attention to sentence styles. Here is an example.

Original sentence:

Sam and Pilar sit on chairs next to each other,
facing the window, talking softly. The
STREELIGHT shining through the letters in the
front window makes patterns on their faces—

Imitation:

David and Chrissie stand next to the barn,
looking at the ponies, saying nothing. The
SUNLIGHT filtering in through the latticework on
the old barn window makes a silhouette on the
floor.

SUGGESTED READING

Beaufoy, S. (1998, Spring). The full monty. *Scenario: The Magazine of Screenwriting Art, 4*(1), 6–45.

Corbett, E. P. J., & Robert, C. (1997). *Style and statement.* New York: Oxford.

Darabont, F. (1996). *The shooting script: The Shawshank Redemption.* New York: Newmarket Press.

Sayles, J. (1996, Summer). Lone star. *Scenario: The Magazine of Screenwriting Art, 2*(2), 6–49.

Trimble, J. R. (2000). *Writing with style* (2nd ed.). New York: Prentice Hall.

Williams, J. M. (1997). *Style: Ten lessons in clarity and grace* (5th ed.). New York: Longman.

I like to write a draft quickly, because then I know the shape of it. Then I can go back and start layering things in and finding connections. For instance, if you discover an aspect of a character on page 90, you can go back and set that up on page 15. Or an action a character makes on page 90, I can imply might have happened on page 15. I love to do that.

—Steve Martin (writer of *Bowfinger*), interviewed by Annie Nocent
Scenario: The Magazine of Screenwriting Art 5.3 (1999/2000), 60.

Selling the Screenplay

For good or ill, there is no one way for an idea to make it to the screen. An approach to success that works for one writer will not work for the next. If it did, there would be no reason to take courses and workshops, to download "how-to" Web sites, or to fill bookshelves with books such as this one. Everyone would "make it" using the same strategies, and everyone would be rich, famous, and dull.

More helpful, I think, is to come to terms with the fact that marketing a screenplay can take all kinds of directions. This chapter lists some of the key players, defines some terms, and provides several potential scenarios with the caveat that, however you achieve success, it will probably be different from what you or anyone else imagined.

First, it is important to **know your audience**: who is (or might be) involved in the selling of your project.

POTENTIAL PLAYERS

These are some of the key personnel involved in the process of marketing screenplays:

Producers
Assistant Producers
Story Editors (for "coverage")
Assistants to Producers (often different from Assistant Producers)
Independents
Connections
Agents
Writers Guild of America

Producer

Producers come from many walks of life. They can be investors (bankers, lawyer, doctors, Wall Street financiers) with some money that they are willing to risk on a very speculative venture: film making. They can be successful actors or directors (Robert Redford, Clint Eastwood, Oprah Winfrey) who have earned a substantial reputation and have the financial clout to take over producing chores. They can be studio executives who have the responsibility for finding a good idea and bringing it to light in a film. They can be independent film makers who have built up financial connections and have the resources and know-how to make a film happen. All of these people have one thing in common: They want people to see and like their films. As an important and necessary consequence, they want to make a return on their investment.

As I have reiterated in earlier chapters, films are very expensive to make. A look at the credits at the end of a film will give you a good idea of some of the obvious costs:

- Salaries (often big ones) for directors, producers, and stars
- Salaries for the rest of the cast
- Salaries for extras, stunt people, animals trainers, tutors for child actors, gofers (miscellaneous assistants)
- Salaries for the crew (camera, grips, gaffers, editors, sound technicians, special effects experts, many of whom are union)
- Location costs (exotic, period, urban, rural)
- Equipment (cameras, dollies, editing rooms and equipment, video equipment, film stock)
- Distribution
- Advertising
- Miscellaneous production and studio costs, which can include anything from finishing guarantees and insurance to company executive and secretarial salaries

The producer is responsible for securing financing and monitoring these costs. Today an extremely low-budget film is $1 million, and that is usually made with cast and crew working for scale or less, on a short production timetable, and with the bare minimum of production costs (no distant or exotic locations, limited special effects, etc.). Most of the films that make it to the movie theaters cost much, much more. Not only is money at stake in the marketing of a film, but jobs and reputations are as well. Producers need to make films that make money to stay in business, even when they are only producing films for the love of movie making.

As I mentioned in earlier chapters, writers need to sell audiences the idea that their screenplay will result in a film that lots of people will want to see. It will make its producers and investors money, hopefully plenty of it. Remember that it is easier and much less costly to turn your idea, treatment, or script down than to put it into development or purchase it outright and have it ultimately fail. It is always safer for a producer to say, "No." So one of the goals of a pitch meeting (a meeting at which you try to sell your idea) is not necessarily to get a go-ahead (although this would be ideal), but rather to avoid getting nixed.

What kinds of films do producers think will make money? The producer's guess is as good as yours, although he may not admit it. Why doesn't anyone know? Because there are too many variables. Among these variables are:

The audience variable. There are numerous, often fluctuating markets: the children's market, the teen market, the young adult market, the intellectual market, the art market, the Baby Boomer market, and so on. What might work for one market may not work for the next, and markets change.

The timing variable. Some films are just not popular at certain moments in time, either to audiences or film producers. Audiences are known to be fickle in terms of film genre; one year the love story will be the rage among Baby Boomers; the next year, it will die miserably with the exact same audience. Westerns, science fiction, and period pieces go in and out of favor.

The packaging variable. Packaging has to do with big names (usually actors and directors) who are associated with the film. But a film can have everything going for it (lots of money, special effects, stars, directors, etc.) and still not work. Big stars are made and fade overnight. Other times, unknown actors can emerge from a film into instant stardom, meaning popularity for themselves and for the film, screenplay, and/or genre.

A producer is a person under a lot of pressure.

Assistants to the Producers

Many producers have assistants who are usually young, ambitious, and often quite smart. Producers rely on their assistants for help in the decision-making process and to do some of the legwork that producers do not have time for. Some of this legwork consists of finding projects, listening to pitches, reviewing projects, talking with screenwriters in the early stages, and suggesting ideas for revisions. An assistant has the ear of the producer. Hence, assistants, like those on a producer's secretarial staff, are good people to be listening to, be friendly to, and get to know.

Story Editors

Story editors are professional readers who are hired by a studio, network, producer, or agency to read the innumerable screenplays (and occasionally treatments) that come through a production or development office. Story editors read anywhere from 7 to 20 (or even more) per week. If your screenplay has been read by a story editor, it has received *coverage*.

A story editor reads the script and writes a brief synopsis (ranging from a paragraph to a page) and a commentary on the screenplay's strengths and weakness (ranging from one to several pages). She will make a recommendation to the producer about whether to reject the screenplay (*pass*), to consider it further (maybe suggesting substantial revisions), or to purchase it immediately. If the story editor rejects the screenplay, the producer will probably never look at the screenplay. In fact, some very busy network executives only read the coverage.

Story editors (sometimes called *readers*) are often writers. They may work at a studio on staff or they may read freelance, getting paid by the script. They are generally quite familiar with the genre of screenplay writing and writing in general, and they usually give your project a fair assessment. Other story editors aspire to producer status and are "paying their dues" in the script department.

Independents

Usually this term refers to someone who is not formally affiliated with a studio, network, or major production house, although they most commonly have plenty of connections.

Often an independent is a producer or an aspiring producer who is willing to take a chance on your screenplay or project, perhaps even option it (secure temporary rights to your screenplay or idea), to *shop it*—that is, to make attempts to find interested investors—at a major production house or studio. An independent may attempt to *package* your project with particular actors, directors, or executive producers to make it as attractive as possible to investors. For example, an independent may option a screenplay, take it to an actor with whom he might have connections (Ed Harris, Gary Busey, Susan Sarandon,

Brad Pitt), and induce him or her to consider it as a potential project. If an actor (or director) of considerable stature expresses interest in this project, it most certainly will help get things moving. Occasionally, name producers, such as Steven Spielberg or George Lucas, may be willing to sign on as an executive producer—that is, they basically endorse the project and lend their name to it, often without taking on an actual producing (or directing) role.

Connections

Most people who live and work in Los Angeles know someone affiliated with the film business. He or she may be a lawyer, an actor, a set designer, an agent, or an assistant editor. If you have connections, use them. The film business operates on the basis of connections, so do not stand on ceremony or false pride. If someone can help you, call her and ask for help. Often a passing acquaintance—someone you met at a party or health club—may be willing to help. If you actually do achieve some success, you may be able to repay that person in kind. Many agents are willing to meet with someone who comes in with a referral, especially if that referral is either a client or someone they know.

If you do not have connections, find ways to make and cultivate them. Move to Los Angeles or New York. Enroll in a film school or scriptwriting class. Enter your screenplay in screenwriting contests. Take a job as a *gofer* or production assistant—a person who works on the shooting set running errands for everybody else. Production assistants (PAs) earn next to nothing, but they make wonderful contacts. If you must, work for nothing—at least for a while. You will learn a lot and make the connections you may need to get in the door someplace.

Agents

Find an agent.

Almost no one in the film business will read a screenplay or treatment that is sent to her cold—whether it is sent by the U.S. Postal Service, Federal Express, or delivered in person. You need someone to present your idea—or shop it—and to represent you and your interests. Some people use a lawyer for this, but most use an agent because good agents make it their business to know who is buying and selling and what various production companies are looking for. Here is what an agent can do for you:

- Give you feedback on the marketability of your project or screenplay
- Arrange for a pitch meeting with a producer

- Shop your screenplay
- Negotiate a deal
- Write up a contract
- Protect your proprietary (including screen credit) and financial interests
- Get you your next deal

How do you get an agent? For first timers, people trying to break into the business, this can be a Catch 22 situation. If a producer is already interested in buying or optioning your material, it is pretty easy to find an agent to represent you. If you are a brand-new name with nothing but a script in your hand, you will have to work at finding representation. It is much more difficult, but not impossible. The irony is that the film business is always looking for something new, although it only trusts people who have a track record.

An excellent place to start is The Writers Guild of America (discussed at some length at the end of this chapter), which maintains a listing of agents and the kinds of projects they represent, including whether they are interested in taking on new clients.

Other resources include books like Callan's (2002) *The Script is Finished, Now What Do I Do? The Scriptwriter's Resource Book and Agent Guide* (Sweden Press) or the *2005 Annual Agency Guide* (Writers' Network) which contain lists of Hollywood agencies and tips from the agents on how to approach that agency with material. Callan suggests the query letter, and this is a good idea. Agents will not respond to an unsolicited script and will generally throw it away, unread. But if you write a brief, sparkling query letter about yourself and your project, and you enclose a stamped, self-addressed envelope, you have a good chance of getting somebody to reply.

In selecting an agent to approach, do your research. A small agency will be inclined to pay more attention to you and your projects; a big agency often has more clout in the industry. Many agencies, at some time or another, will take a chance on a newcomer, but a query letter will help you determine this. Chances are, your query will be read by a junior agent, who, although she may not have the status and power of her "bigger" colleagues, may make up for that lack with her energy and enthusiasm for your project.

PRESENTING YOUR MATERIAL

Most—if not all—stories have been told—not once, but dozens of times. Still, the best advice is to go in with a good story (as I have insisted in earlier chapters). Unless you have directly stolen your plot, characters, and dialogue from another story, your screenplay will be different: The timing is different, the characters are different, and the juxtaposition of circumstances and players is different.

Your presentation can take many forms. You may have to produce nothing in writing (at a pitch meeting); provide a longer, more or less detailed sketch of the story (a treatment); or turn in the actual screenplay. Here is a brief description of each form.

The Pitch

Not everyone who wants to sell an idea to a film producer or investor is fortunate enough to sit down and present her idea. If you are one of the lucky ones, I will sketch out some common practices.

A pitch meeting, usually with an agent or producer and/or their assistants—depending on your status as a writer—is a brief meeting, usually 20 minutes at most (often less), in which you are given the opportunity to present your idea for a screenplay. In this meeting, you should cover:

- A brief description of the setting, ideally an interesting one that may or may not take readers/viewers to an unfamiliar place
- The key characters, who are both intriguing and ones we can care about
- A brief narrative. This is your story, and you should lay out the tension, climax, and plot reversals/unexpected twists that will mark your story as "different" and "interesting."
- The project's market and marketability
- The originality—what makes this project different, exceptional, intriguing, or insightful?

You should discuss your project with confidence, enthusiasm, and vivid detail. Here is the moment to be a good storyteller. You want to convey that you have a great idea with plenty of dramatic potential.

Do not talk too long. You do not have to (or even want to) give your listener every last detail of the plot or a grocery list of the characters. You may not even have an ending. The pitch is essentially a "tease." Simply and forcefully provide enough of the story concept to make a positive impact on your listener. Your listener will usually get a strong impression in the first few minutes, so start with your strongest material—whether it is a great character or an intriguing plot. Do not digress or ramble.

The Treatment

The treatment is a present-tense, carefully written narrative of your film story. The length of a treatment varies widely—ranging from 3 to over 100 pages. Most treatments average between 7 and 15 pages and are designed to give the reader a good sense of your characters, conflict, story, and, perhaps most important, your writing ability with a minimum expenditure of time and effort on your reader's part. Because treatments are cost-effective, they are often used as sales tools. They take less time to read, are less costly to produce (in terms of how much a writer gets paid for one, not necessarily the labor that goes into it), and give the reader an extended synopsis of the project.

A treatment generally begins with a description of the setting, the key players, and the conflict. It should also set a mood or create an atmosphere. Here is an early version of the opening paragraphs of the original *Star Wars* by George Lucas (1973).

```
Deep Space.

The eerie blue-green planet of Aquilae slowly
drifts into view. A small speck, orbiting the
planet, glints in the light of a nearby star.

Suddenly a sleek fighter-type spacecraft settles
ominously into the foreground moving swiftly
toward the orbiting speck. Two more fighters
silently maneuver into battle formation behind the
first and then three more craft glide into view.
The orbiting speck is actually a gargantuan space
fortress which dwarfs the approaching fighters.
Fuel pods are jettisoned. The six fighters break
off into a power dive attack on the huge fortress.
Laser bolts streak from the fighters creating
small explosions on the complex surface of the
fort. Return fire catches one of the fighters and
it bursts into a million pieces. Another of the
craft plows into a gun emplacement jutting from
the fortress causing a hideous series of chain
reaction explosions. The chaos of battle echoes
through the vastness of space.
```

It is the thirty-third century, a period of civil
wars in the galaxy. A rebel princess, with her
family, her retainers, and the clan treasure is
being pursued. If they can cross territory
controlled by the Empire and reach a friendly
planet, they will be saved. The Sovereign knows
this, and posts a reward for the capture of the
princess.

She is being guarded by one of her generals (Luke
Skywalker) and it is he who leads her on the long
and dangerous journey that follows. They take
along with them two hundred pounds of the greatly
treasured "aura spice," and also two Imperial
bureaucrats, whom the general has captured.

Note how this treatment begins with both tension and an exotic atmosphere. It
introduces not only the key conflict, but some of the major characters as well. A
drab beginning, one without excitement, tension, or the promise of something
intriguing, will be the kiss of death for your treatment. The reader may not even
read beyond the first few paragraphs. Work carefully on your opening paragraphs.

Obviously, good openings do not have to include battle sequences. Here is
another treatment example from *The Shining* by Stanley Kubrick.

Main Title sequence. Jack's car driving up high
mountain roads, in Colorado, ending in an approach
point-of-view shot of the Overlook Hotel, which is
set beneath the peak of Mt. Qualo, 25 miles from
Sidewinder, the nearest town.

Jack is playing Spanish study tapes on the car
cassette-radio. Now and then, when he has trouble
repeating a phrase aloud in the gaps left on the
tape, he says things like: "No pissa me off,
babe."

Jack Torrance is hired by Ullman, the manager of
the Overlook, for the job of winter caretaker.

> Ullman warns Jack that a previous caretaker,
> unable to endure the snowbound isolation, killed
> his wife and two young daughters, and then
> committed suicide during a winter at the hotel.
> Despite his warning, Jack is not worried, and in
> fact, looks forward to the quiet and solitude, in
> which he hopes to get some writing done.

In this sequence, Kubrick introduces the main character, provides a character tag through the description of action (Jack's responding to the language tape), and presents strong foreshadowing of the conflict to come. In a screenplay the description can only cover what we see and hear, but in a treatment there can be some minimal laying-out of background material that might help set up the characters, plot, and setting, as shown earlier. Even so, primary attention should be paid to what we actually see and hear, not the characters' thoughts or history.

After this opening, the treatment then continues to outline the story. The story contains specific details that will impart a strong sense of the story, but dialogue is often summarized. For example, in this scene from *The Shining*, Jack is in a scene with George, one of his students:

> Jack, in an unnecessarily tactless and sarcastic
> way, refuses to change the grade and provokes
> George with taunts about "jocks," about his
> father's money and about his stuttering.

However, a writer may provide snippets of the dialogue in order to give the reader a flavor for her characters. The following is from *Star Trek III: Return to Genesis* by Harve Bennett.

> And perhaps he [Sarek], too, has succumbed to
> anger. "But why you?" asks Kirk. "Because," says
> Sarek, "you abandoned my son." Kirk's protests only
> enrage Sarek. He accuses Kirk—and McCoy—of
> criminal ignorance. "Why was Spock's body not
> returned to me? What makes you think he was 'in
> death'? How dare you presume, with your primitive

```
science, to understand Vulcan physiology and the
Vulcan ways!" In short, says Sarek, Spock might
have been in a transcendental state—a state in
which he may still be.
```

Treatments are used to provide the reader with, literally, a *treatment* of your script idea. Before you write, you should have worked out your entire story— your protagonist, antagonist, character tags, conflict, rising tension, climax and resolution, plot peaks, and so on—regardless of whether they appear on paper. Many treatments are written after the screenplay is completed, so at this point your idea should be carefully plotted; it should have a beginning, middle, and end, and it should have specific, well-drawn characters. In your treatment, however, you should **tell no more or no less** than is necessary to flesh out a story. Consequently, although you should include all major characters and subplots, you do not need to deal with minor characters or details that are not particularly consequential to the plot or that slow down a smooth reading of your story.

Some format tips for treatments include the following:

- Your story should be told in present tense.
- Characters' names are capitalized when they first appear.
- Treatments often begin with "FADE IN:" and end with "FADE OUT."
- Rarely are camera movements described in treatments.
- Treatments for feature films are generally about 12 to 15 pages long and are often divided up into three acts. The first act is one quarter of the screenplay, the second act is the middle half, and the third act is the last quarter. The first and last acts should be especially strong in terms of drama; they are the first things a reader encounters and the last thing he or she will remember reading.
- For TV, half-hour sit-com treatments are 2 to 3 pages; 1-hour dramas are 5 to 8 pages.

The following is an example of a rough draft treatment written by a student writer. It is for a short 15-minute film. Although it underwent some changes before it reached the screenplay stage—particularly in the ending and conflict between the protagonist and antagonist—it is a good example of style and format.

Atlanta Blues by Fred Lenhoff

Scene 1

   Toes wiggle contentedly inside two dusty,
blackened, worn leather boots, atop fresh-laid
black asphalt. Sound of water running. View widens
and we see a long, lazy arc of urine spackling
against the new pavement, steam rising in the heat
of a July day in Atlanta. The sun is setting,
casting long shadows behind our contented pisser,
ROBERT SKINNER, known to all as RABBIT. He closes
his eyes and breathes out in relief as the water
flows. Rabbit is mid-20s, wiry, deeply tanned—pre-
cancerous, really—with cold ice-blue eyes. Like his
half brother, JOHNNY SKINNER, or SKINK (10 years
Rabbit's elder, and as attractive as his nickname),
he's a country boy from Winder, Georgia, coming to
grips with sprawling professional-class suburban
Atlanta—its subdivisions, shopping malls, vaguely
colonial place names, and parking lots.

   The latter, parking lots, is what brings Rabbit,
Skink, and the other members of the South Coast
road paving crew to this part of town. They've just
finished paving this subdivision (the sign behind
Rabbit reads "Winchester Common—Distinctive
Townehomes, from the $110s") and are about to wind
it up for the day. The other two permanent members
of the crew are a wizened black man from inner city
Atlanta known only as PLAT and a gangly white
college freshman, KEN MEREDITH, who everyone calls
THE KID. The rest are day laborers, both black and
white.

The mood is festive—like the locker room after the
game. Everyone is tired, dirty, sweaty but
victorious and basking in the afterglow of teamwork
towards a common goal—laying 100,000 square feet of

asphalt. Everyone's talking about tonight's plans—
it's Friday—or bragging about yesterday's exploits
as they wait for the foreman to drive up with the
day's wages—cash for the day laborers, checks for
the regular crew.

Skink sits in the pickup smoking and drinking a
Coke, the door open, one leg hanging out. Plat is
squatting on his haunches, smoking a cigarette and
admiring his work with the asphalt rake. Kid is the
only one still working, cleaning the shovels and
raking in a 10-gallon bucket of diesel fuel. He
focuses on his work, as if afraid of what he might
see if he looks up.

Rabbit banters obscenely back and forth with his
fellows all the while. When he's done urinating, he
stares pointedly at the Kid and mocks him with a
lewd comment. All turn expectantly to the Kid for a
rejoinder, but the Kid says nothing, only blushes,
the red on his cheeks visible even in the setting
sun. In the uncomfortable silence, his
embarrassment seems to spread to the others. Plat
comes to his rescue, and jokes back at Rabbit, and
Rabbit responds, matching obscenity with obscenity.

Scene 2

A dirty Ford pickup, bed filled with tools and
buckets, speeding north on I-85. Skink is driving
with Rabbit riding shotgun and the Kid on the hump.
On the way, Rabbit picked up a six pack of beer,
and he shares it with Skink. He tries to get the
Kid to have one but he won't.

Skink and Rabbit are dropping the Kid off in suburban
Lilburn on their way home. They pass the exit,
however, and the kid starts to protest. Rabbit tells
him not to worry, that tonight they're gonna have

some fun. Rabbit drapes his arm over the Kid and puts
him in a headlock—yeah, fun! He shouts and gives a
Rebel yell, hawks up a gob of mucus and fires it out
the window like a bullet. Then he pops open another
beer, sucks back a mouthful and signs loudly.

Rabbit continues to goad the Kid. Skink finally
tells him to knock it off, leading to a slap fight
between Rabbit and Skink, with the Kid in the
middle, as they fly down the highway. The Kid
stares at the road, petrified.

Scene 3

Rabbit picks up a HOOKER from downtown Winder.
Either she's missing a molar or there's a hug-hunk
of spinach caught between her teeth. She squeezes
in between Rabbit and the Kid. "Hey there, cutie,"
she says to the Kid, "you look like my boy." Rabbit
has a lot of fun with this at the Kid's expense.

At Skink's house (Rabbit is married; they can't go
there), Rabbit, then Skink (both drunk by now) have
sex with the woman in a back room. The Kid tries to
hide out in the kitchen but there's no avoiding the
sounds, the men's groans, the woman's non-committal
exhortations.

"Your turn, baby boy," Rabbit says as he emerges
from the back. "What do you mean, my turn? I don't
want a turn," responds the Kid. "What's that, sissy
boy?" rejoins Rabbit. He gives the Kid an
ultimatum: either have sex with her or he'll have
sex with the Kid. "He'll do it, too," cackles
Skink. The Kid tries to back away, but Rabbit seems
ready to make good on this threat.

"One more chance, Kid," he says and tosses him a
pistol that's sitting on the TV next to the remote.
"Here, use this on her."

"Are you crazy?" says the Kid. One way or the
other, persists Rabbit. The Kid is getting
seriously worried. Shaking, he raises the gun
toward Rabbit who slowly moves toward the boy,
taunting him all the while. Meanwhile Skink has
pulled out a rifle. "You don't wanna do that," he
says to the Kid. Too late, the Kid, at the end of
his rope, aims the gun at Rabbit's leg and pulls
the trigger. Click! It's unloaded.

"Now it's my turn," says Skink. He raises the
rifle, aims it at the Kid and—Click! It's not
loaded either. The Kid has aged 10 years; he's
sweating, breathing ragged, looking around wildly.
Skink and Rabbit are hysterical with laughter. The
woman, who has re-entered the living room, is
laughing, too.

"You should have seen yourself," howls Rabbit.
"Welcome to the crew," he says, grabbing him
roughly around the head and shoulders. "And try not
to take everything so goddamn serious."

The Step Outline

A step outline is a brief outline of all the scenes in your screenplay, with a description—sometimes fairly detailed—of what those scenes entail in terms of characters, action, and conflict. Step outlines are not usually for public consumption. They are for you, the storyteller and, as such, are valuable tools. Although treatments often read like short stories, step outlines—because they break down that story into filmic blocks—make the step from treatment to screenplay that much easier.

How many scenes? A feature film (90–120 minutes) often runs in the neighborhood of 15 to 20 scenes or sequences. A *scene* is a series of shots that take place at the same location, at the same time, with the same characters. For example, *Chinatown* opens with a scene in Jake's office. That scene continues until the setting changes.

Some format tips for step outlines include the following:

- Usually step outlines are numbered by scene. Each scene—usually described in a paragraph—should treat all the action that takes place at the time, at that location, and with those characters. When you change any component, start a new number (and paragraph).
- Scenes can be broken up into shorter paragraphs for readability. But each scene should have only one number.
- Capitalize the names of characters when they first appear.
- Include no background or recounting of the characters' thoughts. Include *only* what we see or hear.
- As in the treatment, dialogue can be treated explicitly or in summary. Usually a combination of the two is both useful and appropriate.

Here is an example of a step outline that includes the first five scenes. Note that the setting and characters are listed up front for ease of reading, and each scene locates the reader and indicates clearly who is involved in the scene and what is going on.

The Boarder
The story takes place in Paris in 1968.
Characters

- ANNA, a Polish woman living in France, aged 45, small in stature and rather homely, but clearly runs the household.

- GEORGES, her French husband, about 50, a lawyer, is fat and balding, says little.

- PHILIPPE, their 22-year-old son; a flippant youth, the kind who knows everything about everything.

- CONSTANCE, aged 20, their independent daughter.

- BARBARA, aged 14, a quiet young American who comes to live at their house while studying in France.

1. It is early morning in a large, elegant apartment on the Left Bank in Paris. Anna and Georges are asleep in their bedroom. Suddenly Anna opens her eyes. She sits up. The scene

shifts to 1940, a Paris train station. A young
Anna (age 15) timidly gets off a train. She is
dressed in country garb and carries one small
suitcase. She is extremely intimidated by the
violent hustle of the station. People stare at
her. She looks up and sees "Room for Rent" on a
sign across the street. We shift back to 1968.
The woman, Anna, is still sitting up in bed. The
phone rings. It is her brother's doctor,
requesting that Anna go see her brother at the
hospital today.

2. It is breakfast time. Anna presides over the
   breakfast in regal fashion. It is wasted on the
   family as they generally ignore her. Constance
   and Philippe moodily gulp down their coffee and
   leave. Georges grunts responses to her
   conversation as he reads the news. She tells him
   that she is picking up their new boarder today.
   She wonders why the doctor called so early.

3. Place de la Concorde. A student demonstration is
   taking place. Students carry signs and placards
   and are shouting at a large, armed group of riot
   police who are nervously ringing the square.

4. Institut Catholique reception area. Barbara
   waits shyly in the large reception room. She is
   the last to be picked up by her homestay French
   family. Finally Anna arrives, looking very
   strange in a large, oversized fur coat on her
   small frame. Barbara is very nervous. She says
   nothing as they drive home in a taxi. Anna
   prattles on about the family and the rules of the
   apartment.

5. Anna goes to the hospital. She cannot find a
   taxi so she descends to the Metro. There are a
   lot of people so she misses a train. She finally
   finds herself seated next to a man she discovers
   to be dead. She cries out, but no one will help
   her.

Thus far, the outline has set up the protagonist, setting, characters, and a foreshadowing of potential conflict. In the scenes that follow, the protagonist will become clear, and the conflict should intensify.

SCREENPLAY SCENARIOS

As has hopefully become apparent, there are as many ways for writers to "break in" to the feature-film industry as there are writers. Perhaps the best resource for learning about some of these ways in is the Writers Guild, mentioned later in this chapter. For now, here are several different scenarios that depict different kinds of things that can happen at the marketing stage of your screenplay. The following scenarios are entirely fictitious, but they are based on real events.

Scenario 1

You have written a screenplay, have moved to Los Angeles, and are ready to shop it. You have no agent so far. You get to know someone at your local health club whose father, a corporate executive, lives in Malibu next door to a well-known and reasonably marketable young actress. You have an idea for a film and think this actress would be perfect in it. You ask your friend if he might be able to arrange for the actress to take a look at your screenplay. The friend agrees to try.

Several weeks later, the friend tells you that the actress, Mariella, will not read a screenplay, but would be willing to read a short treatment. You spend a few days writing up a treatment and send it to Mariella with a cover letter. She reads it and agrees to meet with you at a café in Malibu.

You meet with Mariella and explain more about the project. She tells you she really likes it, and if you can put something together, she would be interested in considering it.

You send out a few query letters to local agents, summarizing your project and Mariella's interest in it. On the basis of her interest, you are able to get a meeting with an agent in a small literary agency in Beverly Hills. You pitch your project; the agent also likes it and is willing to take it on and see what interest she can generate for it. She wants to market it as a treatment initially.

After a month or so, she is able to interest a producer in your treatment. As a result, he is willing to read your screenplay. Actually, one of his assistants reads your screenplay and advises the producer to get a more experienced writer to redo the screenplay, although they will pay you the WGA minimum for your script. Because you are smart and willing to swallow your pride of authorship to get "in the door," you agree to these terms.

Although this scenario seems reasonably promising, it only happens to the lucky few. Usually, you need to do a lot more before finding someone who is willing to back your project. Some goals: get more people interested in your project, write a number of query letters, and meet with quite a few agents. Do not quit. Keep trying.

Scenario 2

Your screenplay, *The Roofer*, has won a screenplay competition in Austin, Texas. Several agents and producers—who are interested in new writers—express an interest in seeing it. After a few weeks, you are able to select an agent, who, in turn, is able to get you a deal with one of the producers. You will be paid, not for *The Roofer*, but to develop a screenplay from a successful novel that the producer has optioned. Because you are a relative newcomer to the business, you will be paid the minimum (according to the Writers Guild of America's contract), but the agent is able to negotiate more money if the screenplay goes into production.

You read the novel. Although you are disappointed not to work on something original, you correctly see this as a wonderful opportunity and agree to do the project. The agent negotiates the contract for you, and you have 4 months to complete the screenplay.

You sit down with the producer and his assistant and go over what they would like to see developed from the novel. You contribute your ideas; you work out some plot and character details and then you are on your way.

Scenario 3

You have been living in Los Angeles for several years and have worked as a production assistant and a story editor. You have sold an idea for a sit-com episode for a short-lived series that died 5 weeks into its season. The idea was never developed into a screenplay or produced. You have had a screenplay optioned by a small production company and are waiting (endlessly) for something to happen with it. You have also won an "honorable mention" at a local screenwriting contest.

Based on your work thus far, you have been able to secure representation with a small, growing writers' agency, and your young agent seems excited about your prospects. You go into his office one afternoon and pitch an idea to him based on another screenplay you have written. He likes it (he likes all your work) and promises to "get it out there." About 3 weeks later, he calls to tell you he has had a nibble and wants you to meet with a studio producer.

The producer meets you at a coffee house in Westwood and tells you he is interested in your project. He wants to see your screenplay. You send it to him. A week later he gets back to you to tell you that the project is not really for him, but he likes your writing and wants to see more of your work. Over the phone, you give him a synopsis of another screenplay you have finished, and he wants you to send it to him. You call your agent and have him send it to the producer.

He likes the screenplay and, what's more, wants to buy it to produce for TV. Some revisions need to be done, but he will hire you to do them. You call your agent and she and the producer negotiate a deal. You will get a bit more than standard minimum (see chap. 5), but will get paid for revising the screenplay for TV.

Versions of this scenario do not happen for everyone, but this last scenario is probably more likely than the other two. The distinguishing feature of this scenario is that the writer has done his homework. He has been working in the business, made some contacts, accumulated knowledge about the film industry, and, at the same time, has been working on his writing. He has completed several screenplays and has not given up. Consequently, he has been able to take advantage of chances that have come his way.

Overview

Even successful writers have to pitch their ideas, write treatments, and generally be salespeople for their own work. This process means meeting people, being good on your feet, getting along, and remaining confident and enthusiastic in the face of continual rejection. Much of the rejection will not be pleasant, but it will teach you things, both about your work and your audience.

THE FOLLOW-THROUGH—AFTER THE SCRIPT IS COMPLETED

You have had your first taste of success. You have a complete script in hand or you have been hired by a producer to write one. You are on your way through the Hollywood maze. What happens next? As you might have guessed, the answer is "any number of things." Fairly consistent in every process—at least at some point—is the story conference, so we will begin there.

The Story Conference

Here is one scenario. You are "in development" at a major studio, working with a producer who has a development deal. This means the studio is paying the producer and providing an office and office staff for him to bring in some ideas and develop them into screenplays and eventually films. The producer has arranged to provide an office for you so that you can work closely together.

You have successfully pitched the idea to the producer, and he has given you a go-ahead on the script. You have been pretty much left to yourself to complete the script while the producer is busy with other projects.

The due date has arrived. You turn in the draft to the producer and wait. After about a week or two, the producer arranges a meeting, and you go in to discuss revisions, if any. You meet in a studio bungalow over Perrier and drip coffee. The producer's assistant is there, and she and the producer have copies of the script and a sheaf of notes.

They begin by saying they *love* the screenplay. The plot is great, the dialogue sparkles, and the characters are wonderful. They have a few suggestions for revisions that they would like to see.

Good producers—good because they have agreed with the basic concept and are familiar with you and your work—often have suggestions that make for an immensely better script. Some of these are substantive plot ideas. Some make the project more marketable, based on prevailing winds and trends and the studio's current management. After all, the producer is, or should be, in a position to know quite a bit about what the studio will accept or reject. Good producers also have good story minds; in fact, they may have some writing skills and may (although this can also be a liability) consider themselves to be writers, too. In any case, the changes they suggest may range from dropping and adding scenes that make story sense to changing the cast of characters to adjusting the beginning, ending, or both.

The more drastic revision ideas often make less sense. Change the main male character into a female. Change the heterosexual love relationship into a homosexual one. Change the Hispanic cop to a Black one. Change the setting from New York to a small town in South Dakota.

Often these changes demonstrate little or no understanding of your premise, of good storytelling, or the value of multidimensional characters. Even so, the producers are the people in charge. Changes must be made, although you have some (albeit limited) room for negotiation.

Treat changes, however large or small, as creative challenges. You want to make this the best script possible; it has your name on it, and your ability to work well with a producer may mean other jobs in the future, both with this producer and other money people this producer knows. Reputations can be made or broken in story conferences. This can be a wonderful occasion to make collaboration work for you. Often you can brainstorm with the producer and his group about potential changes or work out plot problems.

Of course, if you do not make the changes, you may be in breach of contract. Or if you do not make changes that work, the producer may assign another screenwriter to "doctor" the script; this person will take part of the credit. Then again, you may do it all wonderfully and the producer or studio executive still does not like it and kills the project or hires another writer anyway. Frequently, the screenplay that gets produced has so little resemblance to the one the original screenwriter wrote that it is unrecognizable. In some instances, the final product is so bad that the writer has his name removed from the film credits.

Another Story Conference

Let us back up a bit. Let us say you finish the script, present it to the producers, and get a call a few weeks later in which the producer says, "We have to talk."

You hurry over to the production office and sit down with the production staff. They tell you that the script is in real trouble. The story has taken some turns they had not anticipated, and they wonder if you actually can do the kind of substantive revision it needs to be acceptable. They are considering hiring another writer.

First, do not panic. Part of the game they may be playing is to get more work out of you than the contract allows. Your contract does call for a revision, and chances are if you tackle the revision and incorporate at least some of their comments, supplementing them with some new ideas of your own and changing the landscape of the script somewhat (perhaps the chronology, parts of the setting, adding or deleting characters), you might very well be able to accommodate the producers as well as yourself.

However, the requests may be so drastic and so far from what you would feel comfortable doing that you might feel it is the best use of time and energy to get out of the project. This can be done, but negotiations can get sticky. A revision is to be considered as a revision, not a new screenplay. Agents and lawyers are often the ones to work out these situations.

Contractual obligations are important, but also important is your relationship with your producer. Hollywood is a small town—news gets around fast about people who are great to work with and people who are utterly impossible. You want to be in the former category, and sometimes this means going beyond what you are required to do. Even if they do not use the final script, they will re-member that you went the extra mile.

"Polishes"

In the film business, polishes are considered the final revisions. Here the writer merely fixes a few more or less minor parts of the script. It may be as simple as changing the name of a character and adjusting or cutting a small dialogue in a scene. It may also be more substantive, but generally the terms are covered un-der the contract.

THE WRITERS GUILD OF AMERICA

The Writers Guild of America (WGA) is an extraordinarily valuable institu-tion for screenwriters. The mainstream movie industry is a business like any other; the profit motive reigns supreme. It is also an industry that is highly spec-ulative: There is a lot of money involved, but new film companies and alliances appear and disappear with regularity. One of the results of the financial drive and volatility has been the unionization of crafts (actors, director, editors, film crews, etc.) to ensure fairness and equitable compensation—especially where hours and work can be long and unpredictable. Traditionally, the writer has been an undervalued member of the film-making team, both in terms of pres-tige and monetary remuneration (in American cinema) with the producer, di-rector, and actors taking the lion's share of the credit and profits when a film is produced. In 1886, the Berne Treaty was drafted in an effort to protect all art-ists and their art. When film making emerged as a growing business, these rights were extended to writers, directors, and cinematographers. When the treaty became applicable in the United States, writers were dropped out. Now the WGA is undertaking an important effort to get Congress to re-include writers under the terms of the treaty.

Since 1933, the WGA has worked tirelessly for writers to maintain competi-tive and fair payment for goods and services, to guarantee screen credit, and to generally protect the rights of writers. The Guild maintains a collective bar-gaining agreement with producers that is renegotiated every 3 to 4 years. In fact there are two agreements—one with the Alliance of Motion Picture and Tele-vision Producers (AMPTP) and the other with the networks, but there is es-sentially little difference between the two contracts.

These agreements specify minimum standards under which payment to writers for various kinds of work must not go. For example, in 1996, the mini-

mum for the first draft of a screenplay was $40,851 (whether original or an ad-
aptation), and the final revision was $15,314 more. Usually, however, most
working writers get around $150,000 per screenplay. A treatment is $30,639
with no length stipulations. (As I indicated in chap. 4, treatments may be as
long as a book, as short as a page).

The Guild does not negotiate delivery schedule. But writers must be paid a
starting fee of 10% or so. There is also a minimum for options (the WGA negotiates these payments scales, too).

Screen Credit

The great part of the Guild's work is with credit. In fact, the Guild was started
because of credit issues. In the 1930s and 1940s, writers might or might not
have received screen credit. For writers like William Faulkner or F. Scott Fitz-
gerald, established writers in another genre who were brought in to write
screenplays, credit was a given, but for the writers who worked with them, it
was not. In the first WGA agreement in 1941, half of the five-page document
dealt with credit.

Now there is a system for determining credit on cases that are not clear-cut or
are in dispute. Three people (all WGA members and writers) sit on an arbitra-
tion committee. The members of the committee are anonymous; they do not
even know each other. They are given the materials, the authors' statements
about why they feel they deserve the credit they are asking for. The three-com-
mittee members decide. The authors in the dispute have 24 hours to appeal. The
whole process takes 21 days. There are about 100 arbitrations per year.

The WGA only works with sales and employment; they do not get into
copyright issues. This is a legal problem and goes through the courts. Interestingly, copyright is automatically given to novelists, dramatists, and poets, but
not to screenwriters. Screenwriters give up copyright when their screenplays
are produced.

Improving the Status of Writers

More recently, the Guild has fought to make the screenwriter more prominent
in the public eye. There is currently a big campaign to improve public perceptions of what writers do, geared to granting them more creative control and
recognition. The campaign includes:

• Increased publicity for screenwriters

• Increased access to writers and their scripts. For example, the WGA has introduced "coffee houses" at film festivals where scripts are available for people to read and discuss. In addition, the WGA sponsors "afternoons with writers" at local bookstores.

• Marketing screenplays—making both the screenplay and novelization available at movie theaters and bookstores

Other Services

The Guild makes a number of other services available to its members. The WGA

• Oversees a health insurance and pension plan for writers
• Works to combat sexism, racism, and ageism in hiring practices and policies
• Maintains an updated list of writers and their screen credits
• Sponsors film screenings

The Guild also provides a script registration service. Members or nonmembers may "register" their scripts with the Guild by sending in their script accompanied by a nominal fee. Registrations give your script an identification number and establish a registration date on which the writer claims to have written it. Copyrighting is also a good idea, but more complicated, and is done through the copyright office in Washington, DC.

Joining the WGA

For a writer to join the guild, she must accumulate so many units, which are tabulated according to the kind of writing performed or sold. In other words, a writer gets a certain number of units for selling a screenplay, another amount for a treatment, and so on. Any studio or producer may hire a writer who is not a member of the Guild, but after 30 days of employment, she must join the Guild. Dues are 1½% of fees paid to the writer, plus a $2,500 initiation fee.

There are two chapters of the WGA—the Writers Guild East and the Writers Guild West. To contact The Writers Guild:

Writers Guild of America West
8955 Beverly Blvd.
West Hollywood, CA 90048
310-550-1000

Writers Guild of America East
555 W. 57th St.
New York, NY 10019
212-767-7800

The Writers Guild also maintains an excellent Web page with plenty of resources for both the experienced and novice writer. Among other things, the Web page contains:

- Interviews with working writers
- Current news in the industry
- Events and workshops
- Bookstores
- Research sites
- News from the WGA
- Reviews of story software
- Reviews of format software
- Reviews of screenwriting and writing books

Web page: http://www.wga.org

THE MEASURE OF SUCCESS

Uncountable numbers of ideas get pitched in Hollywood every year. Of these ideas, several thousand get put in development (i.e., move from the idea stage to the screenplay stage). Of these, only a small fraction ever makes it to the big (or little) screen. You can work quite successfully for years, making a lot of money, producing very good screenplays, and building a solid reputation without ever seeing your name on a credits list.

Although this fact may be disappointing to the fledgling screenwriter, it is the way things are in the film industry. The selection of which screenplays go forward to production is a very fickle process and highly unpredictable. It may have to do with the personality of the executive in charge of production that year. It may have to do with sagging network ratings on *another* network. Or it may have to do with current events. For years after the Vietnam War, war films were out, no matter how compelling the story. Nobody wanted to see war films, and nobody wanted to risk making them. Even now, Vietnam War films are difficult, although there have been quite a few that have been successful, both critically and financially. Finally, it may just not be your time.

Consequently, find ways to measure your success that do not have to do with reaching "the big time." After you have been writing for a while (regardless of whether you manage to earn a living writing), explore new avenues: TV sitcoms, the cable market, novel writing. Reinvent yourself; try different genres;

explore new styles. Find ways to stretch and evolve as a writer. If indeed you make it big at some point, you can always dust off those old screenplays and maybe find a better, more accepting market.

SUGGESTED READING

Subscribe to *Written By*, a monthly publication by the Writers Guild of America, West (www.wga.org under Publications). Monthly issues feature articles by writers (feature, TV, and documentary) on a range of issues, including how they got started as successful (paid) writers.

PART II

APPLYING DRAMATIC
PRINCIPLES

The second part of the book extends writing for film beyond the original feature screenplay. The first chapter of this section, on adaptations, has perhaps the most obvious connection to the film drama discussed in the first half of the book because most adaptations evolve from works of fiction or nonfiction into traditional feature films. But the inclusion of writing for the documentary, marketing film, and experimental film in this book assumes a strong tie-in to the principles of drama that we have looked at thus far. In other words, dramatic structure and style remain the underpinnings of good films, whether fact or fiction, marketplace or experimental.

One of the biggest differences between the theatrical film and the genres that we examine here is that—with the exception of the adaptation—the writer is more likely to be involved in the production of the film. This necessarily involves her in the full range of film-making arts, including but not limited to preproduction, photography, editing, sound recording, and postproduction. Because this book focuses primarily on writing, some of these elements are beyond the intended scope of this book. These chapters instead provide introductions to these genres and ultimately demonstrate for the aspiring film writer the multiple directions that she can take her writing aspirations.

Adaptations

The big job on the screenplay of The Last Picture Show *was to take everything good out of the book, drop what we had to because of length, keep it as rich as possible, and find the right order of events to tell it.*

—Peter Bogdanovich on story conferences with Larry McMurtry.
Scenario: the Magazine of Screenwriting Art (Winter 1998–1999), 97.

DISTINCTIONS BETWEEN LITERARY FICTION AND SCREENPLAYS

Today many of the movies we see are not from original screenplays, but rather drawn from adaptations of novels, short stories, or plays. A cynic might maintain that the reason for this is that there is nothing new under the sun, and, even if there were something new, very few people have the genius or talent to make it happen on film. Although it is true that there are few really good ideas and these have already surfaced in some shape or form, there is a more pragmatic explanation. The reason that we have so many adaptations is that published fiction or drama is an established commodity. It has already gone through a fairly rigorous review process; someone has already taken a chance on it and, in some way, that chance has paid off in revenues, critical acclaim, or popularity. The fact that a novel has been published, for example, means that someone (who is familiar with literature), somewhere (usually at a publishing house) has determined that people will read (and like) this novel. Because it has been published—or because a play has been performed in a theater—it usually already has an audience. It has been pretested, so to speak.

Second, many of the novels selected to be adapted are already best sellers or have achieved some critical acclaim—*Gone with the Wind* by Margaret Mitchell, *Devil With A Blue Dress* by Walter Mosley, *The Joy Luck Club* by Amy Tan, or *The English Patient* by Michael Ondaatje. Other novels like *The Little Princess, Passage to India, The Lord of the Rings*, or *Emma* are considered literary classics. Still others, *Amadeus* or *Sound of Music*, have been successful on the stage (on Broadway and elsewhere). They carry with them a certain prestige and panache that will, most likely, bring viewers into the movie theaters.

But to be successful, adaptations have to negotiate a fairly precarious ground. Not all novels, short stories, and plays are suitable raw material for the screen. They may be too "heady" or too intellectual, focusing on the interior lives of their characters; they may lack charismatic lead characters (or lead characters at all); the kind of action that plays so well on the screen may be different or even missing in print. Furthermore, many viewers who have read the novel or short story that served as the source for the film come into the theaters expecting to see a filmed version of what they have read: a faithful and fairly accurate portrayal of the original story. People who have these expectations are generally disappointed, and most writers who attempt an exact screen representation of the original material are doomed to fail. Why?

Cinematic Versus Literary Drama

In chapter 1, I talked about many of the differences between literary writing and screenwriting. I also discussed how reading differs from viewing, resulting in important reasons that a screenplay must be what it is in terms of drama, length, characters and characterization, verbal fluency, and impact. To reiterate: The drama of the screenplay must be cinematic. That is, it must include conflict that can be easily conveyed on film, through its sound (usually dialogue) and visuals (images and action). Regardless of whether they recognize it, audiences have certain expectations when they read a book—about chapters, characters, drama—and they have different expectations when they view a film; these must be taken under consideration when considering an adaptation. Perhaps most pointedly, an audience in a movie theater expects to be entertained and engaged almost immediately. Consequently, crucial elements are those we have discussed at length in previous chapters on film structure. These are: a strong conflict, a building tension line that rises to a climax, and identifiable, interesting characters.

THE PROCESS OF ADAPTATION

Securing a Property

There are any number of approaches to adaptation, all of which are fairly circuitous unless you are already the author of the original material. The first step, of course, is to have or acquire the rights to the original material. This may mean buying the property (a story, novel, nonfiction book, or play) outright or optioning the rights to it and "owning" the original material on a temporary basis. For most material published in the last 50 years, the rights are owned by either the author or a related party: the author's family, the author's agent, or a publishing house. Other works are in the *public domain*, meaning that the copyright has expired. Anyone can use public domain material as a source without penalty or cost as long as the original work is acknowledged. The first step is to find out where the copyright stands. Contact the U.S. Copyright Office of the Library of Congress (101 Independence Avenue S.E., Washington, D.C. 20559–6000). To speak with someone there, call (207) 707–3000 or check out the Web site: http://www.copyright.gov/ .

Options. Buying a property outright is risky. It is usually quite expensive (anywhere from $30,000 to millions of dollars) and it is always uncertain whether you will be able to sell the project. If you cannot make a go of it, you are left with a stack of paper that is without much value. An attractive alternative to purchasing an original work is to *option* it. An option is a contractual agreement between a buyer and the person (or organization) who owns the rights to a property that allows the buyer to develop or market the property during a specified time period. Often options are for 6 months to 1 year; sometimes they are renewable by mutual agreement. An option may or may not be costly depending on the property and the deal, ranging from $100 for 3 months to several thousand dollars or more. An option contract contains contingencies for the purchase of the work at the end of the option period. Among these contingencies are: the eventual purchase price, the bonuses if the screenplay goes into production, and the royalties due if there is a profit from film distribution or cable sales.

Other Sources. An option also carries with it some degree of risk. Six months—even a year—is not a long time to write an adaptation and market it—especially if you are a newcomer to the business. Many options end up expiring at the end of the period without a sale, resulting in loss of hundreds or thousands of dollars. Even so, many people believe the option is the safer route to go in adaptations.

Stories from the newspaper or real-life events can also be used as source material. If a news story is published, the story is considered public domain—but you can only use parts of the story that are considered public record (i.e., facts in the news). Other details—say, about the lives and personalities of people involved—are protected under the Right to Privacy. To use these kinds of more personal facts, you need to get permission from the persons involved or risk the legal consequences. You can also get in trouble if you falsely portray a person who has been cast into the public eye, although his story may be public domain. For example, films about Jackie Kennedy Onassis, which were all the rage for several years, underwent considerable scrutiny in studio legal departments. If facts and details were presumed to be in the least bit slanderous or defamed in any way the principle character, chances are there would be litigation. In a made-for-TV project about Jackie's life with Aristotle Onassis that I worked on, the problem was sidestepped by basing the screenplay on a published version of her life. The source material, then, was a book in print, not Jackie Onassis' life directly. The movie rights were purchased by the producer. We were, however, obliged to be quite attentive to our source material and refrain from too much unnecessary invention and speculation. When in doubt, consult a copyright attorney.

Story and Character Selection Process

Once you have secured the rights to a property, you need to select what you want to use and how you want to shape it into a treatment or screenplay. The first thing to do is to read it thoroughly (again and again) and then decide what elements of the story lend themselves to translation to the screen. Here are some things to consider.

What's Visual?

There are some wonderful and highly gripping stories that are not appropriate for the screen because they are not visual. Furthermore, there are parts of stories that are not suitable either. Many literary works make ample use of internal monologues (i.e., characters talking to themselves or, in other words, thinking) that are very difficult to convey well in a screenplay, except by using narration, flashbacks, or another clunky and artificial device. Likewise, the historical background of an event or character is difficult to convey in a film unless the historical facts emerge in the telling of the plot.

Some stories feature people talking—and talking a lot. Most of these films, with the possible exception of *My Dinner with André*, fail miserably if mostly what we see on the screen are "talking heads." You also want to be careful with telephone calls, where you see only one person on the screen, as well as scenes that involve a person talking to herself. Because the screen renders such a complete image (sound, sight, color, shape, movement), what might not seem interminable for a novel may seem deadly on the screen. Films are much *less* forgiving in this sense.

What you do want to include is what is visible—that is, *characters in action*—action that involves movement within interesting settings and action that evokes emotion or passion. Select those stories or elements in those stories that involve:

- Characters doing things
- Well-crafted dramatic dialogue
- Interesting settings
- Movement within the settings

Where's the Story?

Most book-length manuscripts either have more than one story going on or have a story that is very complex. Sometimes these stories are told chronologically, and sometimes they unfold in fits and starts, moving forward and backward in time and space. There are often subplots in novels. Most often, then, the literary plot is layered and fairly elaborate.

A writer attempting an adaptation of an epistolary novel (e.g., John Barth's *Letters*) would have trouble because, although there is a plot, the body of the original is in the form of letters written from one character to another. It is highly textual and, in some ways, highly dramatic, but that drama occurs to some degree between the writer and the reader as the reader tries to link letters, characters, and stories together to unpack what actually happened. *Letters* is just too complex for a feature film.

Often the narrative shifts in fiction are numerous, with the perspective moving in and out of the minds of one or another of the characters, changing points of view, or intertwining motifs. For many readers, this is the beauty of the novel—that it can be so changeable in terms of narrative, speaker, and chronology. But aside from the art film and occasional film classic such as Kurosawa's *Rashomon*, this kind of complexity does not seem to play well for film audiences, and it is really tough to write so it makes sense. In other words, look for original stories that are fairly simple and where the essence of the story (what makes it good reading) is in the action.

Adapting Your Selection

Which Story?

Aristotle points out that good drama must be single in issue, rising to a single climax and coming to a single resolution. This is also true for the film drama, and this, in essence, should be a beauty of the screenplay: Although there may indeed be subplots, they all converge at a climactic point near the end of the film. What emerges should be a single, powerful premise. Therefore, a judicious and sometime ruthless process of selection needs to be made about what to keep and what to jettison from the original material. In fact, some wonderful scenes and plot twists and turns from the original will never make it into the screenplay, and rightly so.

Which Characters?

By the same token, many quite interesting and useable characters that appear in the original material will undoubtedly need to be omitted from the screenplay. Sometimes several characters will be combined into one for the screenplay. Not only will this decision making be motivated by the question of length (you simply cannot afford to have a Dostoevskian cast of characters), but some characters are not as suitable as others for translation to the screen. Characters who are charismatic, have powerful strength of character, and are very empathetic are good choices for those to consider keeping. Characters who are embroiled primarily in internal conflicts, whose weaknesses overwhelm their strengths, or who are simply boring are likely candidates for omission.

The Step Outline

The step outline is an excellent way to move from the idea stage to the screenplay in an adaptation primarily because it forces you to select your scenes in advance. I include an example of a step outline based on an original idea in chapter 6. What follows is a step outline for the adaptation of the short story "The Chrysanthemums" by John Steinbeck (1938). Steinbeck's short story begins with a vivid account of the setting.

```
The high grey-flannel fog of winter closed off the
Salinas Valley from the sky and from all the rest
of the world. On every side it sat like a lid on
the mountains and made of the great valley a closed
pot. (p. 939)
```

The narrative continues with a lengthy description of the main character, Elisa Allen, who is digging with vigorous energy in her garden. She notices her husband talking with some strangers. She has returned to her work when he comes up to her.

> Elisa started at the sound of her husband's voice.
> He had come near quietly and he leaned over the
> wire fence that protected her flower garden from
> cattle and dogs and chickens.
>
> "At it again," he said. "You've got a strong new
> crop coming.'
>
> Elisa straightened her back and pulled on the
> gardening glove again. "Yes. They'll be strong this
> coming year." In her tone and on her face there was
> a little smugness. (p. 940)

Note that this story—at least the selections I have provided here—are nicely adaptable in one respect: They focus on what we see and hear, not what the characters think. The similes in the description of the landscape are not necessarily liabilities because they enhance the image that the reader might get of the setting.

Here is how a student in one of my classes began his step outline of this short story:

> "The Chrysanthemums" an adaptation of a John
> Steinbeck story by E. Mitch Mitchell.
>
> Setting: Salinas Valley, California,1930.
>
> Characters: Elisa Allen (age 35)
>
>   Henry Allen (Elisa's husband, age 40)
>
>   The Pot Fixer (early 40s)
>
> 1. ELISA works in the flower garden near the front
>   of her yard, which borders on the country lane.
>   She occasionally looks up dreamily at the sky
>   and grins a wild grin. HENRY, her husband
>   approaches her. Around him, Elisa's voice,
>   expression and mannerisms become pleasant but
>   serious, a "good little wife." He's sold some

```
cattle; he's going out to gather them in, and
then he's taking her out to dinner. He leaves.
   Arrival of the "POT FIXER," an itinerant
repairman or tinker. Been on the road for
days, driving a beat-up wagon with a sign
advertising repairs to household items. He's
all good nature and smiles when it suits him,
but he turns on and off like a light bulb. Not
a villain, not evil, but manipulative in a way
that's not obvious to Elisa. A bit of verbal
fencing: he tries to drum up business; she
tries to tell him no, she's hard at work.
Fixer finally takes the tack of mentioning the
chrysanthemums, and when he does, she starts to
become engaged.
```

Note that Mitch's step outline is both explicit and spare. The outline is not necessarily a sales tool; rather, it is more for Mitch—a way to flesh out the plot and hone it down to the ingredients he believes are essential to telling the story he wants to tell. First, he wants to introduce the key characters as quickly as feasible. Then he wants to create tension that will eventually build into the conflict that will carry the story. He suggests some of the underlying unease between Henry and Elisa, then introduces the Fixer as the source of genuine conflict. He also wants to understand his characters and build into their portrayals those elements that will be essential to the plot as it unfolds.

The preceding scene continues, and the next scene (or No. 2) begins later in time where the conflict between Elisa and the Fixer escalates. The step outline continues until the entire plot is worked out.

Much of what Mitch wrote in his step outline is Mitch's interpretation of the story and not Steinbeck's actual words or phrases. When the time comes to work the step outline into a treatment, Mitch will have the choice of whether to use what Steinbeck has written, presuming that Mitch has secured the rights to the Steinbeck story. All along he has the choice—and in fact must make some hard decisions—about what to keep in his adaptation and what to omit. Because the story is short, Mitch chooses to keep the three central characters. Another adapter might omit a character, such as Henry, or add characters to enhance the drama.

The Feature Film Adaptation

When Eric Sears and I adapted *The Grassman* by Len Fulton (1974), we were faced with the task of taking a 275-page novel with its numerous characters and its plot complexities and shaping it into a 120-page screenplay. Our partner, Zachary Feuer, had optioned this novel, which takes place during the Wyoming Territory range wars in 1886, because of the interesting characters, particularly an enigmatic preacher named Greak, and the action-packed story. Fulton's novel tells the tale of a particularly bloody war between a powerful cattle family named Finn and outsiders who seek to take control of the land.

We first decided on the story line and climax. Essentially, we wanted to treat the key events leading up to the climactic shoot-out. Then we decided on which characters we wanted to keep. Certainly we wanted to keep Greak, the preacher/gunslinger. He was inscrutable, tough, and unusual. We also decided to keep the narrator, the young Andrew Finn (although we did not have him narrate), who journeys west to visit his relatives on the Finn ranch in Wyoming, but we dropped his friend, Holly, who accompanies him on his visit because we felt she added little to the story we wanted to tell. What she did add, we could fold into Andrew's character. We kept Andrew because he seemed to provide a nice catalyst for the story and a person with whom some viewers could identify as they come to understand the story's conflict. We also eliminated other characters we felt were unnecessary.

Writers who adapt from other sources are entitled to use everything from that source—not only plot and characters, but dialogue and description as well. We liked Fulton's language—we felt it added to the Western-ness of the piece, but found we had to simplify some of his dialectal spelling for readability. For example, characters in the novel often talk like this:

```
Paintrock haint partic'lar, sah. Anythin 'at
moves he's onter now 't seems.
```

Although this may add color and authenticity—quite appropriate for a novel where the reader has the leisure to read and re-read to make sense—it is not for the screenplay; it was just too hard to follow.

In addition to simplifying the plot line, we decided to expand the sexual drama between Greak and the patriarch Ben Finn's daughter, Lindy. In keeping with Greak's original character, we decided not to establish a full-blown sexual relationship between them, but simply to heighten the sexual tension.

After making some dramatic decisions, we put together a temporary step outline so we knew the story we wanted to tell. We omitted scenes, extended scenes that existed in the original, and added brand-new scenes mostly to provide strong transitions.

To demonstrate the difference between one of the original scenes and its counterpart in the screenplay, I have included the following scene from the novel and its adapted counterpart in screenplay format. Note some of the changes we made in the adaptation.

From *Grassman* by Len Fulton

[The protagonist, Greak, has just caught up to Lindy Finn (daughter of Ben Finn, the owner of the Blacktail Ranch) after an impromptu horse race across the plains.]

He found her, then, as the Horn was halfway through the yellow-red sun. She sat, her square shoulders back to him, at the bushy cut of a small dry creek. She was dangling a strip of willow in the bottom sand. From way out he spotted the still, red locks, and he put a gradual muscle to the rein, cutting the cayuse's canter to a lope and then an easy jiggle. Up the draw stood the ghost of the great bay stallion, nothing more now than a late-gelded Injun animal trying to scour cottonwood trash. His ears reclined, his eyes sagged, and his graceful neck bent painfully toward the waterless creek. Yellow lather rolled over his sheen, over flank and barrel, neck and forequarters, moistening the dry ground. Not far way lay all his splendid accoutrements—saddle, breech, bridle. They, too, to the last strap, shone with the stallion's sweat.

Greak threw the Oregon aslant of the creekbed, scissored his trendril let about the horn. He noticed her clothes the fine breeches, the chamois jacket, the high stamped boots with calf vamps all soaked down, stuck with the bay hair of the insane race. Her hair strung together and pasted itself to her clothing.

"Waal," Greak observed easily, "If this here's round-trip contest, it appears it's mine. If it aint that, then y'all have won." He glanced at the horse and she saw him in her side vision.

She laughed mirthlessly and shrugged without turning.

"You call it." She motioned toward the horse with her head. "He was aching for a run. I gave it him."

"That's true, said Greak. "Don't reckon Ah've seen a hoss git so much woof took off him so quick in a long spell."

She now turned to look at him over her shoulder.

"You feel sorry for him?"

"Naw. He'll be a-running' broomtails first peep of day. But Ah do have a special wonder about folks who bog a hoss thataway."

"You think I need preaching to?"

"Waal, reckon most of us could stand that. You? Maybe. Maybe just a lickin'."

Again she laughed carelessly and prodded at the bottom sand with her toe.

Greak looked into the air.

"Nightwind's comin'. Y'all goin' t'rub the shiver off the mustang?"

"When I get back."

"Better be starting' it or yuh won't have no hoss. 'Spect yuh daddy'll come lookin', too."

She shrugged again.

"He's east at the ranch trap. I don't expect him tonight."

"Somebody'll be curious—"

"Johnny Lime, I suppose, might come out here. He wouldn't usually, but having run off a jump ahead of a stranger"—she turned quickly, then stood up in the middle of the creek bed and faced Greak. She inhaled, and her young body pressed outward against her sweat-streaked clothing.

"You are a reverend, aren't you?"

Greak caught his breath. She was an exquisite creature, disheveled as she was.

"Ah tote the word," he said.

She glanced, suddenly tense, at her saddle and equipment on the ground several yards away. A rifle scabbard protruded from the carelessly dumped array of gear.

"Stallion gal," Greak went on, "the thunder in me's loud as in any man, and yuh're a right round filly, Ah'll give yuh that. But my wits been around, too, and have got me a sight farther on the trail. Y'all ain't beyond resistance, if that's why yuh run me out here. Besides," he added, "Gawd's watchin'."

She cocked her head and looked at him curiously. Her lower jaw pouted.

"I'm sorry, Mister," she said.

"This here Lime, he's the top hand?"

She shook her head, sat down again, this time on the far cut of the dry creek, facing him.

"Segundo," she said. "Pancho Guarados is top hand."

"Maybe he'll be along then, instead of segundo."

"No, he's away."

"Then this here segundo's top feller—when the ramrod's vacationin'."

"No, Pancho's with the cattle. He hardly ever vacations."

"Now Ah like that in a topkick. Time spent meanderin' turns the head. A man notices all he's missin', a woman and things. Hurts his punchin'."

"It doesn't Pancho's."

"Y'don't say?"

"Well, not so far. He's been married a few weeks, and except for a little honeymoon in Denver, he's been right on this range." She grinned. Now, thought Greak, she's acting more like the she-child she looks!

"Hard way to make a family," he said, shaking his head. The girl's face shaded a light crimson.

"Juanita, his wife, is a plainswoman," she said proudly. "I'm running the chores while she—she stays with him up at Cold Canyon."

"Cold Canyon?"

"Where the main herd is. We'll—we'll be bringing them south in a few days." Her voice was sober.

Then suddenly she looked up at him, her face alight.

"Do you—do you marry people?" she asked, and Greak almost fell off the saddle. Her blue eyes searched for his hidden ones.

"Ah have been known to do it," he said slowly—Saint Gawd, this wasn't happening! She'd led him into a trap with her hell-racing!

She lowered her eyes.

"What do I have to do?"

"Do? Why, Ah reckon the first thing is to git a man—?"

"That's done. What next?"

"Waal"—for the first time in a long time Greak's words would not take shape in his mind. He was cold-stopped by a gal with enough rods in the fire to put her brand on two ranges! Gawd, what a tangle she had going! And Gawd, here was this Texan's soul, with warts enough already on it, plumb square in the tangle too! While Texas called.

Her face was bright, hopeful; her eyes wide.

Night was on.

"Ah've business west and north," he drawled. "Maybe when Ah pass back through."

And thus he slunk away. (pp. 214–216)

Here is the adaptation.

```
EXT. FINN FLATLANDS - DAY


Still in a slow canter, Greak nudges his pony
toward a strip of low-lying hills. Here the plains
grass has sparsened and blue sage taken over. Greak
is in no hurry. The rhythm of horse and rider is
even and steady, seemingly effortless.

After a moment, Greak turns his pony slightly and
they descend into the cut of a small, dry, creek-
bed. There, the back of her square shoulders
towards him, sits Lindy, dangling a sprig of willow
in the sand.

Greak pulls his horse to a gradual slow trot. Up
the draw stands the great bay stallion—a ghost of
the horse tethered at the Blacktail: ears
reclining, eyes sagging, his graceful neck bent
painfully towards the waterless creek. Yellow
lather rolls over his flank and barrel, his
forequarters, moistening the dry ground. His fancy
saddle and bridle lie on the ground, too, shining
with the stallion's sweat.

Greak slows near Lindy, then stops. Her clothes are
soaked with sweat, stuck with the bay hairs of the
stallion. Her hair is strung together and pasted to
her clothing. Greak scissors his long leg over the
horn of his saddle.

                     GREAK
                  (easily)
             Well, if this here's a round-trip
             contest, it appears it's mine. If it
             ain't, then y'all have won.
                                (CONTINUED)
```

- - - - - - - - - - page break - - - - - - - - - -

CONTINUED:

He glances at the stallion. She turns towards him,
and then resumes her gazing at the river bed. After
a moment, she lets out a mirthless chuckle and
shrugs without turning.

> LINDY
>
> You call it.

She motions toward the stallion with her head.

> LINDY (CONT'D)
>
> He was aching for a run. I gave it to
> him.

> GREAK
>
> That's true. Don't reckon I've seen
> a horse get so much woof taken out
> of him so quick in a long spell.

Lindy turns toward him.

> LINDY
>
> You feel sorry for him?

> GREAK
>
> No. He'll be running broomtails first
> peep of day.
>   (pause)
> But I do have a special wonder about
> folks who bog a horse that way.

> LINDY
>
> You think I need preaching to?

> (CONTINUED)

- - - - - - - - - page break - - - - - - - - - -

CONTINUED:

>   GREAK
> Well, I reckon most of us could stand
> that. You? Maybe just a lickin'.

She glances at Greak. After a long moment,

>   LINDY
> What exactly are you doing out here,
> preacher?

Greak is caught off guard by her question. He looks
at her closely. Then almost ominously,

>   GREAK
> I tote the Word.

Suddenly tense, she looks towards her saddle and
equipment on the ground several yards away. A rifle
scabbard protrudes from the array of gear. Her look
does not escape Greak.

>   GREAK (CONT'D)
> Stallion-gal, I'd believe me I were
> you.

She turns to face him and rises.

>   LINDY
> That some kind of threat, preacher?

Greak laughs outright.

>   (CONTINUED)

- - - - - - - - - - page break - - - - - - - - - -

CONTINUED:

                    GREAK
          Grit ain't what you're lackin'. Nor
          brains in your head. What you're
          missing when God piece you together
          was some of that cowboy sense—
          knowing when to talk, when to clam
          up. When to stay home and when to
          ride your horse.

She turns away from him petulantly and goes up to
the stallion. She takes a rag from her hip pocket
and begins to wipe off the sweat and lather from
the horse's rump.

                    LINDY
              (without looking)
          And who's going to give me that
          licking you say I so rightly deserve?

Greak watches her moving body as she brushes the
horse. He exhales audibly.

                    GREAK
          Your daddy.

                    LINDY
              (without turning)
          He could. But he's no good at
          disciplining. He's tried. Guarados
          does that kind of work for him. The
          rough stuff. And Guarados won't
          touch me. Besides, he's up at Cold
          Canyon.

                              (CONTINUED)

- - - - - - - - - - page break - - - - - - - - - -

CONTINUED:

She is silent a moment as she works. Greak slides
off his pony with his canteen to give his horse
some water on his muzzle. As he turns back to offer
her some, he finds himself looking down the barrel
of her rifle.

                    LINDY
          Just who are you, Mister? No
          preacher, that's for damned sure.

Greak blinks, pauses a moment, then moves undaunted
to wet the muzzle of the stallion. She doesn't stop
him but continues to point her gun.

                    GREAK
                  (dryly)
          Going to shoot me, Stallion-gal?

                    LINDY
                (cocking the rifle)
          I might.

Greak finishes with the horse, then turns. He
stares at her then offers her the canteen. His
expression is cold, serious. She pauses, looks at
the outstretched canteen. She exhales with
exasperation and lowers her rifle. His long arm
lashes out, grabs her and throws her to the slope
of the creek-bed where he pins her down. She
struggles, but he is by far the stronger.

                                        (CONTINUED)

- - - - - - - - - - page break - - - - - - - - - -

CONTINUED:

                    GREAK
        Stallion-gall, the thunder in me's as
        loud as in any man, and you're a right
        round filly, I'll give you that. But my
        wits been around, too, and have got
        me a sight farther on the trail. Y'all
        ain't beyond resistance, if that's why
        you run me out here.

Lindy is breathing hard. A look of fear crosses her
face as he speaks.

                    LINDY
        That's not why I run you out. No *that*
        thought only just occurred to me.

Greak stares at her, then slowly relaxes his hold.
She takes one of his hands, holds it a beat, then
pulls it slowly to her breast. He doesn't try to
move it. They remain that way, transfixed, for a
moment. Then Greak reaches her other hand behind
her neck and draws her to him. He kisses her hard
on the mouth. She responds, holding his lean frame
to her.

Suddenly he breaks away. He rises slowly and goes
to his horse. She also rises, straightening
herself. She takes her saddle and starts to wipe
the sweat and grit from it. He mounts his horse,
then glances at her. She looks up. As she starts to
speak he motions her to silence.

                                        (CONTINUED)

- - - - - - - - - - page break - - - - - - - - - -

```
CONTINUED:

                    GREAK
         I've business, west and north.
         Maybe when I pass back through ....

He turns his horse and goes off. She looks after
him, then picks up her saddle and throws it over
the stallion.

                                        CUT TO:
```

Clearly, there are a number of ways to have handled this scene. Our goal was to structure the scene to make it more suitable for the film medium. Among our aims:

- *To make it shorter*
  In reducing a long novel to a relatively short screenplay, we did not have the luxury of a long scene. We had to get a lot done in a limited amount of space, so we both restructured and abbreviated the original scene.
- *To cut out extraneous, unnecessary or inappropriate description, action, and dialogue*
  We got rid of some of the shot description and broke the rest up into easily readable paragraphs. We also reduced the original dialogue considerably. For example, we eliminated the discussion about who or who was not the top hand at the Finn ranch because we did not consider it absolutely necessary to the scene or story. We cut out anything that smacked of interior monologue, such as what Greak is thinking. In addition (as much for readability as for how it played on the page), we simplified some of the spelling of Greak's heavily accented dialogue because, although it added a lot to the style of the piece, it was too hard to read quickly. We also probably walked a fine line between character and comedy by keeping expressions like "Stallion-gal," but early on in the screenplay, we established certain hallmarks of Greak's dialogue. "Stallion-gal," along with "Saint Gawd," was one of them.
- *To have the scene rise to a sharper climax*
  We felt that the original scene took a long time to get to the climax, and when it came it was too subtle for the screen. Consequently, we increased the tension by adding some potential violence (having Lindy aim the rifle at Greak) and made the scene more overtly sexual (including a kiss).

Overall, we reshaped the scene so it would be less informational or expository and more of a sexual confrontation between Lindy and Greak.

- *To make it more active*
  Adding the hint of violence and sex made the scene more active. There now is more action and a bit less talk, and the talk is more fraught with tension than in the original. There is an important caveat here, however. Violence and sex should never be added gratuitously. They should be part of the fabric of the story and the characterization. In this case, we believe they were.

- *To retain the atmosphere and style of the original material*
  We were very concerned about keeping some of the things we liked about the novel in place. Both Lindy and Greak retain most of their original character, although the scene took a direction that gave the original writer, Len Fulton, some pause (he felt it sacrilegious to have Greak make a pass at Lindy). We used some of the original dialogue—its phrasing, diction, and sequencing—and we did the same for the shot description. The resulting scene is, then, both the same and different.

- *To provide some necessary exposition for scenes to come (e.g., the material about Guarados) in the course of the action*
  Because we had to be necessarily selective about what to include in the screenplay, and because in some cases we added and changed material that was in the original story, it became necessary to include some exposition about Guarados, who later plays a significant role in the land wars. By eliminating other exposition, the few lines about Guarados stand out more than they do in the original.

ADAPTING PLAYS

The adaptation of plays presents another set of problems. Plays are designed to be staged in a theater. Consequently, most of the "action" of the play must either come across in dialogue or action that can appear in a limited and confined space. Changes in setting (time and place) are often constrained by the limitations of the stage crew and complexity of the set. Changes in characters are limited by the number of exits and entrances that the unfolding drama can sustain.

Films are both less personal than plays and more. A film allows for much more flexibility in the distance the viewer gets to the action. In a film, the camera can get very, very close or very far away—at the discretion, most often, of the director. In a play, the distance between members of the audience and the stage is the same throughout the play. The camera dictates what viewers see; it focuses their attention. They are intimately involved in someone else's vision of the story. Playgoers, in contrast, are there in the theater where the action is taking place; this is a quite different form of intimacy and a very powerful one. They share the room with the players; although the set is carefully constructed to create an effect, playgoers have a limited freedom to focus on what they want.

Although unfortunately this does not always happen, transforming a play into a screenplay should involve a complete reconception of the original material. For example, Peter Shaffer's (1984) adaptation of his play, *Amadeus*, involved significant changes in the relationships between the main characters and the addition of new scenes that would broaden the visual scope and take advantage of the medium of film. In contrast, *Glengarry Glen Ross* (1984), which is a very powerful play by David Mamet, is not as successful in its film version (1992)—despite the presence of an all-star cast including Jack Lemmon, Al Pacino, Alec Baldwin, and Kevin Spacey—because it fails to make use of the film medium. The action is confined to several sets and relies primarily on the dialogue. Although some accommodation is made in the shooting of the scenes, the result is primarily talking heads (albeit heads talking dramatically and poignantly).

ADAPTATIONS AND THE CREATIVE PROCESS

Adapting original material for the screen can be tremendously rewarding. It requires a good eye and ear for drama; a strong, judicious sense for what can and should be cut; and scrupulous attention to what will play well both on paper and on the screen.

But the challenge is more than editorial. Good adaptation enables you to put your creative energies to work in a wonderfully collaborative way. Presuming that you have selected strong source material, you are essentially taking the work of another writer and transforming it in ways that will produce a product that is both new and faithful to the original material. You use much of the original material—characters, language, scenes, structure—but you also reshape and reconstitute it so that it makes dramatic sense for filmgoers. The results of working this way can potentially be much richer than one writer working alone—especially (and perhaps only) if you take seriously your role of both screenwriter and adapter.

A Footnote on a Hollywood Phenomenon

There is an interesting (and relatively unacknowledged) phenomenon in Hollywood, at least, that books are more literary, and *literariness*, however it is defined, is admired and respected. Sometimes it is easier to write a novel and sell it for the screen then it is to sell a screenplay. But there is also the risk that you spend 6 months to a year (or 10 years) writing that novel with the intention of making it as a screenwriter and have it fail—both as a novel and as material for a screenplay. Time is wasted. Write what is closest to your heart.

By Hollywood standards, what makes something literary? Hollywood's standards for literariness are only tacitly agreed on and would never hold water with a genuine literary critic. These standards seem to include:

- Rich (but short) shot description
- Unusual characters who speak well (eloquently, powerfully, charismatically)
- A complex plot (that is, all the while, easy to follow, exciting, and cohesive)

These attributes should come as no surprise because these are all elements that we have covered already. The lesson here is not to be afraid to sound a bit "literary" from time to time, but always in the service of your film drama.

APPLICATIONS AND EXERCISES

1. *Keep an eye out for material that would be appropriate for adaptation.* This may be a newspaper account, a magazine article, or a short story, play, or novel in public domain. Alternately, it can be something you might want to invest money into: a first novel by an unknown writer, a short story from a journal or review, and so on. Be aware, however, that you will be competing against producers who are looking for the same thing. Furthermore, if you make choices only off the *New York Times* Best Seller list, you will be vying with established producers and wealthy investors.

Track down the copyright; find out who owns it.

Even if you do not end up entering the game by optioning material, you will still have gained valuable practice at considering possibilities and analyzing your choices for suitability.

2. *Write a step outline from a short story.* Read Ambrose Bierce's short story, "Occurrence at Owl Creek Bridge," and then locate the short film based on the story. It is available on DVD as part of the "Twilight Zone" series. Note the way it has been adapted, especially how it relies on visual storytelling rather than dialogue.

Then select a short story—regardless of its availability—that might be appropriate to adapt. Remember the key elements that make for a good screenplay and make your choice accordingly. For my screenwriting classes, I have had students select from stories like William Faulkner's "A Rose for Emily," John Steinbeck's "The Chrysanthemums," Alice Walker's "Everyday Use," and Sherwood Anderson's "I'm a Fool." (Note that "I'm a Fool" has been made into an hour-long film—an adaptation primarily for literature students—and this can be viewed as a basis for comparison.)

Then try your hand at writing a step outline. For a story that is 10 to 15 pages long, your outline will probably range from 3 to 5 pages. Stick to strict time limits. I have my students write an outline for a 15-minute film (or a 15-minute screenplay) because I want them to get into the practice of making difficult choices on what material to include and what to leave out. Other writers may want to work toward more common time constraints—for example, an hour.

When you have completed the step outline, review your work for the following to make sure you have taken under consideration the following rules:
- Present tense narrative
- Good dramatic structure: conflict, rising tension line, climax, and resolution (despite what is in the original)
- Limited cast of characters
- Reasonable (but not slavish) fidelity to original material
- No interior monologues (no characters' thoughts)
- No description of what takes place before the drama begins
- No flashbacks unless stylistically appropriate

3. *Take a look at some well-known adaptations* of both novels and short stories to see what has been included and what has been left out. Read both the novel and screenplay (or see the film). How has the screenwriter stayed "faithful" to the original and how has she deviated? What works and what doesn't? Here are some possibilities:

> *Seabiscuit* (novel: Laura Hillenbrand; screenplay: Gary Ross)
>
> *The Thin Red Line* (novel: James Jones; screenplay: Terrence Malick)
>
> *The Pianist* (book by Wladyslaw Szpilman; screenplay: Ronald Harwood)
>
> *The Green Mile* (novel: Stephen King; screenplay: Frank Darabont)
>
> *The Talented Mr. Ripley* (novel: Patricia Highsmith; screenplay: Anthony Minghella)
>
> *A Beautiful Mind* (novel: Sylvia Nasar; screenplay: Akiva Goldsmith)

4. For a provocative look at what it takes to adapt a film in Hollywood, take a look at *Adaptation*, written by Charlie Kaufman and Donald Kaufman and adapted from a nonfiction piece, "The Orchid Thief," by Susan Orlean.

SUGGESTED READING

Brady, B. (1994). *Principles of adaptation for film and television.* Austin: University of Texas Press.

Cartmell, D. (1999). *Adaptation from text to screen, screen to text.* Oxford: Routledge.

Fulton, L. (1974). *The grassman.* Berkeley, CA: Thorp Springs Press.

Morrissette, B. (1985). *Novel and film: Essays in two genres.* Chicago: University of Chicago Press.

Seger, L. (1992). *The art of adaptation.* New York: Owl Books.

I was hired to adapt a book called The Orchid Thief, *about orchids and orchid poaching, by a* New Yorker *writer named Susan Orlean. I ended up writing about the process of trying to adapt it. The script is a document of the process of writing it from beginning to end, in which I put myself and my brother in, by name, as the main characters. I called it "Adaptation" because there's a parallel between what I did and the book, which is about the natural history of these flowers. How it's been manipulated by people, but also by natural selection. What's so amazing about orchids is how they trick insects into pollinating them, by looking like insects or by smelling like rotting meat. There's also this play between Darwin and Aristotle because the orchid people talk about Darwin and a screenwriting teacher in the script talks about Aristotle, and the difference between nature and art.*

—Charlie Kaufman (on the film *Adaptation*) interviewed in *Scenario: The Magazine of Screenwriting Art* 5.3 (1999/2000).

The Fact Film:
Documentaries—Form and Format

WHAT IS A DOCUMENTARY FILM?

Documentary films rank among the best films ever made (of course, there are some awful documentaries as well). The good ones can be extraordinarily powerful, dealing with topics ranging from high school to bald eagles to little known harpsichordists; they can be personal and emotional, as in the story of a loved one dying of AIDS; or they can be impersonal and objective, as in a filmed chronicle of the pyramids. The end of this chapter lists some of the classic documentaries and some good resources for finding out more about the genre. Most people who are familiar with regular TV programming and cable networks are familiar with shows like 60 *Minutes* and *Dateline*, the Discovery and History channels. In fact, the cable market offers viewers a veritable smorgasbord of documentary films of differing quality, length, and angle. Even "reality" TV makes a contribution, although its relationship to reality is questionable.

A documentary is essentially a "fact" film; that is, it is a film made about a person, place, event, phenomenon, or experience that exists or has existed (or even may, one day, exist) in the real world. Although the sources for these films are "real," documentaries are always one point of view or one "take" on this reality. They often have an angle to explore, a bone to pick, a point to make—in other words, a premise. Sometimes they are used as political weapons (Michael Moore's *Fahrenheit 9/11*, or *Stolen Honor*, a film depicting Presidential candidate John's Kerry's antiwar activities).

For most documentary films, the scenes are not re-created (as in a docudrama), and the film makers do not use actors or construct sets. Documentary films explore what must be construed as "real," as something that happens in real life. That said, the "reality" of the film is affected—even contaminated—in a variety of ways: the presence of an observer or observers, the presence of the camera, the film maker's goals or values, and the producer's objectives. Although this might seem a liability, in fact this is what makes good documentaries so exciting to make and watch. Documentary films treat "reality," but good films convey a *point of view on that reality* that brings us insight and allows us to immerse ourselves personally, emotionally, or intellectually in a reality that is not our own or is unfamiliar.

Let me elaborate in terms of some precepts:

1. *The point of the film (premise).* Most film makers have a particular point or attitude they want to get across—even though they may not know exactly what that point is at the outset. They may want to save an endangered species, convey the artistry of a musician, or investigate a historic event. Even when the "reality" that film makers actually get on film turns out to be different from what they intended, sometimes substantially so, the final product will still convey a particular stance on the subject. Sometimes this takes the form of an argument, in which the film is an attempt to persuade viewers of the rightness of that position.

2. *The camera's perspective.* The camera takes a particular position vis-à-vis the material being covered. It cannot see everything. It can only record what is visually and audibly available in that particular space and time. Therefore, it is only "seeing" a portion of what is "really" going on. In addition, documentary films undergo a substantial editing process. Much of

what does not illustrate the film maker's point of view will end up on the editing room floor, and so it should. So the film's perspective must be very selective and subjective.

3. *The existence of the camera.* Anyone who has ever tried to act "natural" while being observed by a camera knows how difficult, if not impossible, it is to behave as usual. The camera always influences the scene and action, if only by its presence. A documentary film rarely sees real life exactly "how it is." This is part of what makes it an art form; in many ways, documentaries are views of "crafted" reality.

4. *Verisimilitude.* Even given the "slant" on reality that documentary films necessarily take, they must still convey the idea that what the viewers are seeing is real. Despite that the reality is viewed through a particular lens or point of view, and that it is inevitably altered by the existence of the camera and film makers, it must not appear to be so. It must seem genuine, authentic, and "real."

In other words, despite that documentary films depend on what "really" happens out there in the world, the writer has enormous power to shape that experience in ways that may make a remarkable phenomenon even more remarkable. Unfortunately, this power also means film makers can craft a film in which a remarkable phenomenon is deadly dull to watch. This is what we try to help you avoid in this chapter and the one that follows on writing for the marketplace.

A Collaboration. It should be noted, too, that although I say "one" point of view, documentary film making is as collaborative a venture as dramatic film making. The only difference is the scale. The film crews are smaller, and the film makers have to answer to fewer people. A documentary film crew can consist of as few as two people—the director and the person holding the video camera. Or it can have a larger crew or even several crews consisting of: camera operator, sound technician, director, and assistants. There are often producers, editors, distributors, financial backers, and clients (for whom the film is often made), all of whom may have a say in the production and final product. Even so, the number of people involved is small compared with film crews for feature films.

A Business. Documentary film making is still a business. The films are still made to be seen and liked by as many people as possible, and they are usually designed to make money, directly or indirectly, for the producers. At the very least, they should make back their production costs.

A Subject Matter.   The subject matter also is enormously influential in shaping the outcome. This is particularly true when the subject is a person (Thelonious Monk, Wayne Newton, or Jane Fonda), but events and experiences also have obvious ways of shaping the outcome. Hurricanes and tornadoes do not stand still (and sometimes do not even show up when they are supposed to), murder trials do not always end in the ways the film makers anticipate, and an event that should be exciting to watch may turn out to be a complete and utter bore. If anything, Murphy's Law (that you can count on the worst possible thing happening at the worst possible time in the worst possible way) is even truer of documentary film production than it is of theatrical film production. At least in theatrical films, a director has some control over her actors.

WRITING A DOCUMENTARY FILM

In an important sense, documentary films are less "written" than dramatic films. Because of the nature of the genre—the fact that you never know what you will get on film when you set out to shoot—much of the film is "created" in the editing room. So much of what I say here refers to the whole package: preproduction (planning and writing), production (shooting), and postproduction (editing). In the majority of cases, the same people are involved in the entire process.

There are significant ways in which the documentary film is quite similar to the dramatic film. To keep audiences interested, good documentary films **have a dramatic structure**: rising tension line, a climax, and a resolution. Many of them have a protagonist—a central character or person who serves to focus or anchor the film. More often than not, this person is someone we can identify with, at least on an emotional level. *Hoop Dreams* follows two characters, Arthur Agee and William Gates, through 4 years of high school and a year of college. Arthur and William are the protagonists; the film is told from their points of view, and they drive the action. The film makers want the audience to care about these guys and what happens to them. *Spellbound* is a film about spelling bees, but also about following eight kids as they prepare for and compete in a national spelling bee contest.

It is even more important to have developed your **premise**, especially in the writing stage of a documentary. *Roger and Me*, for example, is a film that argues against certain business practices of General Motors, vividly portraying the disparity in wealth and lifestyle of GM workers and GM management in Flint, Michigan. The film maker, Michael Moore, knew this going in. *Hoop*

Dreams takes a position on the exploitation of inner-city Black youths. *Silverlake Life* makes an important point about love and death as it chronicles the struggles of two gay men as one of the partners dies from AIDS. This is not to say that all films that are classified as documentaries have axes to grind. But the best ones, the most memorable ones, are either produced to make a point—often a controversial one—or to provide an important insight about the world or human nature.

There are as many ways to tell a "fact" film as there are "facts." The idea is to make memorable fact films—ones that an audience will remember for a long time. Good films give us something to think about and that requires several key things.

A Good Topic

Good documentaries have been made about things that are very personal—a family member, a pet, a personal experience—and they have been made about things that are very public—celebrities, famous historical events, easily recognized places. But these films all have certain commonalities.

1. **The topic must be "interesting."** There are a couple of ways to approach this. First, an "interesting" topic is one that reveals something new—something that is not already common knowledge. Just another film chronicling the well-known events of the Civil War will not be very appealing. But a film that reveals the less considered human aspects of the war, puts faces to names, and evokes some attitude about the war that is not part of our everyday knowledge—is interesting.

Alternately, a good documentary film idea might be one that takes a position and argues powerfully for that position in a way that makes an audience think, reconsider, or even be angry. The kinds of short films seen regularly on *60 Minutes* tend to fit in this category. Topics include people falsely accused of crimes, corrupt public officials in this country and elsewhere in the world, corporate abuse of power, and so on.

Third, an interesting topic might be one that evokes compassion and feeling about a person, group of people, race, or species in ways that tap into our sense of humanity. These are ideas that stimulate the emotions perhaps more than the preceding two. For example, the British film *David*, made in 1951, tells the story of the elderly caretaker of a Welsh school and his bid to win a poetry contest. It is a "small" story told not about some cataclysm or celebrity, but rather about an ordinary human being acting extraordinarily.

Paris is Burning is a film that makes you care about Pepper LaBeija, although Pepper's lifestyle may be alien—even distasteful—to some viewers.

In some ways, films that evoke compassion can be quite voyeuristic. *An American Family* produced by Craig Gilbert is a 12-episode film following 7 months in the life of an upper middle-class American family, the Louds, of Santa Barbara. What might otherwise have been a fairly ordinary topic was made extraordinary by virtue of having the camera present in someone's home to witness the rituals and trials of daily life, including the breakup of a marriage. Although reality TV may stretch the limits of the documentary definition, it too pretends to enter the personal lives of ordinary people to see how they respond to love, sex, money, and so on.

2. A good topic must be cinematic; it must make use of the film medium. Good ideas are highly visual; in other words, the message, information, and insight must be able to be conveyed using the features of the cinema: picture and sound. This also should include *action* if the film is about people or *movement* if the film is about events. *Winged Migration,* a film about the migratory patterns of birds, is breathtaking in its combination of cinematography and sound. In fact, one could easily argue that it is the cinematography that makes this film so compelling. Many other examples can be found on the Nature Channel.

Students in my classes often ask how you can make a film have action and movement if it is about an event that occurred in the past, where the film maker will be using chiefly archival material such as photographs and graphics because the people involved in these events are long dead. The answer to this is to MAKE IT VISUAL. This can occur during the filming (through the selective use of camera angles and movements such as pans, and zooms) and the editing (quick cutting, the creation of rhythms and tension). It all starts with a good topic. Ken Burns' epic documentary, *The Civil War,* is about a war—one of those events in human history that is, by its very nature, action packed and dramatic; it is potentially a good, cinematic topic. But it is also a war that took place over 100 years ago. To make it dynamic, he used an array of cinematic tools: hundreds of archival photographs of people and landscapes to help re-create action, footage of actual battle sites as they look today, interviews with historians talking about the events, and narration created from the writing of people who were alive during the war. In other words, he had to get creative.

> But the long and painstaking process had permitted me to refine a filmmaking style that we had been evolving for more than 10 years: the careful use of archival photographs, live modern cinematography, music, narration, and a chorus of

first-person voices that together did more than merely recount a historical story. It was something that also became a kind of "emotional archaeology," trying to unearth the very heart of the American experience; listening to the ghosts and echoes of an almost inexpressibly wise past.

—Interview with Ken Burns (2002), maker of *The Civil War*
(http://www.pbs.org/civilwar/film/)

3. Good documentaries should have some kind of conflict. As with dramatic films, conflict is the key to making films interesting to audiences. Burns' *The Civil War* is an obvious example with clear conflict. But most good documentaries have some strong antagonistic forces working against each other. In *Hoop Dreams*, Arthur and William are both fighting to eventually get into the NBA. Along the way, the tension builds as they work to get on their high school team, try to win games against formidable opponents, attempt to make the grade in school, avoid the hazards of their respective neighborhoods, and so on. The producers also make use of individual basketball games to heighten tension within scenes: Will the underdogs win and get to the state tournament? The antagonistic forces seem indomitable and overwhelming, but both Arthur and William have their own strengths and abilities, some of them personal and some of them athletic, and they fight the good fight—which is why we root for them and empathize with them, whether we are African-American or not, whether we like basketball or not, whether we believe in social justice or not. In *Winged Migration*, the conflict is more subtle, but it is nonetheless present in the elements (hunters, pollution, fatigue) that impede the long seasonal flights that birds take to get where they need to go. The tension in *Capturing the Friedmans* comes from the attempt to determine guilt or innocence in a child molestation case in which the Friedmans (father, Arnold, and son, Jesse) are accused.

One of the reasons that the personal sketches during the TV coverage of the Olympic Games work is because they often portray the barriers that some athletes have had to overcome to make it as far in their sport as they have. These obstacles include the death of a parent or sibling, a potentially crippling or debilitating disease, or, simply, a hard life. Although these clips can be justly criticized (see my comments near the end of this chapter under "Clichés"), they can potentially add tension and conflict to the sporting event in which athletes participate.

Even documentary topics that do not inherently have tension are best served when tension is made a part of their portrayal. For example, one of my students wanted to write a documentary treatment about a wildlife refuge in

New England. His first draft was simply informational, providing facts and statistics about the refuge and the animals it sheltered. Although the treatment conveyed a lot of data and focused some attention on the natural beauty of the place, it was not otherwise very engaging—especially to someone who did not much care. Because his purpose was to invite contributions to the refuge, we worked to inject some conflict and tension into the piece. His second draft made much more of the threats to parks such as poachers, pollution, lack of funding, governmental neglect, and public indifference. The refuge and the animals in it were at tremendous risk. Consequently, his revised script is much more compelling.

A Good Proposal

Note that many writers of documentary films are also their own production crews. Consequently, proposals may include the shooting and postproduction phases of film production. Most documentary film makers start out with a well-developed plan, which they have in mind (and usually on paper) long *before* they ever shoot a frame of film. This is important for several reasons. First, and this should be painfully obvious by now, the plan—especially as it is written up into a *proposal*—is a sales tool. It is a way of showing someone (a producer, backer, or client) just what you have in mind, that you have an interesting perspective on your subject, that you are imaginative, and that you can do what you propose. It is a way for your audience to imagine (and actually visualize) what might be on film. Second, a good plan helps you decide what *you* want to shoot—what kinds of elements, events, or scenes you want to make sure to cover, how you want to shoot and record, who you want in your film, and where you want your camera.

Your proposal then should consist of the following (not necessarily in this order):

1. **Purpose of film.** This section provides a brief overview of what your film will be about or what it is intended to do.

2. **What the film will show, portray, argue.** This is your premise. It should be clearly stated.

3. **Your approach.** This will include your particular slant or perspective on the topic. Here you should pay attention to how this film might differ from films about the same topic or in the same genre.

4. **The style of the film.** You should provide enough specifics to convey a strong sense of what we will see. You may want to discuss structure, narrative (if you have any), and possible scenes. You may even want to include sam-

ples of narrative or representative scenes. Note that although you can only imagine what you will get on film, you need to take an educated guess with an emphasis on verisimilitude. In other words, the proposal cannot sound like fiction. Do not make up people or invent action. Talk about what you expect to film and how you will treat your material.

5. Your expertise. This section should explain why you are especially suited and uniquely positioned to make this film. You may want to include your credentials, or you may simply want to convey why you are an authority on the topic. Other sections of your proposal will convey this indirectly. For example, specifics and details can indicate how knowledgeable you are about your topic.

6. Prospective audience. In some cases, this will be self-evident; in others, you will need to specify your target audience and an explanation of how and at what levels this project will appeal to them or accomplish your goals.

7. Cost. If you do not have a specific budget, then provide a sense of how much the film will cost.

Sometimes there are other elements as well. Alan Rosenthal, author of *Writing, Directing, and Producing Documentary Films and Videos* (1996), suggests adding the following categories to the earlier list, especially if the writer is also the producer:

- Shooting schedule—when, where, and how long actual shooting will take place. This may or may not include time for postproduction or editing.
- Marketing and distribution.
- Film maker's biography and support letters.

Barry Hampe (1997; *Making Documentary Films and Reality Videos*) suggests dividing your proposal into three sections: purpose, approach, and content.

Whatever your format, proposals should be brief and succinct, and yet explicit and concrete enough to give the reader a strong sense of the film. Most producers do not have the time to wade through pages and pages of explanation and treatment, but they do want to know what they are going to get on film for their money.

Research

The documentary's success has much to do with the eight young competitors profiled in the film. Thorough research, analysis of past Bees, and word of mouth let them [producers Blitz and Sean Welch] to several good subjects that best embodied the human stories beyond the mere recitation of words. The final cull is a cross section of Bee culture and American life.

—Mari Sasaon's review of *Spellbound* and interview with writer/director, Jeff Blitz (2003; www.seemagazine.com/Issues/2003/0703/screen5.htm)

If your documentary proposal reveals to the reader what she already knows, you have not done your homework. Almost all good documentary films are products of extensive research. For some kinds of films, this means going to the library or the Internet and/or examining archival material in museums. This is especially important for historical documentaries, but it is just as essential for biographies, current events, exposés, and other kinds of fact films—even of people, places, and things about which you believe you are the expert. For example, a student in one of my classes wanted to do a film on "little people" or "dwarves." Because she had worked with and personally knew people who were dwarves, she felt she had enough material to at least write a proposal. I encouraged her to do more. I suggested she carry out a series of informal interviews as part of her additional research before she revised her proposal. As a consequence, she found a way to treat her topic that was much more detailed and fully formed than it otherwise would have been. Professional film maker, Ken Burns, whose documentary biographies (e.g., on Frank Lloyd Wright, Susan B. Anthony, and Mark Twain) and historical films appear frequently on PBS, spends years researching his subjects.

Research also enables you to add more specificity and color to what might otherwise be dry and superficial. It helps you supply details about locations, people involved, and experiences. Most important, research can be particularly useful in helping you create or revise your stance. Remember that you want to provide insight—a view of a subject that ordinarily we might not be able to see or know. Often you even want to find a way to capture the attention of people who do not much care, but who should care. Your film must make them care. Immersing yourself in your topic helps you do this. Some suggestions about research:

- Don't wait until you have the go ahead to do your research. Do it before you have written a line or made a presentation of any kind.
- Visit locations—even if the event took place in the past.
- Talk to people. Informal interviews are a great way to determine whom you want to feature in your film and whom you do not.
- Read. Use your library; use the Internet. Even novels, if available on your topic, are useful because they provide additional perspectives.

- View films. Often other film makers have made films on the same topic. Use these films to help you get as substantive a picture of your subject as possible.

SAMPLE PROPOSALS

The following are two examples of proposals or treatments. The first is the first draft of the proposal about dwarves. Note that although it provides a good overview on objectives and parameters, it is still fairly vague.

Proposal: "A Day in the Life of a Little Person"
by Katie McConnell
Purpose of the film

1. To focus on the unique challenges faced by adult dwarves in everyday life, including, but not limited to, functioning in the corporate world.

2. To show the emotional and physical obstacles little people must overcome to survive in modern society in the U.S.

3. To foster an attitude of respect for people of small stature.

4. To explore the social prejudices faced by dwarves in a society so concerned with appearance.

5. To debunk myths and assumptions about dwarves.

6. To discuss some of the support groups provided to little people.

7. To educate viewers on the condition of dwarfism and the medical problems often associated with dwarfism in addition to a small stature.

8. To show how a little person interacts socially, thus educating viewers that dwarves are Little People, too.

9. To eliminate the word "midget" from our vernacular.

Approach to the Film

We wish to observe the behavior of an adult of
small stature, preferably a business professional,
in everyday situations. We will explore and
document how an adult dwarf tackles daily tasks
such as getting ready for work, commuting to work,
and tackling the world of work. The film will also
chronicle the behavior and response of others in
the adult dwarf's life, including family members,
coworkers, and strangers.

Filming Situations will include (but are not
limited to):

· The daily routine of an adult dwarf, including
doing daily tasks such as brushing his teeth,
making breakfast, commuting, working.

· The interaction between an adult dwarf and family
members or roommates, between the dwarf and people
on the street, between the dwarf and coworkers.

In the second draft, Katie added more details, including an explanation of how she intended to follow a surgeon (also a little person) through his daily routine as the means of accomplishing some of her goals. Note also that as a sales document, the proposal would be enhanced by addition of some facts about Katie's own expertise—the fact that, although she is not a dwarf herself, she has worked with dwarfs for the past few years and counts several of them among her personal friends. This information would set her up as an authority and give the reader the sense that Katie's perspective is not only authentic, but is also that of an insider.

The film is geared toward informing the general public. Even so, it is wise to have in mind a specific audience that might be able to come up with financial backing. For example, Katie's proposal might be a good project for an organization that funds public service films or for a TV news magazine series. Overall, however, the proposal has a clear sense of purpose and premise, a conflict, and an indication as to how the film will approach the topic—in other words, what we will see on the screen.

Here is another sample of a short documentary proposal by Katherine Ozment that is more fleshed out. Note this proposal/treatment has an overview or introduction that is very valuable in setting up the issues and the importance of the project.

Testing 1-2-3: "Making It" in a Chicago Magnet School
Introduction

In the past four years, the Chicago Public School system has created six regional magnet schools, allowing a record expenditure for their formation and draining much-needed resources from other schools. But while the creation of magnet schools is a common way for cities to provide quality programs for even its poorest students, the very premise of Chicago's magnet schools is new and unusual. Unlike other magnet schools in the U.S. (with the exception of three such schools in New York City), Chicago's regional magnets accept students not based on unusual artistic talents, musical yens or cleverly written essays. Entry to these schools is instead based on test scores. Students must score above the 59th percentile on a grade school exam just to apply to a regional magnet. At City Preparatory High School*—the most expensive school in Chicago's history—only the top one percent of students who took the most recent entrance exam were accepted.

That magnet schools often drain other schools of high achieving students has been well-documented, as has the alleged racism embedded in Chicago's creation of these schools, the most expensive of which tend to favor white, working class families. What no one has looked at yet is what life is like for the students who are accepted into schools like City Prep. Just this year, the school made headlines by capturing the top slot in the Prairie State Exams, making it the number one high school in the state in terms of test scores. What is it like to attend such a school, where expectations for perfect grades and astronomical test scores are

---

*Not the real name of high school

great and failure is not an option? How does it
feel to leave a grade school where you were the
brightest student in your class only to be
surrounded by people as smart as or smarter than
you? And what values of democracy do you learn when
you are separated out from other students because
of a test score and allowed to attend a state-of-
the-art school as a reward?

Purpose
· To examine the costs and benefits of creating a
school made up entirely of high achievers

· To foster understanding for the unique position
of these students

· To explore the possibility that such schools hurt
not just the other public school students who are
left behind, but also the ones who "make it" into
the school

· To question our received notions of "education"
and "achievement"

· To examine the result of creating undemocratic
groups of students within a public school system

Approach
We will film students in classrooms, in school
activities and at home. Students will show us what
it is like to be in a school like this.

Intended Audience
Adults with children, especially those pondering
options for their child's education. It is also
intended for policy-makers, particularly city
school boards considering the creation of magnet
programs.

Content
Filming situations include:
· Classroom Pressure Cooker. Students in various

classrooms answer difficult questions from their teacher, work in groups with other high-achieving classmates, and prepare for tests and making presentations.

· Little Fish in Big Pond. What happens to the psyche of a student who excelled in grade school and comes to find she is just like all the other fish in this pond? We chart the ebb and flow of a first-year student's self-confidence throughout her first year at City Prep.

· Give Me a Break. How do students spend their lunch hour? In the cafeteria, we see who is socializing and who is busy with homework.

· Smells Like Team Spirit? City Prep's version of a pep rally leaves much to be desired by those who are familiar with pep rallies as cheerleaders tossing pom-poms and beefy football players drumming up excitement for the night's game. Just what does a pep rally look like at a school without a football team?

· Great Expectations. Teachers and students hold forth on the "gifted" students in their midst and what is expected of them.

· Swept Under the Rug. What about students who make it into the school and can't compete because of a learning disability, language barrier, or emotional problem?

· The Big Test. Last year, City Prep scored first on the statewide Prairie State Exam, topping other well-known local schools. What goes through the minds of this year's juniors on the morning before and the afternoon after the test?

· Is It Worth It? Students talk about what they hope to get from this experience and whether they think it will be worth the costs. They may compare their experiences to those of their peers who attend other area high schools.

A SAMPLE TREATMENT

Treatments can also serve as proposals. The difference between a proposal and a treatment is that the documentary treatment—much like a dramatic treatment—is told in narrative form and provides a stronger mental picture of what we will see and hear. Sometimes producers want both. Proposals are usually shorter and quicker to read, but treatments may give a clearer indication as to whether this film will appeal to an audience. Sometimes the treatment and proposal are one and the same. The following example is a treatment that could potentially serve as a proposal as well.

Treatment: "My Body My Choice" by Annie Noland

This film chronicles a day in the life of a doctor who, among her other duties, performs abortions in Charlotte, N.C. The film does not pass judgment on this controversial issue, but rather examines the personal story of a doctor who, in both her life and work, must deal with the dangerous fallout from one of the most volatile political and religious controversies of our day.

FADE IN:
  Opening shot is a bumper sticker on the back of a red Acura Legend that reads, "My Body, My Choice." RACHEL WEBER is driving through the streets of Charlotte, North Carolina, on her way to work. Weber is an OB/GYN who performs abortions at the Planned Parenthood on South Kings Drive in Charlotte. As she drives, she talks about how she ended up in her current job. By the time she attended medical school, she knew that she was interested in women's health issues. She decided to become a gynecologist. During her residency, Rachel saw the need for doctors to perform abortions and decided that she could make a difference helping women. As we arrive at Planned Parenthood we see a few straggly protesters with signs, but nothing for Weber to be afraid of.

We follow her through her day. After each appointment, she takes a few minutes to reflect on

her day, her profession, the highs and lows that
she faces. We get to know the NURSING STAFF, a
few PATIENTS who are willing to talk with us, and
the other DOCTORS. We look out the windows of the
clinic to observe the protesters. North Carolina
is one of the most volatile areas of the country
in which to be an abortion provider, and Weber
knows this. The killing of an abortion doctor in
his own kitchen took place not far from here.
ERIC RUDOLPH, a man wanted by the FBI for bombing
an abortion clinic in Alabama, is suspected of
being at large in the mountains of North Carolina.
He has evaded the police for over a year, living as
a fugitive, probably in a cave in the forest.

Rudolph's story is interspersed with Weber's to
show the dangerous environment in which she works.
POLICE OFFICERS talk about the Rudolph case.
RESIDENTS of the small town in which he was last
seen talk about their beliefs and the anti-
abortion sentiment that is prevalent in this part
of the country. The goal in this section is to
contrast perceptions of Weber as an evil villain
with the reality of her humanity drawn from her
day-to-day work and existence.

At the Weber home, husband, NICK, talks about his
wife's profession as their two girls, BRIDGET, 6,
and BRITTANY, 4, make dinner with Rachel. He talks
about the threats the family has received because
of Weber's work, his fears, and about raising
children in this environment. As the girls are
sent to bed, Rachel and Nick talk about the girls'
understanding of what their mother does and about
the juxtaposition of Rachel's life—on the one hand
raising her girls and on the other performing
abortions. How does she reconcile this dichotomy
or does she even feel the need to?

Anti-abortion web sites on the Internet that list
the names of abortion practitioners flash on the
screen. These are widely referred to as "hit
lists" in that many of the web sites provide ideas

and instructions for bombing abortion clinics and killing doctors who provide abortions. The doctor who was killed in his own kitchen has his name listed on such a site. There is currently legislation under consideration to prevent sites of this kind from being posted on the Internet. We will look at a few sites of this kind and juxtapose this with the evening at the Weber household.

Rachel Weber talks to us as she stands at her kitchen window looking out into her back yard. There are trees that surround the edge of the back yard so that the neighbors' homes are not visible. She explains that Nick considered cutting the trees down and putting bulletproof glass into all of the windows in the family home. Weber wouldn't allow it. This scene is intercut with old news footage of the day the doctor was killed standing in his own kitchen, making breakfast for his children. As the news footage rolls, we
                                                   FADE OUT.

Although some may find flaws with the piece, here is a checklist of the elements it contains:

- An overview or introduction;
- A vivid account of the people involved;
- A detailed description of settings;
- A sense of conflict;
- A potential message;
- Specificity—enough to give us a feel of what we will be seeing on the screen and to give us a sense that the writer knows what she is talking about (she has an "inside" view); and
- Generality—enough to allow for the vagaries of real life—and the fact that a producer/director will not ever get on film exactly what she has planned for.

Most important, it conveys both realism and a story, the two key components of many great documentaries.

THE DOCUMENTARY SCREENPLAY

The screenplay for a documentary film is at once similar to the dramatic screenplay and quite different. It is similar in that it sometimes reads with the specificity and detail of an actual film. It may or may not have people (or characters); it
may (and should) be structured so that it has some dramatic tension; and it
should clearly convey a message (or premise). It is different in that it must
sound like the film will deal with real life. In other words, you will need to fi-
nesse it a bit: You want to convey a clear picture of the final film—and a writer
who has done her research can often predict the kinds of scenes she will be able
to get on film—but also want to make it seem real. Thus, you want your script
to be a bit "rough." You may want to paint your scenes in broad strokes—not
necessarily with specific dialogue or narrative (although you can certainly be
specific, especially with the narrator's script), but with summaries or descriptions of what you envision.

Structure

Screenplays differ from treatments in that the screenplay will be much more
precise about the structure of the film—even given that the structural plan is
only tentative. Depending on the topic of the documentary, there is quite a bit
of leeway to how a film is structured. Here are some things to consider.

An Opening Hook

People usually go to see a theatrical feature film because they have some famil-
iarity with or expectations about what they are about to see. They may like the
horror genre or science fiction, and they are eager to get into the theater for a
Stephen King story or the next installment of a Harry Potter film. Alternately,
they may have heard about the film they are about to see, either from a friend or
acquaintance, or they have read a film review. In any case, they are primed (or
have primed themselves) to see the film. In theatrical films, an enchanting, exciting, enticing, or provocative opening is nice, but it is not critical to keep the
audience members in their seats, at least for 20 minutes.

Documentary films are different. Because many people in today's audiences
are not used to seeing documentary films (despite exceptions like *Hoop Dreams*,
Spellbound, Michael Moore films, and the perseverance of PBS and cable TV),
it is a good idea to get a viewer more quickly into the drama of your piece than
for feature films.

As a writer, try to consider the opening of your documentary film as a guide to viewing the rest of the film. It is here that you set the tone, establish the players and the conflict if there is such, and set up a kind of imperative as to why the viewer should actually see the rest of the film. The imperative is sometimes called *the opening hook* because it gets the viewers so immediately involved that they cannot prevent themselves from watching and listening to what you have to say.

Just as in argumentative essays, there are a number of ways to begin—almost always drawn from the subject matter. The best ways involve what is known as the *representative anecdote*—that is, a scene or sketch drawn from the material that typifies your story, suggests the problem you are going to explore, or sets a provocative tone. Here are the openings to some well-known documentaries:

Paris is Burning—First a title to situate the audience: New York, 1987. We see streets filled with pedestrian traffic and we hear a male voice telling us about a conversation with his father in which his father tells him he has three strikes against him—being black, being male, and being gay—and that he's going to have a very hard time. His father continues: "If you are gonna do this, you're gonna have to be stronger than you can ever imagine." The scene shifts to a black gay bar where a fashion show is taking place. The models are all black males dressed as females.

Comment: This opening serves a number of different functions. It sets the scene and the players: New York in the 1980s and a unique sector of the gay community. Second, it reveals the central issue or controversy and the conflict. The featured characters are up against incredible odds; there is significant foreshadowing of conflict to come. In addition, it also sets up the style—a narrative mixed with interviews and contrasted with scenes from "normal" New York. If viewers are not somehow intrigued by this opening, then they should probably not be in the theater.

Unzipped—The film begins with a black-and-white shot of fashion designer Isaac Mizrahi buying a newspaper in New York City. We see the title: Isaac Mizrahi is a fashion designer. He has just shown his 1994 collection. Mizrahi reacts as he reads a bad review in the newspaper. In voice-over, he talks about himself and how he responds. This is followed by a color sequence in which he begins to put together his next collection.

Comment: Stylistically, the film maker, Donald Keeve, sets up the black-and-white/color pattern. He also sets up the conflict: failure for a fashion designer is actually a big failure so Mizrahi has plenty of conflict in his life. We know from this moment on what the film is about, what the issue is, and what the style of the film will be.

Spellbound—The film opens on a boy looking very nervous. He's given a word to spell (*banns*) and he fiddles, fidgets, and talks to himself. Then we see the photos of eight kids on the screen and a title introducing the competition.

Comment: Competitions suggest victory, defeat, conflict, pain, and triumph. Jeffrey Blitz plunges us right into a scene from a spelling bee. He features one of the contestants, Harry, who bumbles his way through his turn. Blitz sets up the conflict, the drama, a lead character, and a tone that is both humorous and agonizing. This is what the film will be about.

Organization

Just as in theatrical feature films, there is a wide variety of ways to structure your film. Some films work through cause and effect or comparison and contrast to make their points. Many good documentary films, however, work through narrative because it is the easiest way to get your audience involved. In other words, good documentaries tell a story. *Hoop Dreams* tells the story of two kids trying to make it to the NBA. *Fog of War* features former U.S. Secretary of Defense Robert McNamara's narrative about his life and experiences working with various U.S. Presidents; it is a largely chronological narrative that leads us from the Depression through Vietnam that is framed around 11 lessons that McNamara has learned about war in his long career. *Unzipped* tells the story of a fashion designer putting together his latest fashion collection. All of these films have messages that transcend their narratives, but the best way to get a message across is to tell a story.

To tell a story, you often have to find a person or people to follow. In one of the earlier proposals (the film about little people), Katie's best option is to find a character or characters about whom she could tell a story: a young man's struggle to get an advanced degree, a woman's struggle to be taken seriously in her workplace, or the day in the life of a child.

Background

As with a dramatic screenplay, it is hard to convey a lot of background material in a documentary screenplay. You can preface your piece with background, for sure, but in the screenplay, you must reveal what the audience needs to know through action or narration (see "Narration"). In *Amandla: A Revolution in Four-Part Harmony*, a film about the music that sustained the anti-apartheid movement in South Africa, background is revealed through a series of interviews where interviewees such as Hugh Masekela, Abdullah Ibrahim, Vusi Mahlasela, and other singers, musicians, and activists reflect on their roles and the history they witnessed; the reflections cue the appearance of archival footage of protests, jails, and landscapes that, in a sense, re-create what the speakers refer to.

Tension Rise and Climax

In looking at the dramatic film, we have explored how tension is created (through conflict) and how the point or premise of the film arises out of the climax. This is no less true for the documentary. If the conflict is not plainly evident from the subject matter, at the very least make sure to frame your storytelling in a way to enhance any conflict. Chances are, if there is no conflict at all, you do not have much of a tale to tell.

Alan Rosenthal (1996) maintains that "a film should have a logical and emotional flow, its level of intensity should vary, its conflicts should be clear and rising in strength, it should hold our interest all the time, and it should build to a compelling climax" (p. 91). This point cannot be overemphasized. If you do not have rising emotional intensity, you will not have a documentary that most people will want to see.

Ending

This is probably the part of your documentary that is the most difficult to predict. More often than not, your material will dictate it, but often the sense of closure will have to be created by you or the director. Real life almost never comes to a definitive sense of closure; it does not have conclusions, happy endings, or even tragic endings. Rather the film must end when you have said what you want to say about your topic, and often you will have to address the sense of ambiguity and open-endedness that is part of your story. *Hoop Dreams* is a good example of this. Neither Arthur nor William meets his goal of being in the NBA, and as the film ends, it is not clear whether either of them ever will. In fact, Arthur, the one with the least going for him, seemed closer to playing NBA-level ball than William. Even so, the film maker's point about the difficult journey that society organizes for kids such as this has been made. The film could end having proved its premise, but without providing a decisive conclusion.

All this ambiguity notwithstanding, you must indicate in a screenplay what you *expect* your ending will be. It does not necessarily have to be specific. If you had written the screenplay for *Roger and Me*, you might have simply indicated that the film ends at the annual stockholders convention or in a final interview between Roger Smith (CEO of General Motors) and Michael Moore. What is important here is that you convey a clear idea of what you want to say with the film and how you are going to say it.

NOTES ON STYLE IN DOCUMENTARY WRITING

Because your proposal, treatment, or screenplay will often make the difference between getting your film made or not, or between actually getting to talk to a producer or financial backer or not, it is of utmost importance that you think about your writing style.

Tedious as these tips may be to follow, they make the difference between sitting in your room with a good (but dead) idea and getting your project off the ground:

1. **Pay attention to style.** As we've discussed in earlier chapters, style can refer to a range of considerations, including wording, sentencing, and other language choices. The rule of thumb here, as well as in feature films, is to write to your audience. Gear your prose to be readable and understandable to whomever will be reading it. Do not aim too high (i.e., too much jargon or prose that sounds too erudite) or too low (i.e., too casual or colloquial a tone, overuse of slang, sentence fragments, or cutesy language).

With the language you do use, try to create mental pictures. To do this, use words that are *concrete and specific*—especially in descriptions of setting, people, or events. Use adjectives where they will help the reader visualize what you are describing. Use imagery or figurative language (metaphors, similes, or analogies) to enrich your language and further enhance the image you want to convey to your reader. As should be clear by now, in writing for film, your language becomes doubly important because you are writing for a visual medium without the benefit of access to pictures to convey what you want your reader to see. Write to create both strong visuals and a strong vision.

2. **Use the medium** (visual artistry, audio artistry, verbal artistry). Along the same lines as No. 1, describe what we will potentially see and hear. Although you have certain license in documentary writing to convey background information and to justify why the film should be made, ultimately the reader wants to get a clear sense of what she will see on the screen. Give her that strong sense. Do not force her to ask, "But what am I seeing?!"

3. **Revise for mechanics and usage.** Just as in writing for feature films, you want to appear literate and competent. The most direct route to being written off as a novice is to present material that is riddled with spelling and proofreading mistakes, problems with tense and sentence structure, and punctuation that draw attention to themselves. You want the reader to read what you say, not focus attention on your mechanics.

DIALOGUE AND NARRATION

Unless you are writing a docudrama or some kind of documentary re-creation, you will have two principle ways to use talk: interviews and narration. The general rule of thumb for both is: Less **is more**.

Interviews

For many topics, the interview may be the main source of information. Sometimes the people you interview will be fascinating speakers or have an incredible and highly exciting tale to tell. Even so, watching a talking head for several minutes is a liability. It is essentially static, makes poor use of the film medium, and is quite risky in that it may alienate or bore your audience. Try to come up with alternative visuals that work to either represent what your speaker is talking about or serve as counterpoint.

Skill in interviewing is largely determined by knowing **what questions to ask**. Knowing a good deal about the subject's background helps shape questions that are appropriate and bound to elicit full responses. Plan your interview: Generate a list of questions that will enable you to get rich responses. Avoid questions where it is easy to answer "yes" or "no." Rather, try to ask open-ended questions: "Tell me about how your upbringing contributed to the kinds of music you enjoy composing?" or "What do you consider to be important influences in your musical career?" Then, as the subject talks, be prepared with follow-up questions that allow you to probe more deeply: "How did you transition from African music to the kinds of music you now like to produce?" or "Can you describe some of the difficulties you've had in getting your music accepted by mainstream audiences?"

If for some reason you have discovered that your exciting speaker is quite the contrary when speaking to a camera (e.g., goofy or boring), you may need to find someone else. This is another reason to do your research: You will have backup ideas when something goes awry (as it always will).

It is worth taking a look at some of the TV newsmagazines like *60 Minutes, Dateline,* or *20/20.* Rarely does a speaker remain on the screen for more than 10 to 15 seconds. The film will most likely return to that speaker if he is a key player, but it will not hold on him. The program will usually cut away either to what the speaker is talking about or to a setting that is related to the interview: hotel, factory, battlefield, or cityscape. Interviews alone will not carry your film, nor should they.

Narration

If you can tell your story *without* narration, do so. Aside from talking heads, little is more irritating in a documentary film than a talky or preachy narrator, especially when things are evident from the visual track, the audio track (natural sound), or the context of the film. Most novice writers tend to overdo narration, providing far more background and commentary than audiences need, resulting in a kind of academic lecture, which generally has the same effect on viewers as lectures do on students: Everyone except (usually) the lecturer falls asleep.

What narration should do is provide links where otherwise there would be none. *Hoop Dreams* does this well. There is only minimal use of an anonymous narrative, and this is only to set the scene—where and only where setting the scene helps the audience understand. For example, when we see Arthur's mother dressed in white and attending a ceremony, the narrator lets us know that she is getting ready to graduate from a nurse's aid program. Otherwise, the film lets the characters, actions, and settings do the talking, and they do so very effectively.

One of the important hallmarks of a good film writer, as I mentioned in previous chapters, is *subtlety.* If your story is a good one, if your subject is worth talking about, chances are you can simply allow the narrative to unfold on the screen with little commentary. Too much commentary, in fact, can kill the beauty of the tale you are trying to tell, whereas indirectness or reticence can let the readers/viewers come to discoveries about your material seemingly on their own. This route is far more effective because then readers/viewers feel like they have undertaken the journey without a guide—and this is far more exciting than feeling like you are being led by the nose.

If you do choose to use narration, you have some choices:

The narrator with personality. This style is both imaginative and creative. Michael Moore's narration in *Roger and Me, Bowling for Columbine,* and *Fahrenheit 9/11* is funky, quirky, and many times outrageous. He begins *Roger and*

Me with, "I was kind of a strange kid," and through the film we get a view of his personality, his brand of polite insubordination, his use of irony, and his dedication to the people of Flint, Michigan. For this film, the narrator is also the protagonist, working on behalf of the people (autoworkers and townspeople) he is trying to help.

The invisible narrator. This narrator is the one who is so anonymous and so sparingly used that the audience is not even aware he (or she) is there. He does not call attention to himself in any way; he does not speak too long; he does not comment too much. In a word, he is "invisible." This is perfect. Most people I ask about *Hoop Dreams* insist there is no narrator. They are wrong, but the film makers had it right.

The subject as narrator. In Wim Wenders' *Buena Vista Social Club*, he lets the Cuban musicians whom he is chronicling speak. Although he has clearly asked them questions, they tell their stories. Except for Ry Cooder, who serves a pivotal role because he brought the group together for the original album of the same name, the musicians speak in Spanish that is subtitled. Even when the speaker's language is stilted, the subject telling his own story lends both authenticity and personality to the overall story that each speaker helps to tell.

SCREENPLAY FORMAT

Although documentary screenplays can look a lot like dramatic screenplays, here are two samples from screenplays that are quite common. The first format—the double-column approach—is perhaps used most often because it enables a clear explanation of how the audio and visual will work together. The second is easier to format and block out on the page, but can be more difficult to read. Both are quite acceptable, as is the standard format for the feature script.

```
SAMPLE 1 - DOUBLE-COLUMN

MAHARA-JI

VISUAL                              AUDIO

OVER BLACK, we see a series
of posters, still photos of
Mahara-Ji and some small
altars in private homes,
```

SEPARATED BY DISSOLVES. In the last shot, CAMERA HOLDS on small altar where incense is burning.
(SEQUENCE: 10—15 seconds)

Slow-moving rock hymn of praise—an original tune played by Jiva, a rock band inspired by Mahara-Ji. MUSIC CONTINUES OVER TITLES AND CREDITS.

                    DISSOLVE TO:

INT. LARGE MEETING HALL, FULL AND MEDIUM SHOTS OF CROWD - NIGHT.

A large meeting hall is filled to capacity. The majority of the people are young (ages 15—25). They are mainly seated on the floor, although some are standing up in the back or seated in chairs along the sides of the room. THEY ALL FACE THE SAME DIRECTION

Noise of crowd—a quiet hum, interspersed with sounds of people greeting one another. CONTINUES UNTIL SPECIFIED.

MEDIUM SHOTS - INDIVIDUALS

People seated on the floor. People greeting one another with hugs. People taking off their shoes and sitting down. People walking back and forth to find seats.

A "DEVOTEE" talks about his experience—how he first heard of Mahara-Ji, then "attained knowledge" and how his life is better for it. He speaks to devotees and nondevotees alike in simple terms with ease and with joy, explaining how he was touched by the divine light.

MEDIUM SHOT - ELEVATED PLATFORM IN FRONG - BAND (JIVA)

Band is setting up.
(SEQUENCE: 2 minutes)

Note that:

• Visuals are loosely styled after shot description in the feature script format, with shooting directions, principle characters, and important props capitalized. They are generally indicated so we can visualize what we might see. As with the dramatic screenplay, it is important for the readers to be able to quickly locate where they are. Slug lines are often very effective at doing this.

• Visuals are grouped into easily identifiable sequences. Length of sequences should be indicated.

• Audio should be lined up with visuals so that it is easy to see what sounds go with what visuals. Work for readability. Avoid overly long paragraphs. Use plenty of white space.

• When moving to the next page, avoid breaking up scenes or, if you must do so, try to break the scene at a natural pause.

• For dialogue or narration, it is smart to capitalize the speaker's name. With narration or voice-over, you may have a good sense of what will be said. Go ahead and say it. Example:

VISUAL	AUDIO
B&W photograph of Charles Johnson	NARRATOR: Charles was born in Virginia around the turn of the century.

Sometimes documentary ideas lend themselves to differing kinds of script formats. Here is another format that is occasionally used.

SAMPLE 2 - FULL PAGE

2000 Days

Minutes

      1. A CHILD'S INTRODUCTION

(2)
      a) AN AMBULANCE SPEEDS DOWN A CITY STREET. IT GOES INTO THE DRIVEWAY OF CHILDREN'S ORTHOPEDIC HOSPITAL AND MEDICAL CENTER (COHMC) IN SEATTLE. IT STOPS IN FRONT OF THE ENTRY. A CHILD IS TAKEN OUT AND IS WHEELED DOWN THE HALLS INTO THE EMERGENCY ROOM. DOOR SHUTS. TITLE, *2000 DAYS*, IS SUPERIMPOSED.

      Sounds of ambulance radio. A voice estimates arrival time and communicates to hospital. City sounds, siren. Team working on child inside the ambulance. Hospital sounds. A doctor quickly quizzes parent as child is wheeled down the hall.

(1)
      b) INSIDE EMERGENCY ROOM, DOCTORS WORK ON CHILD

      Sounds of doctors discussing vital signs, ordering medication, oxygen.

(1)

c) SHOTS OF WAITING ROOM, COLOR MURAL, CHILDREN'S MOBILES HANGING FROM CEILING. A VOLUNTEER PLAYS WITH A CHILD IN A GURNEY. CHRISTMAS DECORATIONS ABOUND. CHRISTMAS TREE IN LOBBY WITH HAND-MADE DECORATIONS. CHRISTMAS TREE IN FRONT OF HOSPITAL AT EMERGENCY ENTRANCE. SHOT OF BAMBINO, SYMBOL OF COHMC.

Ambient sounds, subdued.

($\frac{1}{2}$)

d) EMERGENCY ROOM. DOCTORS STILL WORKING.

e) PARENTS IN CONFERENCE IN ADMITTING DEPARTMENT. SHOT OF STAFF MEMBER THEY TALK TO.

($\frac{1}{2}$)

Parents discuss what happened to child and briefly provide information about child's medical history.

(1)

(f) EMERGENCY ROOM. DOCTORS FINISH UP. A DOCTOR TAKES OFF MASK AND COMES OUT OF ROOM. HE FINDS PARENTS.

Doctor says that the child will be admitted into the hospital.

2. <u>WHO CARES ABOUT A CHILDREN'S HOSPITAL?</u>

(2)

a) SHOTS OF TEENAGE WARD. YOUNG PATIENTS IN WHEELCHAIRS IN RECREATION ROOM WITH CD PLAYERS, MOBILES, BOOKS, A POOL TABLE, GAMES. SHOTS OF ROOMS WITH LARGE GLASS WINDOWS THAT LOOK OUT ONTO HALL. PATIENTS IN BEDS - SUFFERING, CHEERFUL, INDIFFERENT.

(sequence continues)

Note that:

- Here the visuals are all capitalized to distinguish them clearly from the audio, which is lowercase.
- Sequence time is indicated in left-hand column. Again designing your screenplay in sequences often enhances the sense of structure and improves readability.
- Paragraphs should be short so that the visual and audio are easy to follow and it is clear what audio goes with what visual.
- Narration can be inserted any number of ways, including traditional dialogue format as in:

f) EMERGENCY ROOM. DOCTORS FINISH UP. A DOCTOR
TAKES OFF MASK AND COMES OUT OF ROOM. HE FINDS
PARENTS.

Doctor says that the child will be admitted
into the hospital.

                    NARRATOR
          This is COH, a children's
          hospital.

Or it can appear within the audio as in:

f) EMERGENCY ROOM. DOCTORS FINISH UP. A DOCTOR
TAKES OFF MASK AND COMES OUT OF ROOM. HE FINDS
PARENTS.

Doctor says that the child will be admitted
into the hospital.

NARRATOR: This is COH, a children's hospital.

What to Put in and What to Leave Out

This is probably the most troubling issue for writers who are new to the documentary format. You do not want to invent scenes, characters, and dialogue. However, you do want to convey what you suspect you will get on film because this information conveys your premise, point, and assertions. Consider the following example:

VISUAL	AUDIO
INT. CHEESY'S PUB - NIGHT	
The bartender Delores Brown serves a drink to Butch Rogers.	DELORES: That's your last one, Butch. You've had fives drinks too many. I just can't letcha have another.
He grabs her by the collar and yells at her, then shoves her roughly backwards. A bottle behind her falls and shatters on the floor.	BUTCH: You good-for-nothing dame. I pays my money. I drinks as much as I damn well please.

Of course, because you have done your research and know that Butch frequents the bar and often drinks too much, forcing Delores to cut him off from time to time, you can predict that you will probably be able to get this on film (with everyone's permission, of course). However, it sounds a little like fiction; it does not sound real. Here is an alternative

VISUAL	AUDIO
INT. CHEESY'S PUB - NIGHT	
The bartender Delores Brown serves drinks to some of her regular customers. One of them is Butch Rogers. Tonight, she refuses to pour a drink for Butch and he gets mad.	Delores cuts Butch off, telling him he's had enough for the evening. Butch gets angry. DELORES (V.O.) talks about how hard it is to tangle with her patrons over their drinking. After all of these years, most of them are her friends. But she sees it as part of her job.

Essentially the same information is conveyed (perhaps more with the voice-over), but in the second version the feel is more documentary than dramatic.

It is quite likely that when the camera and sound equipment are set up, you will be unable to get what you want on film. But at this stage, that is beside the point. What the screenplay must convey is the substance of the film, which is a result of your research and vision. If you are too vague, you will not be able to get your point across. It you are too literal, the script will not ring true.

Relationship Between Visual and Audio

One of the biggest and most rewarding challenges of writing for film is attending to how the visual works with the audio. With the incredible potential that documentaries have for conveying information, emotions, and ideas, it behooves the documentary writer to pay attention to the interplay of sight and sound. With *sound tracks* consisting of conversation, interviews, narration, sound effects, natural sound, and music and *visual tracks* consisting of movement, color, shape, and camera angles, you have an astonishing array of options.

Working again with the precept that less is more, keep your ideas for your audio and visual tracks simple, paying attention to variation and rhythm as much as getting across information. Make use of the concept of counterpoint, where the audio does not merely reiterate what we see, but rather works in juxtaposition, adding new information.

TROUBLESHOOTING

Once you have completed your draft and are looking to revise and fine-tune your treatments or scripts, it is useful to go through a checklist of potential problems. These will help you revise.

Long-Windedness

Not only is there a problem with too much explanation, but many of your sequences go on longer than they can be sustained. As with the feature treatments and proposals, no active producer or financial backer worth her salt has a lot of time on her hands to read and read and read. Cut any explanations that you absolutely do not need.

Cohesion

One sequence should lead logically to another. This does not necessarily mean there should be a linear chronology, although this helps. It does mean that there should be a clear connection between one part of the film and the next—especially where one sequence follows another. This can be done in a variety of ways, including working to anticipate what the reader or viewer will want to know next (and providing it) or adding transitional titles.

Development

Make sure your screenplay story goes somewhere. Avoid repeating the same point again and again. Instead, we (as readers and potential viewers) should continue to learn as we move through the screenplay or treatment.

For example, in *Buena Vista Social Club*, we see a series of interviews with rediscovered Cuban folk musicians. Each musician tells his story, and many of these stories are similar—men born in the early to mid-1900s who became musicians. This could be potentially tedious, but the film develops in two ways. First, it shows us more and more of a Cuba that few of us know, and, second, the narrative line pulls these musicians all together to play to sold-out audiences in Amsterdam and New York—a kind of re-creation of a rising tension line shaped through intercutting.

Cliché, Artificiality, or Affectation

A very good example of overkill is the unending stream of tear-jerking minidocumentaries that can appear during the TV coverage of the Olympic Games. There seem to be countless (because there are, literally, too many to count, and the Olympics go on almost nonstop for 17 days) film segments dealing with athletes' "dreams for Olympic gold" as they struggle to overcome overwhelming odds: polio, asthma, or the death of a father/sister/brother/mentor/pet. It is almost as if the producers do not believe the sport will have enough drawing power or will be exciting enough to hold an audience's attention. Aside from the amount of coverage, the problem also stems from the choice of focus (attempting to make a big struggle out of a small problem) and overkill (hammering away at the loss of an athlete's sibling so that viewers may feel that their emotions have been manipulated). That said, segments about training regimens or personal lives can add depth and complexity to the competition and bring viewers who are not familiar with individual sports up to speed. For example, in the 2004 Olympics in Athens, NBC presented interesting backstories that featured athletes who train in less-than-ideal conditions (Iraq, Romania, Russia) and still come to compete.

Too Many Trivial Details

Details and statistics can be powerfully persuasive, but be careful in every stage (proposal, treatment, and screenplay) of overuse. A few choice facts can work well, but more than a few can be an utter bore in a visual medium. Because viewers need to attend to what they see on the fly, so to speak (usually they cannot rewind to get something they have missed or forgotten), most statistics quickly pass by unless they are especially salient. To make something salient, you will want to avoid crowding it with other statistics and details. Besides statistics do not tell your story. People and events do. Let them.

Lack of Power

Probably the worst thing a writer can do is write or attach herself to a project that has no power. If you believe you have a good project (see my earlier definitions of a *good* topic) and it still lacks power, try a new approach:

- Tell the story in a different way or order.
- Find a person in your story that the audience can identify with and tell the story from his perspective. If you have used someone already and it does not seem to work, try someone else.
- Make your project more dramatic by emphasizing conflicts or antagonistic forces.
- Come up with more exciting, more dramatic visuals.
- Capitalize on the unexpected. Where something can occur that is new, different, or unforeseen, use it.
- Make sure your film is about something. Ask yourself: Does this have a clear point? Then answer the question.

I want to elaborate on this last point because it is very important. *Silverlake Life* follows the perspective *not* of the dying man, but of his partner, the survivor. It is an interesting twist. The film is about what it is like to be the survivor. The film has conflict; the antagonists are the disease, the men's families, governmental agencies, and public perceptions. The tension comes from how the two men fight death. Finally, however, the film is about something more than death, AIDS, and the gay lifestyle. It is about love, humor, and humanity, and that is what good documentaries are: They are about specific subjects and struggles, but they also have universal appeal.

AUDIENCE

A final note about your audience. Writing for documentary films must always take under consideration the clients (the financial backers). Occasionally, your client will give you carte blanche and let you come up with whatever you would like, but this is rare. More often than not, your client wants to get something specific across to a particular viewing audience, and chances are he will have an idea—sometimes vague, sometimes quite specific—about how he wants that done. Your job is, first and foremost, to listen. What are his goals? What seem to be his likes and dislikes? What have been his past experiences, if any, with documentaries? In other words, what are the client's expectations?

I once had a client who wanted a film made about an elderly patron of the arts who established an artists' retreat south of Los Angeles. Because the patron was getting on in years, time was critically important. But the approach was equally important to the financial backer. It had to focus on certain characteristics and aspects of the retreat. Furthermore, the backer had had bad experiences with previous film makers and was very wary. But she also wanted guidance and ideas as to how to do the documentary. She wanted it to be "creative," and she was asking several film makers to submit proposals. This scenario is fairly typical, if it can be said that any documentary scenario is typical. The process asks for a mix of compromise and creative challenge—a blend of meeting the client's needs and inventing a workable, cinematic project that reflects well on everyone.

All in all, the documentary is a wonderfully powerful art form—and should be just that, taking a part of the world we know and providing insight about it for all to share.

APPLICATIONS AND EXERCISES

1. Pick a topic from each category: person, place, thing, event, or experience. Assess strengths and weakness as a good topic for a documentary film based on the criteria listed under "A Good Topic" in this chapter.

2. See several documentary films (more and more video stores feature documentaries, or you might subscribe to a service such as Netflix that has a wide variety of films to rent). Select a film, outline it, and then diagram the dramatic structure. See if you can determine protagonist, antagonist, conflict, climax, and resolution. What is the premise?

3. Pick a segment from one of the TV shows such as *60 Minutes* or *Dateline*, or a short documentary from a cable channel. If you had proposed that segment to a producer, what would your proposal have looked like? Write a short treatment (2–3 pages) for that segment, as if it had not yet been produced.

4. Draft a short 20-minute documentary of your own and run it through the checklist provided earlier.

FOR VIEWING

One chapter in a book cannot prepare you to make good documentary films; I have only tried to provide an introduction. Documentaries vary enormously; the ways of producing documentary films differ as widely as the topics they chronicle. If you are seriously interested in becoming a documentary film maker, see films. Read books about how to make films. Familiarize yourself with funding opportunities. As a starting point, listed next are some films to see and books to take a look at.

Documentary Films

The following is a brief (and hardly inclusive) list of classic documentary films in order of year produced. Some were nominated or have won Academy Awards; others are considered classics of the genre.

- *Nanook of the North* (Robert Flaherty) 1922
- *Man of Aran* (Flaherty) 1934—the Aran Islands shark fishermen
- *Louisiana Story* (Flaherty) 1948
- *Triumph of the Will* (Leni Reifenstahl) 1935
- *The Plow that Broke the Plains* (Pare Lorentz) 1936—dust storms that turn farmland into desert
- *Thursday's Children* (Lindsay Anderson) 1954—school for deaf children
- *Lonely Boy* (Frederick Wiseman) 1961—about Wayne Newton
- *Jane* (Donn Pennebaker) 1962—about Jane Fonda
- *Showman* (Maysles Bros) 1962
- *Happy Mother's Day* (Richard Leacock) 1963—about the Fischer quintuplets
- *Don't Look Back* (Donn Pennebaker & R. Leacock) 1966—about Bob Dylan
- *High School* (Wiseman) 1968
- *Monterey Pop* (Pennebaker) 1968
- *Law and Order* (Wiseman) 1969
- *Salesman* (Maysles) 1969—about door-to-door salesmen
- *Gimme Shelter* (Maysles) 1970
- *Hospital* (Wiseman) 1970
- *Grey Gardens* (Maysles Bros.) 1975—portrait of two eccentric women
- *Harlan County USA* (Barbara Kopple) 1976—about unions
- *Scared Straight* (Arnold Shapiro) 1978—prison program designed to scare juvenile offenders
- *From Mao to Mozart (Isaac Stern Visits China)* 1980
- *Say Amen, Somebody* (Murray Lerner) 1980—beginnings of gospel music
- *Hearts and Minds* (Peter Davis) 1984
- *Roger and Me* (Michael Moore) 1989
- *Civil War* (Ken Burns) 1990
- *American Dream* (Kopple) 1990—about working conditions at Hormel
- *Paris is Burning* (Jennie Livingston) 1990
- *A Brief History of Time* (Errol Morris) 1991
- *Silverlake Life: The View From Here* (Tom Joslin & Peter Friedman) 1992
- *Hoop Dreams* (1994)
- *Unzipped* (Douglas Keeve) 1994
- *When We Were Kings* (Leon Gast) 1996—about Mohammed Ali
- *Waco: Rules of Engagement* (William Gazecki) 1997

- *4 Little Girls* (Spike Lee) 1997
- *Buena Vista Social Club* (Wim Wenders) 1998—about Cuban folk music
- *Jazz* (Ken Burns, PBS) 2001
- *Capturing the Friedmans* (Andrew Jarecki) 2003
- *Amandla: A Revolution in Four Part Harmony* (Lee Hirsch) 2002
- *Lost in LaMancha* (Keith Fulton & Louis Pepe) 2002
- *Johnstown Flood* (Mark Bussler) 2003
- *The Fog of War—Eleven Lessons from the Life of Robert S. McNamara* (Errol Morris) 2003
- *Chernobyl Heart* (Maryann DeLeo) 2003—about the effects of Chernobyl radiation on Belarus
- *Winged Migration* (Jacques Perrin) 2003
- *The Elegant Universe* (Brian Greene) NOVA 2003—explanation of major scientific concepts
- *Spellbound* (2003)
- *Super Size Me* (Morgan Spurlock) 2004
- *Fahrenheit 9/11* (Michael Moore) 2004

Public TV is one of the remaining free resources for good documentaries. Some documentary channels on cable include: Discovery, Biography, History, Animal Planet, The Learning Channel, Science, and National Geographic.

The International Documentary Association (IDA) is a nonprofit organization listing funding opportunities, jobs, festivals for documentary films, and projects. It is a terrific resource. The Web site is: http://www.documentary.org/resources/index.php. *Wired* magazine also has information and commentary on documentary films, among a host of other interesting articles for those interested in film and media

SUGGESTED READING:

Barnouw, E. (1993). *Documentary: A history of the non-fiction film*. New York and Oxford: Oxford University Press.

Grant, B. K., & Sloniowski, J. (Eds.). (1998). *Documenting the documentary: Close readings of documentary film and video*. Detroit: Wayne State University Press.

Hampe, B. (1997). *Making documentary films and reality videos*. New York: Henry Holt.

Rosenthal, A. (1996). *Writing, directing, and producing documentary films and videos*. Carbondale: Southern Illinois University Press.

I think that all of my films reflect my sensibilities and interests. I think that all good filmmaking—documentary and otherwise—incorporates something of the person making it and his relationship to the subject matter and to the film. I like to think that there's a lot of me in Fast, Cheap & Out of Control *and a lot of me in [*Mr. Death*]. On the simplest level, the films reflect my concerns or my obsessions. But I like to think that what keeps me going in these films is that there is something that I don't know about these people and about the subject matter of the film itself, that there's some mystery left to be explored.*

—Errol Morris (Fast, Cheap & Out of Control) in an interview
with William H. Phillips, March 20, 1998.
http://www.bedfordstmartins.com/phillips-film-1e/home.htm

Marketplace: Screenplays for Films That Inform, Explain, and Sell

If we can't create something useful or beautiful ... we shall certainly create something else: trouble, for instance. (p. xi)

—Lajos Egri, *The Art of Dramatic Writing* (1960).

Much of what we have discussed in the previous chapter about documentary films is directly applicable to writing for what could be loosely defined as *the business market*. In fact it is often difficult (and sometimes pointless) to distinguish between a documentary film and a film for the world of business. Even so, films written for the business world keep countless screenwriters and film makers gainfully employed at writing that can be interesting and creative. Thus, it is useful to spend some time looking at how to write for this arena.

What is *the marketplace?* In some ways, this term is a misnomer because not all marketplace films are designed to sell products and services. For the purposes of discussion, films that fit into this category can be:

- Informational or how-to films for: (a) government (how to clean your firearm or defuse a land mine), (b) business (how to dress for success or talk to Japanese clients), and (c) products or services (how to clean your gutters);
- Public service announcements (how important it is to talk to your kids about drugs, why not to smoke cigarettes, how great teachers are);
- Sales films (why to buy a powerful modem from CompuSell, how well the CarrotChopper works); and

241

- Outright commercials (why you should sign up with AT&T or use Pampers diapers).

In addition, with the capability of computers to display moving images, the potential market for films for electronic media (films for the Internet) has only begun to be tapped. Clearly there will be an increasing need for people who can write for this market—people with both ideas and a solid grasp for writing for the screen—who can put together a script that will dazzle, delight, sell, inform, and, most important, persuade. Ad agencies already have a raft of creative people who dream up wonderful ideas for persuading people through their ads in magazines and on TV that their product is worth buying. Freelance writers are already kept gainfully employed by companies that want a video that informs, promises, or persuades.

Note the emphasis I have placed on persuasion. At the heart of this whole enterprise of writing for the marketplace is getting someone else to believe what you have to promote. The bulk of this chapter, then, is designed to help you persuade people—not only to buy your script, but to believe what you have to say in that script and then act on it: They will want to buy into—literally and figuratively—whatever product, service, or message you promote.

Know your genre. Films for the marketplace have different aims and do different things. They are seen in different forums: corporate conferences, industry conventions, accompaniments to high-priced consumer products, political meetings, and so on. It is valuable to keep track of your overriding purpose in making the film. Here are your options:

- Instructing (providing information, techniques, and strategies that will help someone do something or be something),
- Explaining (much like instructing),
- Evaluating (providing a critical eye and attempting to persuade your viewers that your criticisms are valid),
- Proposing (explaining, evaluating, and then proposing so that your viewers will actually do or believe something that they haven't before),
- Arguing (taking a position that divides your audience, and getting people who do not already believe you to see and believe your side), and
- Selling (making people part with something that is extremely valuable to them—their money).

I have listed these in a rough order, proceeding from the least difficult to the most. In the most difficult cases, you want your viewers not only to do or believe what you say, but to go out and change an aspect of their lives or spend money. Consequently, you need to be much more rigorous in attending to your viewers, creating an appropriate stance, and laying out the approach of your film.

THE COMMUNICATION TRIANGLE

Let us say you have been assigned to write a script that will persuade an audience of medical professionals to use a particular technique when handling hazardous medical wastes. As with many persuasive projects like this one, one of the best ways to approach your project is to consider the rhetorical or communication triangle.

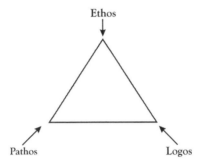

Pathos—Your Audience

First and foremost, you want to consider whom you are writing for. Yes, you are writing for your client, but both you and your client want the film to be successful, so you need to pay serious attention to your target audience—or the audience you want most to reach with your message. Here are some questions to consider:

- Who is your audience?
  - ✓ Age (e.g., teenagers, middle age, elderly)?
  - ✓ Gender?
  - ✓ Race?
  - ✓ Socioeconomic status (e.g., wealthy, working class, etc.)?
  - ✓ Politics (conservative, liberal)?
  - ✓ Geographical location (East Coast, Midwest, city, suburban, rural)?
  - ✓ Cultural difference (can encompass all of these aspects)?
- Why would they care about your film?

- What would make them care?
- What do they already know about the topic?
- What do they need to know?
- What do they probably feel and think before the film, and what do you want them to feel and think after the film?

These questions certainly are not the only ones you could ask or need to ask. But they get at the fact that you are gearing your script toward people who have certain prejudices, values, tastes, and lifestyles, and taking this under consideration will give you a strong advantage over writers who simply write for "whomever is out there." Above all, this analysis will help you break through the **boredom threshold** while making a film that is appropriate. You need to take care here. Video Arts (www.videoarts.com) produces a number of very funny training videos, some of which feature actor John Cleese. As humorous and entertaining as these videos are, they may not be appropriate for audiences who prefer more serious approaches to business management.

In some ways, this consideration of audience is similar to understanding your audience when you write for feature films. But because audiences can be much more specific and narrowly defined when you are writing for a marketplace, it becomes strategically much more crucial to know everything you can about your target audience.

Functional, Useful, and Immediate.   Most people in the professional/ business world—the world of the marketplace—do not have a lot of free time on their hands. Furthermore, for people—anyone—to learn something new, instructions need to be functional and directly useful. Ideally they must be put to use almost immediately for the information to be retained. For example, I have a video on how to use my laptop. It is a nicely produced video that is easy to follow, but if I do not plan to use my laptop in the near future (like in the next day or so), it is not particularly useful to watch. In fact the video is only really useable if I have my laptop in front of me so I can follow the instructions step by step and can put the information to use right away, reinforcing what has just been explained.

Although these precepts about utility and immediacy seem painfully obvious, many marketing or information films provide material that people may or may not use (or even care about). Most of us can probably recall being forced to sit through a film that had very little relevance to what we were interested in, or was so boring and tedious—or even silly—that it was dreadful to watch. This problem often happens at school where "enforced viewing" sometimes seems to be a staple. When I was in graduate school, I saw a film on how to run a writing tutorial. The roles were played by amateur actors portraying students; the dialogue was didactic and stilted. I did not learn much about writing tutorials; instead I remember thinking that this goofy piece was a colossal waste of time—both to make and to watch, despite its good intentions.

That said, there is surprising anecdotal evidence about people who have watched films on CPR or earthquake preparedness that are so skillfully made that viewers can recall what they have seen and have used the essential information in an emergency. These films are effective in ways that make a strong impression on the viewer. This is the kind of script you should try to write.

How do you write something impacting? Here are some ideas that incorporate the precept of knowing your audience.

Be an amateur psychologist. What would motivate your audience to believe what you have to say? What are the goals of your viewers? What are their prejudices? Where are their blind spots? What do they really want in life? What are they likely to find boring or silly? For example, ads can be powerful, but miss their target. The 1987 public service ad (PSA) sponsored by the Partnership for a Drug-Free America featured two eggs sizzling in a frying pan with the narration: "This is your brain on drugs. Get the picture?" The ad was geared toward kids to warn them off drugs. Although the PSA was very popular and became very famous, it was more successful with parents. The teenagers often found it to be a joke because it did not match their experience with drugs in their lives (see http://cnnstudentnews.cnn.com/fyi/interactive/news/brain/brain.on.drugs.html#1). It is very useful to talk to people who might make up your target audience. Get to know them. Ask questions about what is important to them. Ask questions about the kinds of film they would like to see.

Use people in your film. Because human beings are, at their core, highly egocentric, they like to see people like themselves on film. Alternately, they like to see kids and animals (although this is less universal than egocentrism). A PSA on gun violence distributed by the Ad Council features a young boy who talks about the penalty he pays having to live without his older brother, who is in prison for 7 years on gun possession. Incorporate someone in your film who your audience can identify and empathize with.

Tell a story. A lot of writing for the marketplace will not be conducive to telling a story, and stories can sometimes appear affected and pretentious. Even so, where it is possible, shape your message around a narrative. Stories are much easier to remember than straightforward information or instruction because they are more engaging. In a PSA on bullying, the Ad Council created a scenario in which a child is being bullied on the playground. Another child calls out to an animated character called McGruff to find out what to do. McGruff gives him instructions, which the child follows, encouraging other kids on the playground to do the same. Problem solved (see Bullying Prevention, "Bullying Hotline"—www.adcouncil.org).

Be funny. The motto of Video Arts (producer of John Cleese training videos) is the following (from its Web site): "Fun is good. Especially in the world of learning. Entertain your audience and you'll find something rather interesting happens. People remember what they've learnt" (www.videoarts.com). In their video "Meetings Bloody Meetings," for example, the producers use British humor to give advice on how to make meetings short, productive, and less frequent. In this segment, Cleese tries to supervise a meeting in which nobody seems to be able to decide anything, including determining what decisions need to be made. In "Customers from Hell," Cleese plays several types of salesmen—one a cheese salesman for a woman who insists on Italian cheese and then cruelly demeans him for not being able to find it. In the next clip, he plays a shoe salesman whose customer cannot stop sharing her personal story as to why she is looking for a shoe cleanser.

To return to our original example, what does an audience of medical professionals care about? One can safely assume that medical professionals care about their patients. So you might write a film where we get to know a patient (a real person) and can follow the routines that the film is promoting through a kind of narrative (or story). That way the target audience has the opportunity to empathize with both the patient and the featured medical professional. It is likely that medical professionals also care about their status and sense of professionalism. Alternately, you may want to feature an actual medical professional (someone like them) and tell your story from her perspective.

Some might argue that it seems much easier and more straightforward to simply TELL your medical professional audience what to do with hazardous wastes by making your film a fact film. But you take a risk that they will not remember or will not care—not because they are negligent or indifferent, but because the "facts" denuded of their personal appeal do not always stick.

Ethos—The Film's Stance or Position

Ethos has to do with establishing credibility and a good rapport with your target audience. Most people are persuaded by someone they know and trust. If the person who is doing the persuading is a stranger, it is very important that he convince us of a number of things:

- That he is honorable and tells the truth as he knows it;
- That he is an authority, either through research or training or experience;
- That he has our best interests at heart and can identify with us and our concerns; and
- That he is likeable.

There are a number of ways to create a strong ethos or stance. Here are some suggestions.

Sound Honest and Trustworthy.   There is an art to "sounding honest," and it is that art form that requires some attention. In recent years, many people have developed a healthy skepticism about politicians and salespeople. They often seem glib and phony, clearly telling their audiences what they think we want to hear and then changing positions when the time seems right. We know they have an ulterior motive (to get elected or sell a product) and that they do not always (or even rarely) work in our best interest. They are, in a word, self-serving.

Lesson 1. The film should sound like the film maker knows what she is talking about. Get your facts right. Although you do not necessarily have to have experts talking on the screen (some experts can be really boring), you do need to come across as having authority.

If you do use authorities on a subject, identify them and their qualifications in a subtitle (Dr. X, cancer researcher at the Fred Hutchinson Cancer Center, or Dr. Y, professor of ancient history at the University of Athens). In using authorities, you will in turn convey that you are in control of your project—that you know who should be listened to and you have a strong sense of your subject. To select your authorities and to get your facts right, you will need to do your research. This is another good reason to read, undertake interviews, and see related films. It is a good thing to know far more than you will use in your film.

Lesson 2. Do not talk down (or up) to your viewers. Use terms and vocabulary that will demonstrate to your audience that you are familiar with their field (jargon, technical terms may be quite appropriate), but also terms and vocabulary that you know your audience will understand.

Make sure you know the standard pronunciation of each word you use (so you can convey this to your narrator if you have one). Even small mistakes in pronunciation can deflate an entire argument. Medical terms, for example, can be difficult for a lay person to pronounce. Get them right.

Lesson 3. Avoid clichés, both in what you say in your film and how you say it. People who can avoid clichés tend to sound more honest. By definition, a *cliché* is a phrase or expression that has been used too much; it has either lost all its meaning or means different things to different people. A good **slogan** is different than a cliché. A *slogan* is a memorable phrase or sentence that sums up your message. Good slogans gradually become clichés; just start with a slogan (you will have no control over how it devolves). For example, in the antidrug campaign that was so popular some years ago, the phrase "Just Say No" was so overused it became the butt of jokes and eventually lost its power.

Consider the following slogans from PSAs. A PSA from Tolerance.org features a group of kids talking about what tolerance means to them, then in a series of quick shots each child repeats the slogan: "Tolerance: Honor the differences." It has the following qualities: It works well in conjunction with the images (each child is of a different race or ethnicity), it is easy to remember; and it is not too cute. At the end of the PSA, singer Alanis Morissette says, "Picture a world of respect," another slogan. This works in much the same way as the first: It is memorable and works with the visuals.

Morgan Freeman narrates another PSA produced for the National Resources Conservation Services (http://www.nrcs.usda.gov/feature/highlights/freemanpsa.html). The PSA features a series of images that show wildlife and mountains, over which Freeman asks viewers to become Earth Team volunteers to help preserve the natural environment. At the end of the PSA, he says, "… because there's just no place like home." This is a cliché for sure. But it works here because it does not refer to our individual homes, but to our planet. It is used in a way that is different.

It is hard to know what might sound cliché to an audience that you do not know much about—hence, we return to the value of doing your research. Using our example of medical researchers, it would be inappropriate and even laughable to use the expression "Cleanliness is next to Godliness" with this audience. It would just sound silly.

Select the Right Tone. You have a range of options here: informal, formal, colloquial, familiar, academic, sarcastic, ironic, or humorous. Again, selecting a tone will depend both on your audience and your topic or issue. It will also depend on what kind of stance you want to take.

A formal and academic tone (one you would use for a teacher or within school) is the most difficult to sustain because it can sound preachy and overbearing, especially for long educational or informational films. Still this type of tone also sounds the most objective and can often make use of logic, facts, and statistics that are enormously persuasive.

An informal tone is easier on most audiences because it tends to be more conversational. It sounds like real people talking. The speakers sound more approachable and honest (even if they are not), and they are easier to identify with.

Lately, a number of PSAs have featured TV, film, music, and sports stars (David Schwimmer, Anthony Edwards, Oakland Raider Rich Gannon, Ming Na) who advocate connecting with your kids or staying off drugs. These ads are often didactic and preachy, but they get away with it because the celebrity uses informal language and his or her celebrity status to make the audience connection.

However, a recent public service announcement by the Centers for Disease Control and Prevention (http://www.cdc.gov/flu/0405psas.htm) features Dr. Julie L. Gerberding talking to the camera about getting a flu shot. Although she is a clearly an expert, making her speech credible and informative, the ad is also merely a "talking head," making poor use of the film medium and reducing the ad to the conveying of important but essentially colorless information.

One final note on tone: Sarcasm and irony can be risky. Sarcasm especially can alienate your audience and is best avoided. Using irony presumes your viewers will "get" the irony, which they may or may not. If they do not, you will be conveying a message that is opposite the one you intended. Both sarcasm and irony also presume your audience will also be of a frame of mind where irony will work persuasively. But if your audience does not agree with your point of view, irony can backfire, and you will end up looking like an amateur or an idiot.

When it works well, a humorous tone can be marvelous, getting your audience involved and persuaded as well as entertained: the classical ideal. But as most comedians and humor writers know, humor is very difficult. What is funny to one audience will not be funny to the next, and it requires delicate and skillful writer to pull it off.

Logos: Your Argument or Pitch

You have got a handle on your audience. You understand that you need to set an appropriate stance. Now you need to structure your argument and script to accomplish your aims. Here are some tools—some of which I have already mentioned in the context of audience or authorial stance—that are commonly used to persuade. Do not feel compelled to use every one; do not feel compelled to use one throughout your film. Your script will be better if you select the kinds of methods that will best convey your central ideas.

- *Use audio and visuals to convey your message.*

The following is a PSA created for the Arab American Institute to promote tolerance. The message is carried through the narration, but the visuals capitalize on the emotional aspect of the 9/11 terrorist attacks. The narration on its own does not carry the impact; rather the visual (and the music "America the Beautiful") makes this spot work.

"Americans Stand United"
Arab-American Institute PSA—
http://www.aaiusa.org/psa.htm
Created by the Ad Council and the Brokaw Agency

VISUAL	AUDIO
TIME LAPSE PHOTO of New York City skyline. The spot where the World Trade Towers stood is clearly visible. The sky gradually lightens as we move from the beginning to the end of the spot.	MUSIC IN: "America the Beautiful"—guitar.
TITLE SCROLLS UP on the left-hand side of the screen. In the background, a visual echo of the title rises up to fill the space where the south tower once stood: In a war on terror, some say we can't see who our enemies are. But there is	NARRATOR: In a war on terror, some say we can't see who our enemies are. But there is one enemy we can see very clearly. It's a defaced neighborhood mosque, an Arab-American storekeeper in fear of reprisal ...

one enemy we can see very
clearly. It's a defaced
neighborhood mosque, an
Arab-American storekeeper
in fear of reprisal

TITLE HOLDS and alongside
it, on the right-hand side
of the screen, second title
scrolls up. In the
background, a VISUAL ECHO
OF THE TITLE RISES UP to
fill the area where the
north tower once stood:

A Muslim child bullied
because she is different.
Hate is our enemy. And when
we start to hate other
Americans, we have lost
everything. Hate has taken
enough from us already.
Don't let it take you.

Title fades out, but the
Trade Towers (now made of
words) remain.

Title fades in: Americans
Stand United

Sponsor's logo: Arab-
American Institute

FADE OUT

... a Muslim child bullied
because she is different.
Hate is our enemy. And when
we start to hate other
Americans, we have lost
everything. Hate has taken
enough from us already.
Don't let it take you.

MUSIC FADES OUT.

- *Appeal to pity*

A common method of persuading your audience is to appeal to emotions.
The bombing of the Pentagon and the World Trade Center Towers elicited
powerful emotions that the previous commercial taps into though the visual
and music.

- *Compare and contrast*

This is a very good tool for making your point much more vividly and for
persuading the audience of the rightness of your points in comparison with

less convincing ideas. Compare one way of doing a job with another, less productive approach.

- *Give a representative (and compelling) example and then generalize*

This could be a scene or episode—real or dramatized—an interview, or a setting. A 4-year-old in Alaska calls her aging grandmother in Texas to tell her about something special and makes her day. What does this say about good telephone service?

- *Start with generalization and then move into (compelling) examples*

This is essentially the opposite of the preceding tip. Sometimes it helps to set up background material and general ideas before you move into examples. Providing some context about cross-cultural communication might help lay some groundwork for an example of an American businesswoman dealing with a businessman from Beijing.

- *Use testimony*

We have covered an important aspect of this in the use of authorities and experts. In addition, statistics and quotations are, where appropriate, quite persuasive. If Michael Jordan talks about the value of education, kids are more inclined to listen than if the Secretary of Education says the same thing.

- *Explain relevant facts, details, and circumstances*

When and where appropriate, elaborate on the circumstances that control or contribute to your essential points. If you are explaining how to use an inhaler for asthma, it is useful to cover what to do if your viewer experiences side effects.

- *Make your pitch indirectly*

Try to sell the audience on your ideas without seeming like you are doing the selling. One of the best kinds of persuasion occurs when you have guided the audience members to a conclusion that they feel they have arrived at on their own.

Here is an example from a PSA designed by BBDO Atlanta for the Peace Corps recruitment. The spot is essentially a series of questions with an implied answer—one to which the viewer is steered (by the visuals and Matthew McConaghy) to respond positively.

Peace Corps PSA
http://www.peacecorps.gov/index.cfm?shell=resource.
media.psaShowVideo&vd=psaE&bwd=whbe

VISUAL	AUDIO
FADE IN:	MUSIC IN
SLOW TRACKING SHOT across the palm of a hand. The wrinkles of the palm are plainly visible.	NARRATOR: How far would you go to help someone?
CAMERA TRACKS ALONG A STREET to including a CLOSE SHOT of a man's feet as they step off a curb and into a street.	Would you go to the end of your driveway?
TRACKING SHOT across a freeway overpass. Traffic is seen on the freeway below.	Would you cross the street?
MAP SHOT - CAMERA TRACKS a red line drawn long streets of Los Angeles.	Would you cross an ocean?
LONG SHOT - An airplane takes off.	
MAP SHOT - CAMERA TRACKS along the shoreline of a map of South America.	To a place 6,000 miles from home?
ARIAL SHOT - A densely vegetated jungle. Rivers, trees, mountains.	And how long would you go?
CAMERA TRACKS ACROSS THE FOLLOWING SHOTS:	
STILL SHOT - A group of fishermen pull a net onshore	Would you go for a week?
	A month?
STILL SHOT - A group of refugees stand in line for food.	A year?
STILL SHOT - Two busses. A man stretches his hand out the window of one bus, reaching for the hand of a man in the second bus.	Would you go for two years?

STILL SHOT - A PEACE CORPS VOLUNTEER works in a field with a local farmer.	Would you go if you could use your knowledge to teach someone, and in the process maybe learn something yourself?
MEDIUM SHOT - A CHILD stands in front of a chalk board.	
SLOW PAN across the palm of a hand (same as first shot).	Life is calling. How far will you go? Peace Corps.
PEACE CORPS LOGO IS SUPERED OVER BLACK.	MUSIC OUT
TITLE: Life is calling. How far will you go?	

Produced by BBDO Atlanta, narrated by Matthew McConaghy.

A Note on Style.   Throughout this book, we have noted the importance of style in your presentations—whether in a proposal, treatment, or script. Attention to style is as true in marketplace writing, where stale, dull prose can kill a project and where lively, precise, and clear prose can elevate a project to new heights not anticipated by your sponsor. In fact the reason you were hired is to come up with material that your sponsor was not able to.

FORMAT

There is no "correct" format for marketplaces scripts partly because of the diversity of needs, goals, and topics, and partly because there simply is no single way of producing these kinds of films. Sometimes it is more appropriate to write a proposal (see documentary proposals in chap. 8). Sometimes a company contracts a writer to craft a script that has a particular story line or focus. For example, a Florida hospital wanted an easy way to show kids how to use an asthma monitor. They contacted Ballistic Pixel Lab to create a film using pixellated characters ("Max and Buddy the Bear") that would appeal to children. The screenplay for this film—which told a story—looked like a typical screenplay for a dramatic film, with shots, scene description, and dialogue. (For a sample of

the film that was produced, see http://ballisticpixel.com/creations/html/
creations_main.htm.)

Other times, the script is a brief outline that indicates audio, visuals, timing, and structure with a brief overview. The following is a PSA about the connection between literacy and democracy. The intended audience is a general
TV viewership during prime time on a national network. With no dialogue or
narration—in other words, working entirely with impressionistic images—the treatment/script aims to connect in the public mind the relationship among reading, writing, and democracy. Although I plan on producing
the PSA myself, it will most likely be sponsored by another entity (in this case,
a group such as ProLiteracy Worldwide or the Council of Writing Program
Administrators), so the script has to be clear and represent the views of the
sponsor.

Literacy Spot #1

Title: Celebrate democracy

This is the treatment for a 60-second public
service announcement that forms part of a series of
literacy spots, the ultimate goal of which is
highlight the fact that literacy is key to a truly
democratic society.

Sequence #1—Empty Spaces (15 seconds)

  a. An empty garden

  b. A city square early on a Sunday morning. Empty
     except for a flock of birds

  c. An empty library

  d. An empty hallway in a public building
     (courthouse, town hall, chamber of commerce)

  e. An empty classroom

  f. An empty computer classroom

Sequence #2 (20 seconds)

  a. A child reading in bed

  b. Students talking on campus

  c. Students working around a computer

  d. A person reading in a park

```
   e. People reading a newspaper together and
      discussing issues
```

```
Sequence #3 (15 seconds)
```

```
   a. Students filling a hallway
   b. A political rally in a downtown square
   c. A polling station with people coming in and out
   d. A parade on the 4th of July, flags waving, kids
      and adult marching
```

```
TITLE APPEARS OVER BLACK: Celebrate democracy.
Support reading and writing in your home, in your
neighborhood, in your community. (10 seconds)
```

Note that I have not indicated any audio in this piece. Music will be added later, but in this instance the kind of music will depend on the visuals and how the piece hangs together. Double-column format (as in the prior examples) is also a simple way to convey visual and audio.

FINDING A MARKET

Most films for the marketplace originate with a client, so the market is already in place before the writer or film maker is brought in. In other circumstances, such as PSAs, a writer may come up with an idea that cries out to be made, but it is not clear where the market might be. There are innumerable different markets—which will necessarily determine how you structure and market your film. Here are some possibilities:

Public TV

Cable channels

Local TV stations

Public or private agencies that specialize in your topic area

Government (local, state, or federal)

Philanthropic societies

Corporations

For a group, agency, or corporation to invest money in a film, there must be a compelling reason to do so. In other words, investing in the film must benefit the financial backers in some way. This need not be directly financial. Corporations are often interested in making films that improve public relations. Hence, we have oil companies that are willing to invest in environmental films. We have philanthropic societies that are interested in films that feature immigrant populations such as the Hmong living in Minnesota. We have TV stations that wish to provide PSAs on the dangers of smoking. The Ad Council (www.adcouncil.org) is a great resource. A nonprofit group that makes use of volunteer talent, the Ad Council has taken the lead in organizing media campaigns on topics such as childhood cancer, parental involvement in schools, and AIDS/HIV prevention, all designed to benefit the public. As such, it produces and distributes PSAs for other nonprofit and government organizations.

A FINAL COMMENT

If we can only get you to buy into one precept in this entire chapter, it is that this genre of film writing can and should be **anything but dull or routine**. If the film is boring, your audience will snooze through it. If you are creative and inventive, and you design a project that is appropriate to your audience and goal, your audience might just enjoy watching your film as much as you did writing or making it.

APPLICATIONS AND EXERCISES

1. *Audience Analysis.* Select a topic for a PSA, particularly in an area about which you know a good deal. Examples might include: ski or water safety, using the Internet, designing a garden, or dealing with clients. Develop an audience profile based on the list of questions cited earlier. How would you approach this audience in a way that would be both appealing and persuasive?

2. *Stance.* Building on the preceding example, draft a list of ways in which you might create a persuasive stance for that audience. When you are finished, keep the ideas that are most appropriate for the film medium (that make compelling use of sound and visual) and throw the rest out.

3. *Structure.* Select a business or marketplace film that you have seen that is informational and dull. Come up with another version that would make the film much more appealing to its intended audience. Write up a proposal for this film.

Here are some films I have seen that I think need new writers with more creative visions:

- A film promoting birth control for adolescents
- A film that demonstrates baby care for teen mothers
- A film that advertises a neighborhood adult literacy site
- A film that sells feminine hygiene products
- A film for a product that helps prevent premature baldness in men
- A film that demonstrates intercultural communication in business

4. *Finding a Market*. Come up with an idea for a PSA. Look at the information kit for designing a PSA (http://www.adcouncil.org/pdf/official.pdf) and try to answer the questions posed in the materials about goals, target audience, and funding.

Introduction
to the Experimental Film

I see each film/video project as a "first film" with its own cinematic language, one that the viewer learns and engages with as the piece unfolds. This language is shaped by the particular mechanics of each medium, in the same way verbal language is shaped by the mechanics of the human mouth. Thus each film charts the possibility of a pre-cinema experience, one that might have evolved had not narrative and commerce been cinema's prevailing motivational forces.

—Experimental film maker Scott Stark from his Web site,
http://www.hi-beam.net/mkr/ss/ss-bio.html, Retrieved October 15, 2005.

In this final chapter, we venture into a realm of screenwriting that, until recently, fewer people have entered into as a profession primarily because there appears to be a smaller market and audience. But with the advent of the Internet and new, affordable technologies and software, it is getting easier and easier to write, design, and produce these films for the cyberspace market. In addition, cable TV—for example, MTV—opens up vast opportunities for the writer-film maker to make nontraditional films for nontraditional markets. Finally, perhaps even more than the documentary film or marketing film, the experimental film blurs the boundaries between writer and film maker. In other words, the people who write or design the films also make the films. Although this chapter does not provide specific information on the technical aspects of production, it does explore the writing of the experimental film, broadly construed, so that films that you produce in this genre will make dramatic sense to your viewers.

Experimental, avant-garde, or abstract films have filled an important role in the entire enterprise of movie making. These kinds of films provide the opportunity to explore the medium of film, to push the filmic envelope beyond tradition and convention, and to realize some of the potential of film that has not commonly been tapped.

The avant-garde film has both a rich history and an exciting future. Many years ago, Arthur Knight (1957), a film critic, historian, and, for many years, a professor of cinema at the University of Southern California film school, wrote

> The willingness to experiment, to try out new forms, new techniques and ideas, is as vital to the arts as it is to science. Today, through an unfortunate limiting of the word, experiment in film has come to be associated almost exclusively with the efforts of small avant-garde coteries working quite apart from the main stream of motion-picture production. In the truest sense, however, Griffith was experimenting when he pushed his camera closer to the actors than the conventions of the day accepted, when he lit, photographed and edited his scenes in ways no other director had dreamed of. (p. 257)

Many screenwriters today, as well as many producers and even more studio executives—caught up as they are in the business of film that involves primarily the making of money and the acquisition of status—are either unaware of the history of experimentation that has fueled the best films, or choose to ignore or devalue it. Between the 1960s and 1990, experimental films were, more often than not, viewed as oddities by underground film makers from New York or esoteric sketches by students and novices, to be seen only at film festivals.

This life on the margins has not been an entirely bad thing. To really innovate and experiment—particularly in a medium that is as expensive as film is—it is crucial that the work *not* be mainstream, but rather that film makers work from outside—on the fringes. But one need only browse through the growing number of Internet sites and avant-garde film festivals or witness the proliferation of computer media, including games and gaming, to get a sense of the creative ways new film makers are using the media. Many of these films (gaming may be an exception) do not make a lot of money yet. Their funding often comes from the sale of advertising (on Web sites) or from national or international foundations such as National Endowment for the Humanities (NEH) or the Canadian Film Board. But the increase in digital cinema departments at colleges and universities, and the availability of fancy digital technology, make this kind of film making possible for more and more people. Thus, although I only devote one chapter to this kind of film writing, this is a promising area for film writers to explore.

The history of film, as Knight pointed out, is of course rich in experimentation. Here are some thoughts from some of most innovative of our predecessors who, even in decades ago, were critical of conventional film making—both its slavish adulation of realism and its mediocrity.

> All technical refinements discourage me. Perfect photography, larger screens, hi-fi sound, all make it possible for mediocrities slavishly to reproduce nature; and this reproduction bores me. What interests me is the interpretation of life by an artist. (Renoir, 1967, p. 287)

> Mystery is a basic element of all works of art. It is generally lacking on the screen. Writers, directors and producers take good care in avoiding anything that may upset us. They keep the marvelous window on the liberating world of poetry shut. (Buñuel, 1967, p. 175)

> The screen is a dangerous and wonderful instrument if a free spirit uses it. It is the superior way of expressing the world of dreams, emotions, and instinct. The cinema seems to have been invented for the expression of the subconscious, so profoundly is it rooted in poetry. Nevertheless, it almost never pursues these ends. (Buñuel, 1960, pp. 41–42)

Here are some other experimental film makers to look for as you familiarize yourself with the genre: Scott Bartlett, Hans Richter, Stan Brakhage, Maya Deren, Charles and Ray Eames, Jack Smith, Oskar Fishinger, Kenneth Anger, Bryan Gordon, Scott Stark, John Waters, Lars Von Trier, Ron Fricke, François Miron, James Broughton, Jon Jost, and Nina Menkes.

WHAT IS AN EXPERIMENTAL FILM?

Just as there has been no consistent market for the experimental, avant-garde, or abstract film, there is likewise no consistent definition. In general, these kinds of films defy or work against the traditional narrative film that we find so frequently in theatrical films. Often, as in the films of the New Wave in France in the 1960s, they focus the viewers' attention on cinematic form and style by shunning the linear narrative. If there is any common denominator, experimental film makers assume that the film medium is like no other and that they should exploit that difference to the fullest extent and in as many ways as possible.

As a result, most experimental films make wonderful, playful, and inventive use of the movie elements. They are highly visual, using movement, shape, color, shot size, and pattern, and they integrate their visuals with the creative use of sound (dialogue, music, sound effects) to expand and explore what it means to be cinematic. To watch an experimental film is to inhabit a world that is different from the realistic imitations of everyday life that we usually experience at the movie theater. These films invite us to enter the often bizarre, ethereal, strange, dazzling, and sometimes horrific vision of the film maker.

Experimental films, strictly speaking then, are both *experiments* with the cinematic medium and with conceptions of experience, limited by the human imagination and by what audiences can or will accept. Experimental films can be abstract, animated, Dadaist, and surreal. They can be created using claymation, pixellation, or drawing directly on film. They can employ computer-generated graphics and special effects. They are often considered avant-garde—in other words, ahead of their time, unconventional, and oppositional. To provide a sense of the range of categories into which experimental films fall, here are some examples.

Dadaism.   This is an avant-garde movement that began in Germany in the 1920s, but was popularized in France during the same decades. Its principle feature was art that communicated anarchy. In so doing, dadaist art explored and exploited the medium of film (among other art forms) to disrupt conventions and tradition. Among these film makers was Man Ray who laid objects (buttons, tacks, nails) on film, which he then exposed and spliced together. One of the masterpieces of Dadaist film is *Ballet Mécanique* by cubist painter, Ferdinand Léger. Made in 1924, this film is a kind of dance created by the synchronized intercutting of realistic and abstract. A girl on a swing moves back and forth, and this is intercut with close shots of mechanical parts—gears, levers, pendulums, and egg beaters. In the displacement of these objects from their real-life contexts or in isolating their movements or component parts, they take on a life of their own. The patterns and juxtapositions involve a kind of play in which film makers worked to create new cadences and new ways of framing ordinary reality. Other Dadaist films to see are René Clair's *Entr'acte* (1924) and *Emak Bakia, A Cinépoem* (1926) by Man Ray.

Surrealism.   An outgrowth of Dadaism, surrealism had a more political purpose—its proponents often lashed out at organized religion, particularly Catholicism, politics, and bourgeois attitudes and customs. Surrealist films clearly rejected copying objective reality. In fact under the influence of some of Sigmund Freud's ideas, surrealists were keenly interested in the world of dreams and nightmares.

Among the best-known surrealist films is *Un Chien Andalou* (*Andalusian Dog*), made in 1929 by Luis Buñuel and Salvador Dali. This film consists of a nightmarish series of images depicting violence (such as the slitting of an eye-ball with a razor, an amputated hand) and attempts to evoke horror (a dead cow, ants emerging from a hand) and perverse sexuality (an attempted rape). These images are interspersed with images that have an almost lyrical qual-ity—a woman at a balcony, a man riding a bicycle. The attempt is to subvert the idea of logical order and foil attempts on the part of an audience to "make sense," at least on a rational level. Other surreal films to see include Alberto Cavalcanti's *Rien que les Heures* (1926), Joris Iven's *Rain* (1924), and Buñuel and Dali's *L'Age d'Or* (1930).

Expressionism (Especially German Expressionism).   This genre deals with the highly subjective view of reality. Many expressionist films (particularly German ones) are dark and highly stylized—for example, *The Cabinet of Dr. Caligari* (1919), written by Hans Janowitz and Carl Mayer, *Nosferatu* (1922), written by F. N. Murnau from the novel by Bram Stoker—both of which deal with madness and murder—and *Metropolis* (1926), written by Fritz Lang and Thea Von Harbou, about a futuristic and mechanistic city. Expressionism had a great deal of influence on the modern horror film and film noir.

Abstract.   An abstract film uses graphic elements that may or may not be recognizable as part of the world around us. Abstract film makers may use shapes, lines, textures, and movement to convey feelings and sensations; they may distill parts of living figures (human, animal, or plant) or inanimate objects (rocks, buildings, water) into their work to highlight geometric shapes or fluid motion.

The distinction between the abstract film and more traditional types of films is akin to the difference between modern art and classical or representative art, which uses representations of the physical world. Thus, abstract films are usu-ally intended to convey meaning in ways that may defy logical explanation. They may or may not tell a story or make a point.

Certainly many of the Dadist and surreal films use abstraction (*Rain* and *Ballet Mécanique*). But abstraction is not limited to the 1920s, nor does it necessarily consist of traditional cinematography. A master of painting on film, Stan Brakhage, made films such as *Night Music* (1986) and *Study in Color and Black and White* (1993) by painting forms, colors, and shapes directly onto the film's emulsion. The films, which have no soundtrack, are interesting experiments in the relationship among form, color, contrast, and rhythm.

Poetic Essays.   Because experimental films deliberately break rules and work against convention and tradition, there are numerous kinds of films that are difficult to classify or do not belong to a particular school or artistic movement. For example, the film trilogy *Qatsi* by Godfrey Reggio (director/producer/writer) and Philip Glass (musical score) consists of three feature-length films that visually chronicle the destructive impact of the modern world on the environment. The first two segments, *Koyaanisqatsi* (*Life in Turmoil*) (1982), and *Powaqqatsi* (*Life in Transition*) (1987), treat the theme of modernization entirely through visuals of the world in action: men working, planes taking off, buildings being demolished, and people cultivating crops, all set to a modernistic musical score by Glass. The third, *Naqoyqatsi* (*Life as War*, [2002]), looks at the transition to technology. There is no dialogue, only a subtitle here and there to frame the sequences. The result is a sensual treatment of the subject, a poem on film if you will—one that appeals to the senses more than the intellect.

Animation, Claymation, Pixellation, Computer Graphics.   These are some techniques that can be used in designing experimental films (and they have certainly been used in the making of conventional films as well). **Animated** films clearly have a sizeable commercial market, but experimental animation is the precursor. Walt Disney is one of the best known of the early innovators, both in the study of movement (*Snow White*, [1938], *Bambi*, [1942]) and his more avant-garde films (although it may be heresy to call Disney avant-garde), such as *Fantasia* (1940) and *Fanstasia/2000*. *Fantasia* consists of images set to music—the images often involve the movement of shapes and their transformations into realistic figures (fairies, birds, etc.) and vice versa.

Today, computers have the capability of achieving effects that 20 years ago required tedious hand manipulation. For example, *pixellation* is a process by which static elements are moved by hand and filmed frame by frame to give the illusion of movement. *Claymation* is one of the best-known examples of this, where clay figures appear to come to life. This became a popular way to animate films; examples range from the animation of raisins dancing to the tune of "I Heard It Through the Grapevine" to theatrical films. Naturally the process has become much more complex, resulting in the production of computer-generated graphics as in *Toy Story* (1995), *Antz* (1998), *James and the Giant Peach* (1996), *A Bug's Life* (1998), and *The Incredibles* (2004), to name just a few.

In the ways I have defined *experimental* earlier in this chapter, many of the films mentioned are only experimental in the experiments they make with the medium and in special effects. They still depend on narrative to carry an audience and are not particularly daring or innovative in the treatment of themes and ideas. Furthermore, the potential in **computer graphics** is only beginning to be tapped, in terms of exploiting the medium, communicating ideas and concepts in new ways, and artistic creation.

Macromedia Flash and Shockwave.　Web sites that house experimental and avant-garde films are continuing to proliferate. There are thousands of movies made using readily available video software such as Macromedia Flash and Shockwave, many of which are cinematically exciting, inventive, and terrific to watch. Many of these sites come and go quickly, so to become familiar with these films, plan to spend a few hours browsing. Check out the following movie host sites:

> http://jelly.b3ta.com/
> http://mempool.com/
> http://computer.howtuffworks.com/web-animation3.htm
> http://flashmagazine.com
> http://bestflashanimationsite.com

Here is a brief sampling of some films:

> www.rockstargames.com/upload/swf/winners/multimedia/drewcope.swf
> www.wired.com/animation/collection
> www.verylowsodium.com/fanimutation/exuberance.php

WRITING AND DESIGNING AN EXPERIMENTAL FILM

At first glance, an outsider might think these films are made without a script or plan. You have a great idea; you go out and shoot some footage and maybe you digitize and play with it on a computer, stringing it together with some voice-over or music.

Although this may be true for some films, most good film makers start with more than a vision or focal point; they craft a well-articulated plan. For example, Godfrey Reggio, the author of the *Qatsi* films, starts his projects with what Reggio calls "talking pieces" or "dramaturgical shapings." A dramaturgical shaping is an elaborated narrative that describes the subject and how it is to be realized in a cinematic form. For example, *Naqoyqatsi*, the last film of the trilogy, began as a kind of treatment—compiled in a small binder—that articulated the films's three movements. Each movement was divided into sequences in which subtopics that Reggio wanted to treat are listed, often with images (photographs, graphics). In the first sequence in Movement 1, Reggio lists "new icons," "civilized equations," and "world wide web." A few pages later, these are broken down into descriptions of the particular images he wanted to explore visually (e.g., numerical codes, the first electrical computers, global surfing). He wrote an accompanying text that helped give substance to his vision—elaborating, elucidating, and exploring. The piece ultimately tells a cinematic story intended to appeal to the human senses and emotions. For example, the text in Movement 1 begins with:

```
Humans are terrestrial beings evolved from the
living earth, our host of origin and context. Today
we dwell on a lunar surface of stone, cement,
asphalt glass, iron, steel, plastic, and composite
mediums. The living environment is replaced by a
manufactured milieu, an engineered host—synthetic
nature. In a real sense, we are off-planet.

With our origin based in the natural order, should
this context radically change, the mysterious
nature of the human being shall also radically
change—a change that will reflect the
transformation of nature itself/at a turning point
or vanishing point. The roots of this transcendence
are human, reaching back in history a mere several
hundred years. (Reggio, p. 3)
```

This "script-treatment" (Reggio) also specifies in detail the images he has in mind (e.g., war and battle images, weather images, people engaging in endurance sports, robots) and the accompanying soundtrack, including music and sound effects that help shape the flow of images. For instance, Reggio lists colors, kinds of stock footage he will use, and even lenses and camera points of view.

Completed long before the crew gets together, this narrative provides a way to approach the actual process of making his films in which everyone understands the goals from the outset and collaborates in making these goals evolve onto film. Reggio's crews are large, perhaps larger than for most experimental films, but not as large as most feature films. He films all over the world with crews from different countries, and he has a postproduction crew of around 30 people. With all the expense associated with making films, it is imperative that he start with a well-articulated plan, which he uses as a point of departure.

In addition, this plan is based on a good deal of research. Reggio and his line producers travel extensively, scouting locations, photographing them, seeking out shooting permissions, and so on. As with the other kinds of films we have explored (particularly documentary), research is key to helping the film come together.

WHAT IS A GOOD IDEA
FOR AN EXPERIMENTAL FILM?

Many experimental film makers have important things to say about the world in their films. Having something to say is a good place to start. Unlike traditional dramatic films, however, experimental films comment on the world in a different way, and that different way is limited only by the medium.

Where to start? Film maker Ingmar Bergman (1960) said, "I would say that there is no art form that has so much in common with film as music" (p. xii). In some ways, all good films are like music. However, because experimental films usually have nontraditional narrative guiding the viewer, attention to musical structure may be one way to ensure that your film coheres and make sense— not in a logical way, but in a sensory or emotional way.

WORK WITH THE MEDIUM

Instead of a focus on a linear narrative, identifiable characters, and message, shift your attention to the form. In film, form consists of a visual track and a sound track. The creativity comes in exploiting the manifold options for putting it all together, including manipulation of the image, motion, point of view, rhythm (tension), and sound. Here are a few considerations:

Image

This consists of attention to what is on the screen at a given moment. What is the design of the screen space? How is that space used? It can be filled with elements. For example, a frame of Stan Brakhage's painting of filmstrips may contain blotches of color overlain with scratches. Or the frame can contain a sweep of color against a black background. Here are some examples of image design elements:

- Shapes (round, angular, large, small)
- Lines (straight, jagged, circular, complex, simple)
- Color (single color, matching colors, multiple colors)
- Pattern (simple, complex, realistic, abstract)
- Texture (smooth, opaque, rough, scratchy)

What is often underused, much like silence in narrative films, is blank space: a simple diagonal line, a person's hand, a bit of dust. Blank space can emphasize what elements you do have on the screen.

Movement

Motion can be conveyed in a variety of ways: within the screen space, from shot to shot, or from sequence to sequence. Within the screen space, movement can be slow or fast: or movement can be from side to side or forward and backwards, creating the illusion of depth. Depth can also be manipulated using computer graphics to simulate rapid movement in space. Motion backward and forward can produce the equivalent of a roller coaster ride.

Elements and shapes can move in the same direction or different directions. They can also follow circular directions and can seem to explode, implode, appear, and disappear.

Cutting or editing can set up movement from shot-to-shot or sequence to sequence. A person moves one direction in one shot, then something moves the opposite direction in the next. Or try a series of long, slow zooms or short, quick tilts. Quick cuts simulate speed; long shots can slow down the tempo.

Sound

The sound track can inform what is going on in the visuals, as in a piece of music setting the beat for editing cuts and the movement within shots. It can act as a counterpoint, complementing or even contrasting with the visuals. Or it can do both, setting up patterns in which the sound and visual shadow one another, only to be disrupted at a certain point, jolting the viewer out of complacency.

The screenplay example (*The T-Shirt*) that I include in this chapter is a good example of counterpoint and patterns. The writer has used sounds that do not seem to match the visuals (sounds of a zipper, ripping Velcro, and wind matched with images of human shapes and machines), yet they are patterned sufficiently to create a language—a fairly consistent one—that belongs to this film.

Tension

The building and releasing of tension is sometimes the only way you can keep an audience with you. In experimental films, tension can be created a variety of ways other than through a traditional narrative. Generally, tension is created by a sense of conflict—by a force running counter to another force. This conflict can be generated thematically or stylistically by sweeps of line and color, by cinematic representations of crescendo and decrescendo, through pianissimo and fortissimo. Here are some examples of tools you can consider:

- Crescendo: sounds getting louder, images moving more quickly, shorter and shorter cuts
- Pianissimo: lyrical music, soft, low sounds of birds, slow cuts, slow movement on-screen
- Fortissimo: strong colors, especially reds and oranges, quick cuts, rapid movement

The musical imagery is telling. Your work should be music, but on film.

Cohesiveness

Experimental films do not necessarily need to follow the same rules for unity and coherence that dramatic or documentary films do. In fact many film makers work to edit out any sign of cohesion that may inadvertently appear in the script or rough cut. Even so, I believe that the best kinds of experimental films—the most watchable and memorable films—produce a sense of an organic whole in their cinematic play. After all, the purpose behind many experimental films is to reflect something about human existence or the world, even if it is anarchy—life's confusions, paradoxes, ironies, ambiguity, and chaos. These themes are best conveyed through the setting up of rhythms and patterns, created through recurring characters, visuals, or motifs. Many have a soundtrack that links the visuals together. These elements are often able to help the viewer connect to the material she sees on the screen. She may not be able to make intellectual sense, but she can be taken on a journey that has a clear path (or paths).

MARKET

At the present time, you probably will not get rich making experimental films. It is, rather, a labor of love and dedication to one's art. Even so, you want your film to be produced (so you may need money) and seen (so you will need an audience).

The Internet is a rich resource for avant-garde film makers. A number of Web sites have information about grants, competitions, and many other funding opportunities. A good starting place is the Hamiltro Productions Web site (http://www.panix.com/~hamiltro/links/) or Professor Randall Halle's Web site for his class on avant-garde film at the University of Rochester (http://www.courses.rochester.edu/halle/Links/Film.html). These sites include digital, experimental, and Web film resources; film sites; Web essays; online film sites and links to underground and digital film festivals; and film schools. Flicker (http://www.hi-beam.net/cgi-bin/flicker.pl) is an example of a Web site that caters to "alternative" film makers. It provides a way to view films and get your work seen; it also offers interviews and information about alternative films and film makers.

Funding

Because many of the experimental films that are filmed do not make much money—nor are they intended to—these are necessarily low-budget films, usually financed by a film-making cooperative or the film-makers. Occasionally, funding can come through arts grants, such as the National Endowment for the Arts, the Canadian Film Board, PBS, and, depending on the topic, charitable trusts; sometimes they can be made through film institutes or schools such as the American Film Institute (see Appendix for a list of film schools). There is also a growing Internet market in Web design where people increasingly need audiovisual ideas that do the same kinds of things that experimental or abstract films do: say things in new ways while creatively exploiting the audiovisual medium. Commonly, an experimental film maker funds her own films and then works to make the money back though festivals, awards, and grants. Sometimes a patron will step in or, as Godfrey Reggio (interview, 2004) put it, someone who does the right thing for the wrong reasons—or someone who does the right thing despite advice from counsel and financial advisors.

Film Festivals.   Well-established film festivals occur every year (Sundance, Cannes, and Deauville). These are difficult to get into and are primarily (but not exclusively) interested in feature-length films. There are also festivals that appear for a short time, use up money and goodwill, and then disappear. In between these two extremes are thousands of opportunities. Almost every major city has a film festival, some of them traditional, many of them featuring underground or avant-garde films; there are festivals for films by women, gay and lesbian festivals, and animation festivals. Some of the festivals invite submissions in video, 16 mm, or 35 mm. Underground film festivals often look for films to project in real time (during the festival) and in electronic time (digitally, on the Web). Check out some of the online databases for film festivals that offer opportunities to experimental film makers (e.g., http://www.filmscouts.com/scripts/festdb.cfm).

Here is a brief sampling of the festivals in the United States that have an experimental category for competition:

> Breckrenridge Film Festival (Colorado)
> Chicago Underground Film Festival
> Cinequest (San Jose Film Festival)
> Cleveland International Film Festival
> Columbus International Film Festival
> Dallas International Film Festival
> FilmFest D.C.
> Los Angeles Alternative Film Festival
> Los Angeles Independent Film Festival.
> New York Film Festival
> New York Expo of Short Film and Video
> Poetry Film Festival (San Francisco)
> Seattle Underground Film Festival
> Vancouver Underground Film Festival

Many festivals have Web sites. If they do not, a brief check of the Internet will provide a contact, an address, and relevant information.

Art Houses. These are venues that serve a range of functions. Often they are distribution houses for art films. They have small, but loyal followings, and generally if you can get your film booked into an art house theater, it will get seen. Art houses also serve other functions. For example, Facets in Chicago has an enormous video library; it screens films and markets videos and other film paraphernalia.

Music Videos. This constitutes a booming market for experimental-style film writing. Music videos tend to be highly experimental because they are aimed for a youth market that craves innovation. In addition, they are films set to music; thus, they have structure and design based on the piece of music, and this serves as a jumping-off point for novelty.

Commercials. Some commercials make far better use of visual magic than feature films or documentaries. Because they must sell a product or an idea in 30 to 60 seconds, they must maximize cinematic impact. Consequently, many commercials—although they could rarely be classified as experimental—use innovative photography, cutting, and special effects. Commercials producers are always on the lookout for novelty.

Cyberspace. I have already mentioned this, but it bears repeating. With the advent of digital photography, the venue for moving pictures has expanded well beyond the movie house or the TV screen. This industry is growing at such a rate that much discussion of it here would be out of date at the publication of this book. Suffice it to say, this may be *the* big market for all kinds of films—traditional, documentary, and experimental. It is also a market for the moving image in all of its forms, particularly special effects.

FORM AND FORMAT

Because film makers are working with a film genre that flouts convention and consciously works against traditional film narrative, one might assume that the writing format would follow suit and result in treatments and screenplays that are nontraditional. This is undoubtedly true. A screenplay for painting on film is often just a series of notes or experiments that unfold as the painter works. But as we saw with the Qatsi films, many film makers—especially those who aspire to an audience beyond the Internet—do a great deal of writing before the project gets off the ground. Film stock is expensive, whether used for Hollywood or experimental films. Film and video equipment is expensive as well. Film crews—even nonunion—are expensive to hire. It will save you time and money and result in a more cohesive artistic product if you take the time to write your film—so you see where you are going and where you have been.

Furthermore, although most experimental films do not have a producer in the traditional sense (a person whose primary task is to provide funding), there is often an important use for a proposal, a treatment, or a screenplay. That is, many experimental films need (or could desperately use) funding. Sometimes you will have to fund them yourself. But if you are applying for a grant through the National Endowment for the Arts or another agency or corporation that supports artistic endeavors in multiple media, you will need a detailed description (proposal, outline, treatment, storyboard sequence, or even script). Consequently, it is worth thinking about how you might block out your project.

Because experimental films tend to rely more on visuals and sound (and less on dialogue and story), the difficulty of writing this project increases exponentially. It is not easy to describe a scene where colors and shapes roam about, where lightning zaps across the screen, or where a human head appears and then disappears. It requires attention to detail and a strong sense of specificity. Writing forces you to be explicit about what you see and hear. As you write, continue to ask yourself: What do we see now? What do we hear now? If you cannot answer those questions, you may not yet have a very strong idea of what is going on in your film.

Here is a sample treatment by Eric Sundquist. It is the first section of a treatment for a 15-minute film.

Breaking Glass by Eric Sundquist

The television screen is a safety barrier. It is a thing that keeps us distant from murder, sex, drugs, and the occasional beer commercial, while allowing us to be voyeurs. What if the glass were just glass, and what was behind really only a few feet away instead of somewhere in the past on a sound stage?

It begins—with the draining of the flat black ink that fills the space behind the screen. The innards of the television are revealed. The picture tube slopes back into its electrode-emitting socket. It is slick, smooth, and gray. The muffled sound of a screw gun is heard. The tube rocks a bit as if someone is tugging at it from below and suddenly it cracks off from the front glass and drops through the bottom of the television cabinet. The view is now much clearer. The back ends of the speakers and a multitude of wires all dripping with the last of the black ink are seen. A woman's hand appears. It is beautiful. It reaches in from the hole where the tube was and begins yanking out the wires. The sounds of electricity popping and plastic cracking are heard. The hand reaches back to yank out the left speaker, then the right. Both the woman's

hands reach in to finger the edges of the glass,
searching for a crack. They disappear and the sound
of breathing is heard. Suddenly a scraggly woman's
head appears inside the TV cabinet. We see the back
of her head, then she turns to peer at us through
the glass. She screams and spittle sticks to the
glass. She is frightened by what she sees and seems
to be stuck. One of her hands sneaks in and helps
pry her free. She drops back into the hole and her
screaming becomes distant.

A male voice is heard coming from the hole. "Where
did you see it? Just tell me where? What the hell
were you doing in there? I'll fix it." Suddenly a
shotgun barrel is thrust through the hole and
smacks into the glass. It loudly taps the glass a
few times and then a deafening roar is heard as it
goes off. The glass cracks in the upper left corner
where the barrel was pressing. Dark smoke fills the
box and the barrel slides back into the dark.

As the smoke dissipates, the sound of heavy
breathing is heard. The sound comes closer and a
mangy dog's head thrusts up in the box. The dog's
tongue licks the woman's spittle off the glass and
adds streaks of saliva that blur the view. The dog
then notices something beyond the glass and snarls
a warning. It begins to bark and tries to attack.
Paws smack the glass. The attack stops with a yelp
and the sound of running water.

Notice that the more precise and specific the language is, the easier the treatment is to follow and visualize.

Another example, this time of an entire treatment by Tim Green, demonstrates how a film might work with a piece of music.

Abstract Film Treatment: "Fratres"

Introduction: There is a piece of contemporary
classical music called "Fratres" by Arvo Part, a
composer from Estonia. Part is known for his
unusual, haunting music, which has a strange,
ethereal quality about it. When listening to this

piece I have always imagined images of an enduring
loneliness in the midst of bustling activity, and
for my screenplay I have an idea of a sequence of
events that would attempt to visually represent
this sort of feeling. Part's piece, about 8 minutes
long, is dominated by a low droning sound humming
beneath long violin chords ... this is occasionally
punctuated by sharp, fast violin solos, which last
about 1 minute each. I envision a series of visual
images where the vastness and emptiness of a modern
city are echoed in the isolation of a "modern urban
man" who is seen obliquely throughout the film.

1. Dawn (2 minutes)

(_Audio_: The opening chords of "Fratres" are long,
quiet, slow, and meditative, played around the high
register of the violin, accompanied by a steady
drone beneath.)

Visual: An extreme close-up of gently waving water,
deep blue and dark, slow-motion. The camera slowly
pans up to reveal the horizon of a large lake,
extending as far as the eye can see, dimly lit.
Some stars are still visible in the sky above.

CUT TO:
In a long, unbroken shot, we see dawn breaking over
the lake's horizon, the colors gradually growing
into defined oranges, reds, and yellows. The camera
slowly cranes back to reveal that we are seeing
this in a reflection from a window in the middle of
a glass-walled building in downtown Chicago. This
long track backwards continues until we see a
crowded cityscape of buildings, all reflecting the
colors of dawn.

CUT TO:
A series of shots of completely empty downtown
settings in the gray morning light: Doors are
locked. Streets are utterly empty. Shop windows are
closed, blinds are drawn. Interspersed among these
shots are still shots of a man lying in bed—but
only parts are shown: an ear against a pillow. A

curve in the man's foot. A hand hanging down off of the front of the bed. The scene continually cuts between shots of the empty downtown streets, and the "disembodied" parts of the sleeping man.

2. Awake (1 minute)

(<u>Audio</u>: The quiet equilibrium of the first two minutes is broken suddenly by the appearance of the first violin solo, played fast and loose, with many notes in rapid succession. There is a great sense of urgency to this music)

<u>Visual</u>: Lights come on in rapid-fire succession along window fronts in the downtown buildings. Time-lapse images of freeways as they rapidly go from complete emptiness to packed traffic jams, headlights gleaming.

CUT TO:
Images of an alarm clock's digital display flashes. The man's hand reaches for it. Another hand reaches for a light switch. Lights go on all over his house in quick succession, in the kitchen, in the bathroom, in the microwave as breakfast is heated up.

CUT TO:
Water splashes onto store fronts. Street cleaners use hoses to spray away trash and dirt from the roads. Mops splash onto store floors.

CUT TO:
From behind, we see the man leaning over a sink splashing water onto his face. Close-up of the hands bringing the water to the face—But, we never see his full face, it is always partially obscured.

3. Work (2 minutes)

(<u>Audio</u>: At this point the song returns to a similar sequence of long, slow, deliberate violin chords, though much louder this time.)

Visual: Images of the city at work. A crowded
downtown, traffic jams. Close-ups of moving bus
wheels, trains roaring over tracks, skyscrapers
gleaming in the sun.

CUT TO:
Interspersed among these images, disembodied shots
of the man at work: papers are filed, a computer
monitor flicks on, meetings are held, he nods. A
succession of faces appear before him: bosses,
companions, friends, strangers, deliverymen, etc.
... we see all of them from slightly above and
behind his head which is visible in the frame. None
make eye contact, all seem detached and hurried.

4. Loss (1 minute)

(Audio: The sharp violin solo returns, but this
time it is played extremely high, almost
uncomfortably so. It is fast and loose again, but
almost shrieking at the high end of the register)

Visual: A clock shows 5:00. The resulting images
are a rush of activity as people bustle all over
the city—sidewalks are jammed, doors are closed one
after another, lights flick off in offices, people
run to catch trains, cabs nearly crash into each
other, a few near-misses as pedestrians cross the
street erratically. All is drab, grays and blues,
washed-out and nondescript.

CUT TO:
Throughout these scenes we see the man, cut in
between the rapidly appearing images of urban
bustle, moving slowly through the crowded
sidewalks. From behind his head, the camera turns
with him onto a side street and finds it completely
empty. He stops, and just over his head we can see
the outline of the lake bathed in deep red sunlight
from the setting sun, an oasis of color among the
drab buildings. The man begins to run straight down
the empty street towards the lake in the distance.

```
CUT TO:
The solitary figure runs at full speed down the
middle of the street, flanked on left and right by
the massive buildings as the light slowly dims. The
camera cranes back slowly, causing the figure to
slowly diminish as he continues to run away from
the viewer.
```

5. Night (2 minutes)

```
(Audio: The last 2 minutes of the piece are a
return to similarly haunting, slow violin chords as
the beginning, beginning loudly, then gradually
fading away to silence.)
```

```
Visual: High overhead shot of the city stretching
into the distance, as if from the top of the
tallest building downtown. We see the sun setting
over the horizon as the freeways remain full of red
lights.
```

```
CUT TO:
Return to the high overhead shot of the city/
suburbs stretching out into the distance, now most
of the light has gone, and in the dusk we see the
twinkling of thousands of lights begin to grow
brighter.
```

```
CUT TO:
Shot identical to the one beginning the piece, a
slow-motion close-up of undulating water, deep and
dark blue, as the light slowly fades away to black.
```

If you do work with a screenplay, the most suitable is often the double-column approach because it allows a reader to clearly see how the visual works with the audio. Here are the first few pages of an experimental screenplay by an undergraduate student, Andy Sherman, from DePaul University. Notice how he tries to be very precise about what we are seeing and hearing. In general, he is quite successful. As you read the following pages, see if you can determine any place where you cannot visualize or hear what is going on.

The T-Shirt by Andy Sherman

VISUAL	AUDIO
BLACK SCREEN	
A bathroom warm-air hand dryer fills the entire screen.	A tent zipper opens up. The metal of it jingles.
CUT TO:	
A unicellular organism swims around in a solution in slow motion.	Snaps can be heard snapping and unsnapping in a rhythmic pattern.
CUT TO:	
An eye-level shot follows an older man in shorts mowing his lawn in the morning.	The zipper is moved in short bursts as the snaps continue to keep a rhythm.
CUT TO:	
A stainless steel grill's surface is clean and dry. Small plumes of smoke rise from the surface in slow motion. A grill spatula then slathers oil on the surface. Still in slow motion, the oil bubbles. A fist filled with uncooked hash browns then comes in from the top of the frame and hangs there.	The zipper/snap rhythm section continues to intensify as long strips of Velcro are heard pulling apart.
	All sounds stop abruptly.
(SEQUENCE: 1 minute)	
BLACK SCREEN	The sound of wind in a sail rippling in the breeze can be heard.
POV from the angle of a T-shirt is established by	

watching a dryer door open
from the inside.

Motherly ARMS enter the
dryer and LIFT THE CAMERA
up from just outside the
left and right edges of the
frame. The middle-aged,
dark-haired woman lifts the
camera up and out of the
dyer and over to a counter.

The zipper bursts begin
again very slowly.

As she does this, pieces of
blue cloth occasionally in
her hands can be seen as
her hands come into view
for short moments. The view
from the counter is similar
to one of a person laying
down, looking up.

Burlap and canvas rub
against each other softly.

MOTHER hovers above the
center of the frame. She
folds one sleeve over the
camera, which partially
blocks the screen.

She then folds the other
sleeve over the CAMERA and
the screen is completely
covered.

The sounds all stop
abruptly again.

(SEQUENCE: 1 Minute)

BLACK SCREEN

A grease gun is placed into
the joint of a bulldozer.
Slowly it is pumped, and
blue grease squeezes out of
the edges of the joint.

The wind in a sail can be
heard, only more intensely
this time. It continues on.

       CUT TO:

OVERHEAD SHOT of a truck
stop diner table with four
truckers eating breakfast
and pointing at each other
as they talk.

Belt buckle sounds join the
wind in the sail.

WHY BOTHER?

For writers who aspire to become writers for the Hollywood or conventional film, what is the point of even considering experimental films, much less spending time writing them? I believe there are three reasons.

1. First, even as an exercise, experimental film making is a wonderful opportunity to examine closely the relationship between sound and sight. Meaning can be created at intellectual, emotional, and sensory levels. Focused attention to this translates into better films in any genre: feature, documentary, marketplace, and so on.

2. Writing experimental films forces you to attend to ways of getting ideas across clearly and explicitly in writing. Although you can sometimes get away with vagueness in a theatrical film, it is much harder in an experimental film. In all genres, the audience must be able—from the writing alone—to see and hear what might be on the screen

3. Experimental film writing provides the opportunity to work at creating drama through the cinematic elements.

EXPERIMENTAL FILMS AS ART

In important ways, experimental films are, as a genre, most like poetry. Good poetry is read to be experienced; it is not read for information. Therefore, readers attend to the play of words, sounds, rhythms, and patterns. Similarly, art films are viewed to focus attention on the experience of the film and the elements that create that experience.

One could argue, then, that of all the film genres, the experimental/abstract genre most closely approaches a pure concept of "art." The overriding goal of experimental film makers is not necessarily to make money or persuade, but to produce something that has an emotional and sensory impact on the viewers. Of course, what is and what is not art is, and should be, highly debatable.

APPLICATIONS AND EXERCISES

1. Find a video store that rents experimental or avant-garde films (the popular ones in video stores seem to be *Chien Andalou*, films by Maya Deren, a film from the *Qatsi trilogy, Best of the Fests*, and films by Kenneth Anger) and immerse yourself in sensory overload. See if you can identify

the structure of each. Are there any commonalities to these films? How are they different?

2. A storyboard is a series of sketches that portray key scenes in your film. Find a short poem and storyboard it. Then describe (in writing) your storyboard.

3. Pick a 3-minute song (preferably one that does not tell a story) and write a screenplay for an abstract film to accompany the visuals. Remember to describe the visuals clearly (this will not be easy) so that a reader can "see" what you have in mind.

4. Write a treatment or screenplay for a dream you remember, especially a nightmare. As you revise it, take out everything that "makes sense." Leave in everything that is visually interesting, exciting, or provocative.

SUGGESTED READING

History and Theory

Geduld, H. M. (Ed.). (1969). *Filmmakers on filmmaking: Statements on their art by thirty directors*. Indianapolis, IN: Indiana University Press.
Knight, A. (1957). *The liveliest art*. New York: Mentor.
Mast, G., Cohen, M., & Braudy, L. (1992). *Film theory and criticism*. Oxford, England: Oxford University Press.

Practical

Brenneis, L. (2003). *Final Cut Pro 4 for Mac OS X (Visual QuickPro Guide)* (1st ed.). Berkeley, CA: Peachpit Press.
Collier, M. (2001). *The IFILM digital video filmmaker's gandbook*. Los Angeles: Lone Eagle Publishing Company.
Sheridan, S. (2004). *Developing digital short films*. Berkeley, CA: New Riders Press.
Stubbs, L., & Rodriguez, R. (2000). *Making independent films: Advice from the filmmakers*. New York: Allworth Press.
Weynand, D. (2003). *Apple Pro training series: Final Cut Pro 4*. Berkeley, CA: Peachpit Press.

Also: Some of the best reading you can do for this genre is on the Internet. See some of the sites mentioned in this chapter.

Epilogue

I would like to end this book by borrowing a quotation that Godfrey Reggio uses in many of the courses he teaches. The quotation is from Goethe's *Faust*. It applies to the full spectrum of screenwriting I have discussed in this book, and the sentiment it expresses is the reason you should go out and write your film, despite all odds.

> Until one is committed, there is hesitancy, the chance to draw back, always ineffectiveness. Concerning all acts of initiative and creation, there is one elementary truth, the ignorance of which kills countless ideas and splendid plans: that the moment one definitely commits oneself, then providence moves too. All sorts of things occur to help one that would never otherwise have occurred. A whole stream of events issues from the decision, raising in one's favor all manner of unforeseen incidents and meetings and material assistance, which no man could have dreamed would have come his way. Whatever you do, or dream you can, begin it. Boldness has genius, power and magic in it. Begin it now. (Reggio, interview, 2004)

So, if you feel strongly enough that the craft of screenwriting is for you and you are tough enough to work against both the odds and people telling you that you will not make it, go for it. Begin it now.

Appendix

WRITING FOR TELEVISION—SUGGESTED READING

Brody, L. (2003). *Television writing from the inside out: Your channel to success.* New York: Applause Books.

Dimaggio, M. (1990). *How to write for television.* New York: Simon & Schuster.

Goldberg, L., & Rabkin, W. (2003). *Successful television writing.* New York: Wiley.

Rannow, J. (2000). *Writing television comedy.* New York: Allsworth Press.

Smith, E. S. (1999). *Writing television sitcoms.* New York: Perigee Books.

Webber, M. (2002). *Gardner's guide to television scriptwriting: The writer's road.* Washington, DC: Garth Gardner.

SCRIPTWRITING SOFTWARE

There are dozens of software programs available to help in your screenwriting. Some will help you format your work, and some will help with story invention, design, and structure. The Writer's Guild of America's (WGA's) Web site (www.wga.org) contains a review by Robert M. Goodman of recommendations and descriptions of some of the best-known programs for both PC and Mac environments. The WGA updates this site regularly. Before you buy (these programs vary widely in price and what they will do—from $25–$400), do your homework.

For **script formatting programs**, check out compatibility with your computer system, ease of use, vendor support, upgrade potential, and drawbacks.

Some vendors can send you a sample so you can try it out or no charge or for a low fee. Here are some of the leaders in script formatting programs:

Parnassus Software ScriptWerx ($129)—www.scriptwerx.com
Scriptware ($299.95)—www.scriptware.com
Script Wizard ($69)—www.warrenassoc.com/scriptwizard1.htm
ScriptWright ($129)—www.kois.com (for MS Word)
Final Draft ($229)—www.finaldraft.com
Movie Magic Screenwriter 4.6 ($249)—www.screenplay.com

There are others and new ones come out frequently, so check out a number of programs and reviews before you invest.

Although I am not a big fan of **storytelling software**, they can be enormously helpful if used judiciously. None of the programs can do the work for you, but they can all function in some measure as coach and guide. These programs vary enormously in what they do, so you need to pay attention to how you work and how the program can help you. Some are fairly simple (Plots Unlimited), and others are more complex (Dramatica). Still others offer question-and-answer formats to guide you through the revision process (Collaborator). Check out Robert M. Goodman's reviews on http://www.wga.org/tools/ScriptSoftware/index2.html#StoryCraft. Here is a brief list.

Plots Unlimited ($199)—www.www.ashleywilde.com
StoryVision ($199)—www.members.aol.com/storvisn/vision.html
Writer's Blocks ($149)—www.writersblocks.com
Truby's Blockbuster ($295)—www.truby.com
Collaborator III Plus—www.collaborator.com
Dramatica ($149 and $399)—www.screenplay.com
StoryCraft ($99)—www.writerspage.com

FILM SCHOOLS

Most film schools offer concentrations in screenwriting. Even if they do not, writing for film is almost always an integral part of the program, and it is well worth it for any screenwriter to know intimately how a film is produced. Film schools can do three things for you:

1. They can provide experience in screenwriting in particular and film making in general.

2. They can help you decide whether you are cut out for it.
3. They can help you make valuable contacts in the field.

At the current time, there are over 60 schools in the United States and Canada that feature films schools, programs, or media arts degrees, and there are even more if you look worldwide. Of these, there are six that are currently considered top rate. These have established, full-time graduate programs of study geared toward preparing individuals to enter the field of film and TV. These schools are:

- University of Southern California
- University of California at Los Angeles
- American Film Institute
- Florida State University
- New York State University—Interactive Telecommunications Program
- Columbia University

Schools in areas where films are currently produced (especially New York and Los Angeles) have the added advantage of connections to the industry. Because contacts are a critical part of getting your first break in the feature film business, attending a school located in these cities is well worth considering.

Other Film School Resources

- *Complete Guide to American Film Schools*—Ernest Pintoff. New York: Penguin, 1994
- *Film School Confidential: Insider's Guide to Film Schools*—Tom Edgar and Karin Kelly. New York: Putnam, 1997.
- http://dir.yahoo.com/Entertainment/Movies_and_Film/Film_Schools/ College_and_University_Departments_and_Programs/University-Based Film Studies Programs

Universities with Film Programs

Aberystwyth University, Wales
Brooklyn College (New York)—Department of Film
Colorado Film Video Instructional Studios
Columbia University, School of the Arts—Film Program
Concordia University (Canada)

Franklin and Marshall College, Pennsylvania—Department of Theatre, Dance and Film

Hollins University (Roanoke, Virginia)—Screenwriting and film studies

Loyola Marymount University (Film Production)

Melbourne University's Summer School in Filmmaking

New York University, Department of Cinema Studies

Northern School of Film and Television—Leeds, UK

Rutgers University (New Jersey)—Film Studies Program

San Diego State University—Television, Film, and New Media Production Programs

Scottsdale Community College—Film Program

Stanford University (California)—Graduate Program in Documentary Film and Video

State University of New York at Purchase—Conservatory of Theatre Arts and Film

University of Alabama—Telecommunication and Film Department

University of Barcelona (Spain)—Cinema Studies

University of California at Berkeley—Film Studies Program

University of California at Long Beach—Film and Electronic Arts

University of California at Santa Cruz—Film and Video Department

University of Kansas—Department of Theatre and Film

University of Southampton (UK)—Film Studies

University of Southern Maine

University of Toronto, Innis College, Canada—Cinema Studies

University of Utah—Film Department

University of Waikato (New Zealand)—Film and Television Studies

University of Warwick (UK)—Film and Television Studies

University of Westminster (London)—Film and Video and Photographic Arts

University of Wisconsin (Milwaukee)

Watkins College Film School (Nashville)

Commercial or Nonuniversity-Based Instruction

1. Filmmaker's Central School of Cinema (Los Angeles)—www.onlinefmc.com
2. Los Angeles Film School—www.lafilm.com
3. London Film Academy—www.londonfilmacademy.com
4. New York Film Academy—www.nyfa.com

5. School of Film and Television—www.filmandtelevision.com
6. Seattle Film Institute—www.seattlefilminstitute.com
7. Toronto Film College—www.torontofilmcollege.com
8. Vancouver Film School—Canada—www.vfs.com
9. Victoria Film School—British Columbia—www.vicfilm.com

Other Useful Listings

- Directories of Film Schools/Careers in Moving Image Preservation—www.lcweb.loc.gov/films/schools.html
- Film School Directory from Next Frame—www.temple.edu/ufva/dirs/text52usa.htm
- Film and Communication Studies Program in Canada—www.film.queensu.ca/fsac/schools.html
- Library of Annotated Films Schools—annotated by students—www.filmmaker.com/loafs/

General References

2005 annual agency guide. (2004). Beverly Hills: Writers Network/Fade In Magazine.

Aristotle (1955). *Poetics*. In *Aristotle's theory of poetry and fine art* (4th ed.) (S. H. Butcher, trans.). New York: Dover Publications, Inc. (Original work published in 330 B.C.)

Beaufroy, S. (1998, Spring). The full monty [Screenplay]. *Scenario: The Magazine of Screenwriting Art, 4*(1), 6–41.

Bennett, H. (1982). *Star trek III: Return to genesis* [Film treatment]. Hollywood, CA: Script City.

Bergman, I. (1960). Introduction, *Four screenplays of Ingmar Bergman* (p. xii). New York: Simon and Schuster.

Blacker, I. (1986). *The elements of screenwriting*. New York: Macmillan.

Bogdanovich, P. (1998/1999, Winter). "On Story Conferences with Larry McMurtry." *Scenario: The Magazine of Screenwriting Art*, 97.

Bowden, D., & Sears, E. (1985). *Jungleland* [Unproduced screenplay].

Brady, B. (1994). *Principles of adaptation for film and television*. Austin: University of Texas Press.

Brenneis, L. (2003). *Final Cut Pro 4 for Mac OS X (Visual QuickPro Guide)* (1st ed.). Berkeley, CA: Peachpit Press.

Brooke, R., Mirtz, R., & Evans, R. (1994). *Small Groups in Writing Workshops: Invitations to a Writer's Life*. Urbana, IL: National Council of Teachers of English.

Buñuel, L. (Summer, 1960). [Interview]. *Film culture, 21*, 41–42.

Burns, K. (2002). Why I decided to make *The civil war*. Retrieved on October 10, 2005 from www.pbs.org/civilwar/film/

Callan, K. (2002). *The Script is Finished, Now What Do I Do?* Studio City: Sweden Press.

Cartmell, D. (1999). *Adaptation from text to screen, screen to text*. Oxford: Routledge.

Cole, H., & Haag, J. (1990). *The complete guide to standard script formats*. North Hollywood, CA: CMC Publishing.

Collier, M. (2001). *The IFILM digital video filmmaker's handbook*. Los Angeles: Lone Eagle Publishing Company.

Corbett, E., & Connors, R. (1997). *Style and statement.* New York: Oxford UP.

Darabont, F. (1996). *Shawshank Redemption: The Shooting Script* [Screenplay]. New York: Newmarket Press.

Dickey, J. (1970). *Deliverance.* Boston: Houghton Mifflin.

Dickey, J. (2003/1982). *Deliverance: A screenplay by James Dickey from his novel* [Screenplay]. Ipswich, Suffolk: Screenpress Publishing Company, 2003. Originally published in 1982.

Dunne, J. G. (1997). *Monster: Living off the big screen.* New York: Random House.

Egri, L. (1960). *The art of dramatic writing.* New York: Simon and Schuster.

Fielding, H. (n.d.). *Q & A with Helen Fielding.* [Interview with Alan Waldman]. Retrieved Oct. 10, 2005 from www.wga.org

Fulton, L. (1974). *Grassman.* Berkeley: Thorp Springs Press.

Geduld, H. M. (Ed.). (1969). *Filmmakers on filmmaking: Statements on their art by thirty directors.* Indianapolis, IN: Indiana University Press.

Goldman. W. (1989). *Adventures in the screen trade.* New York: Warner Books.

Hampe, B. (1997). *Making documentary films and reality videos.* New York: Owl Books/Henry Holt and Company.

Kaufman, C. (1999–2000). [Interview]. *Scenario: The Magazine of Screenwriting Art, (5)*3.

Khouri, C. (n.d.). [interview with Syd Fields]. Retrieved October 10, 2005 from www.sydfield.com/interviews_calliekhouri.htm

Knight, A. (1957). *The liveliest art.* New York: Mentor.

Kubrick, S. (1978). *The shining* [Film treatment]. Hollywood, CA: Script City.

Lawrence, D. H. (2003). *The prussian officer and other stories* (orig. 1914). Retrieved October 10, 2005 from etext.library.adelaide.edu.au/l/lawrence/dh/prussian/chapter1.html

Lucas, G. (1973). *The star wars* [Film Treatment]. Retrieved on October 10, 2005 from www.scifiscripts.com/scripts/StarWarsTreatment.txt

Mamet, D. (1984/1996). Glengarry Glen Ross [play]. *Mamet Plays.* London: Methuen Publishing Ltd.

Martin, S. (1999/2000). [Interview with Annie Nocenti]. *Scenario: The Magazine of Screenwriting Art, 3*(5), 60.

Mast, G., Cohen, M., & Braudy, L. (1992). *Film theory and criticism.* Oxford, England: Oxford University Press.

McMurtry, L. (1966). *The last picture show.* New York: Touchstone.

McMurtry, L., & Bogdanovich, P. (1998/1999, Winter). The last picture show screenplay [Screenplay]. *Scenario: The Magazine of Screenwriting Art, (4)*4, 59–97.

Mehring, M. (1990). *The screenplay: A blend of film form and context.* Boston: Focal Press.

Moore, M. (2003). [interview with Bill Maher]. Retrieved on October 10, 2005 from www.wga.org/craft/interviews/moore/html

Morris, E. (1998, March 20). [Interview with William H. Phillips]. Retrieved on October 10, 2005 from www.bedfordstmartins.com/phillips-film-1e/morris1.htm

Morrissette, B. (1985). *Novel and film: Essays in two genres.* Chicago: University of Chicago Press.

Orlean, S. (1998). *The orchid thief.* New York: Random House.

Sasoan, M. (2003). Phenomenon, P-H-E-N ... *Spellbound* director roots out emotion in sleeper surprise. Retrieved on August 5, 2005 from www.seemagazine.com/Issues/2003/0703/screen5.htm

Sayles, J. (1996). [Interview with Tod Lippy]. *Scenario: The Magazine of Screenwriting Art, 52.*

Seger, L. (1992). *The art of adaptation*. New York: Owl Books.

Shanley, J. P. (1993). Interview with Richard Roeper. *1993 writer's yearbook* (Vol. 64). Writer's Digest Publications. Retrieved on September 12, 2004 from www.writersdigest.com

Sheridan, S. (2004). *Developing digital short films*. Berkeley, CA: New Riders Press.

Stark, S. (n.d.). Retrieved October 10, 2005 from www.hi-beam.net/mkr/ss/ss-bio.html

Steinbeck, J. (1989, original 1938). The chrysanthemums. In McLaughlin, T. (Ed.). *Literature: The power of language* (pp. 939–940). New York: Harcourt Brace Jovanovich.

Stubbs, L., & Rodriguez, R. (2000). *Making independent films: Advice from the filmmakers*. New York: Allworth Press.

Reggio, G. (2000). *The electric dream: Naqoyqatsi* [Working Scenario]. Santa Fe: Institute for Regional Education.

Trimble, J. (2000). *Writing and style* (2nd ed.). New York: Prentice Hall.

Weynand, D. (2003). *Apple Pro training series: Final Cut Pro 4*. Berkeley, CA: Peachpit Press.

Williams, J. M. (1997). *Style: Ten lessons in clarity and grace* (5th ed.). New York: Longman.

Film References—Feature Films

Aykroyd, D., & Ramis, H. (1984). *Ghostbusters* [Motion Picture]. United States: Columbia/Tristar Pictures.

Beaufoy, S. (1997). *The full monty* [Motion Picture]. United States: Twentieth Century Fox.

Campion, J. (1993). *The piano* [Motion Picture]. United States: Miramax.

Coppola, F. F. (1974). *The conversation* [Motion Picture]. United States: Paramount Studios.

Coppola, S. (2003). *Lost in translation* [Motion Picture]. United States: Universal Studios.

Darabont, F. (screenwriter), (from the novel by S. King) (1999). *The green mile* [Motion Picture]. United States: Warner Brothers.

Darabont, F. (screenwriter), (from the story by S. King) (1994). *Shawshank redemption* [Motion Picture]. United States: Castle Rock.

Dickey, J. (screenwriter) (1972). *Deliverance* [Motion Picture]. United States: Warner Brothers.

Duncan, P. S. (1996). *Mr. Holland's opus* [Motion Picture]. United States: Hollywood Pictures.

Dworet, L., & Pool, R. R. (1995). *Outbreak* [Motion Picture]. United States: Warner Brothers.

Kasdan, L., & Kasdan, M. (1991). *Grand canyon* [Motion Picture]. United States: Twentieth Century Fox.

Kaufman, C., & Kaufman, D. (screenwriter), (from the book by S. Orlean) (2002). *Adaptation* [Motion Picture]. United States: Columbia/Tristar.

Khouri, C. (1991). *Thelma and Louise* [Motion Picture]. United States: MGM/United Artists Studios.

LaGravenese, R., & Chandler, E. (screenwriter), (from the novel by F. H. Burnett) (1995). *The little princess* [Motion Picture]. United States: Warner Brothers.

Luedtke, K. (screenwriter), (from the memoirs of I. Dinesen) (1985). *Out of Africa* [Motion Picture]. United States: Universal Studios.

Mamet, D. (screenplay/play) (1992). *Glengarry Glen Ross* [Motion Picture]. United States: Artisan Entertainment.

Mamet, D. (screenwriter), (from the novel by B. Reed) (1982). *The verdict* [Motion Picture]. United States: Twentieth Century Fox.

Masius, J. (1986). *Ferris Bueller's day off* [Motion Picture]. United States: Paramount Studios.

McMurtry, L., & Bogdanovich, P. (screenplay), (from the novel by L. McMurtry) (1971). *The last picture show* [Motion Picture]. United States: Columbia/Tristar.

Minghella, A. (screenwriter), (from the novel by M. Ondaatje) (1996). *The English patient* [Motion Picture]. United States: Miramax.

Rubin, B. J. (1990). *Jacob's ladder* [Motion Picture]. United States: Artisan Entertainment.

Sayles, J. (1996). *Lone star* [Motion Picture]. United States: Castle Rock.

Shaffer, P. (screenplay/play) (1984). *Amadeus* [Motion Picture]. United States: Warner Brothers.

Sorkin, A. (1995). *The American President* [Motion Picture]. United States: Castle Rock.

Stuart, J., & Twohy, D. (screenwriters) (from the story by D. Twohy) (1993). *The fugitive* [Motion Picture]. United States: Warner Brothers.

Tarantino, Q. (2004). *Kill Bill* [Motion Picture]. United States: Miramar.

Towne, R. (1974). *Chinatown* [Motion Picture]. United States: Paramount Studios.

Weir, P. (1990). *Green card* [Motion Picture]. United States: Disney Studios.

Zaillian, S. (screenwriter), (from the book by T. Keneally) (1993). *Schindler's list* [Motion Picture]. United States: Universal Studios.

Documentary Films

Blitz, J. (2002). *Spellbound* [Documentary Film]. United States: Columbia/Tristar.

Burns, K., & Burns, R. (1990). *The Civil War* [Documentary Film]. United States: Public Broadcasting Service.

Dickson, P. (1951). *David* [Documentary Film]. Great Britain: Panamint Cinema.

Gilbert, C. (1973). *An American family* [Documentary Film]. United States: Public Broadcasting Service.

Hirsch, L. (2002). *Amandla: A revolution in four-part harmony* [Documentary Film]. United States: Artisan.

James, S., Marx, F., & Gilbert, P. (1994). *Hoop dreams* [Documentary Film]. United States: Kartemquin Films.

Jarecki, A. (2003). *Capturing the Friedmans* [Documentary Film]. United States: HBO.

Joslin, T., Massi, M., & Friedman, P. (1993). *Silverlake life: The view from here* [Documentary Film]. United States: Zeitgeist Films.

Keeve, D. (1995). *Unzipped* [Documentary Film]. United States: Miramax.

Livingston, J. (1990). *Paris is burning* [Documentary Film]. United States: Fox Lorber.

Moore, M. (1989). *Roger and me* [Documentary Film]. United States: Warner Brothers.

Moore, M. (2002). *Bowling for Columbine* [Documentary Film]. United States: United Artists, Alliance Atlantis, & Dog Eat Dog Films.

Moore, M. (2004). *Fahrenheit 9/11* [Documentary Film]. United States: Columbia/Tristar.

Morris, E. (2003). *Fog of war* [Documentary Film]. United States: Sony Pictures Classics.

Perrin, J. (2001). *Winged migration* [Documentary Film]. United States: Sony Pictures Classics.

Sherwood, C. (2004). *Stolen honor* [Documentary Film]. United States: Red, White & Blue Productions.

Wenders, W. (1999). *Buena Vista social club* [Documentary Film]. United States: Road Moves & Berlin: Filmproduktion.

Information Films, Videos and Websites

Advertising Council. (2003). Website retrieved July 3, 2005 from www.adcouncil.org

Americans stand united. [Public Service Announcement]. Retrieved July 3, 2005 from www.aaiusa.org/psa.htm

Because there's just no place like home. [Public Service Announcement]. Retrieved March 1, 2005 from www.nrcs.usda.gov/feature/highlights/freemanpsa.html

Bullying prevention. [Public Service Announcement]. Retrieved July 3, 2005 from www.adcouncil.org

Getting a flu shot. (October 26, 2004) [Public Service Announcement]. Retrieved December 10, 2004 from www.cdc.gov/flu/0405psas.htm

Life is calling. [Public Service Announcement]. Retrieved November 20, 2004 from www.cdc.gov/flu/0405psas.htm

Max and Buddy the bear. [Public Service Announcement]. United States: Ballistic Pixel Lab. Retrieved March 15, 2005 from www.ballisticpixel.com/creations/html/creations_main.htm

Meetings, bloody meetings [Business Education Film]. Retrieved on July 3, 2005 from www.rctm.com/Products/celebritiesgurus/johncleese/5618.htm

Picture a world of respect. [Public Service Announcement]. Retrieved July 3, 2005 from www.tolerance.org/about/psa/05-2002/#

This is your brain on drugs. CNNfyi.com. (2000). Retrieved October 14, 2005 from www.cnn.com/fyi/interactive/news/brain/brain.on.drugs.html

Tolerance: Honor the differences. [Public Service Announcement]. Retrieved March 1, 2005 from www.tolerance.org/about/psa/05-2002/#

Video Arts. Retrieved October 14, 2005 from www.videoarts.com/

Experimental, Abstract, and Animated Films and Websites

Alcott, T., Weitz, C., & Weitz, P. (1998) *Antz* [Animated Film]. United States: Dreamworks.

Bird, B. (2004). *The incredibles* [Animated Film]. United States: Disney/Pixar.

Blair, L. et al. (1940). *Fantasia* [Animated Film]. United States: Disney

Brakhage, S. (1986). *Night Music* [Experimental Film]. United States: Stan Brakhage and Light Cone Video.

Brakhage, S. (1993). *Study in color and black and white* [Experimental Film]. United States: Stan Brakhage and Light Cone Video.

Buñuel, L., & Dali, S. (1929). *Chien andalou* [Experimental Film]. France: Luis Buñuel-Salvador Dali production.

Buñuel, L., & Dali, S. (1930). *L'age d'or* [Experimental Film]. France: Kino International.

Cavalcanti, A. (1926). *Rien que les heures* [Experimental Film]. France: Neofilm Productions.

Clair, R., & Picabia, F. (1924). *Entr'acte* [Experimental Film]. France: Criterion Collection.

Flicker. [Website]. Retrieved March 1, 2005 from www.hi-beam.net/cgi-bin/flicker.pl

Halle, R. [Experimental Film Links]. Retrieved March 1, 2005 from www.courses.rochester.edu/halle/Links/Film.html. Rochester: University of Rochester.

Hamiltro Productions. Retrieved March 10, 2005 from www.panix.com/~hamiltro/

Iven, J., & Franken, M. (1929). *Rain* [Experimental Film]. Holland: Capi-Holland Productions.

Janowitz. H., & Mayer, C. (1920). *Cabinet of Dr. Caligari* [Experimental Film]. German: Decla Film-Ges Holz & Company Productions.

Kirkpatrick, K. et al. (screenwriter), & Dahl, R. (from his story) (1996). *James and the Giant Peach*. [Animated Film]. United States: Disney.

Lang, F., & Von Harbou, T. (1926). *Metropolis* [Experimental Film]. Germany: Universum Film Aktiengesellschaft.

Lasseter, J. et al. (1998). *A Bug's Life* [Animated Film]. United States: Disney/Pixar.

Leger, F. (1924). *Ballet mécanique* [Experimental Film]. France.

Morey, L. (adaptation), (from the story by F. Salten) (1942). *Bambi* [Animated Film]. United States: Disney.

Murnau F. W. (1922). *Nosferatu: A symphony of terror* [Experimental Film]. Germany: Prana-film Production.

Ray, M. (1926). *Emak Bakia, a cinépoem* [Experimental Film]. France.

Reggio, G. (1982). *Koyaanisqatsi [Life in turmoil]* [Feature Film]. United States: Institute for Regional Education.

Reggio, G. (1987). *Powaqqatsi [Life in transition]* [Feature Film]. United States: MGM/United Artists.

Reggio, G. (2002). *Naqoyqatsi [Life as war]* [Feature Film]. United States: Miramax and Qatsi Productions.

Sears, T. et al. (1938). *Snow White and the seven dwarves* [Animated Film]. United States: Disney.

Thomas, O. et al. (2000). *Fantasia/2000* [Animated Film]. United States: Disney.

Whedon, J. et al. (screenplay), (from the story by J. Lasseter et al.) (1995). *Toy Story* [Animated Film]. United States: Disney.

Author Index

Subject Index